ALGEBRAIC STRUCTURES

This book is in the

ADDISON-WESLEY SERIES IN MATHEMATICS

———

LYNN H. LOOMIS
Consulting Editor

ALGEBRAIC STRUCTURES

SERGE LANG

Columbia University, New York, New York

ADDISON-WESLEY PUBLISHING COMPANY

Reading, Massachusetts · Menlo Park, California · London · Don Mills, Ontario

Second Printing — September 1968

Partially supported by NSF Grant GP5-303

Foreword

This book, together with *Linear Algebra*, constitutes a curriculum for an algebra program addressed to undergraduates.

The separation of the linear algebra from the other basic algebraic structures fits all existing tendencies affecting undergraduate teaching, and I agree with these tendencies. I have made the present book self-contained logically, but it is probably better if students take the linear algebra course *before* being introduced to the more abstract notions of groups, rings, and fields, and the systematic development of their basic abstract properties. There is of course some overlap with the book *Linear Algebra*, since in that book I wanted to point out certain facts concerning groups of matrices, and rings of endomorphisms. The emphasis here is, however, quite different.

A course in algebra is also the proper place to introduce students to the general language currently in use in mathematics concerning sets and mappings, up to and including Zorn's lemma. In this spirit, I have included a chapter on sets and cardinal numbers which is much more extensive than is the custom. One reason is that the statements proved here are not easy to find in the literature, disjoint from highly technical books on set theory. Thus Chapter VII will provide attractive extra material if time is available. This part of the book, together with the appendix, and the construction of the real and complex numbers, also can be viewed as a short course on the naive foundations of the basic mathematical objects.

Elementary introductory texts in mathematics, like the present one, should be simple and always provide concrete examples together with the development of the abstractions (which explains using the real and complex numbers as examples before they are treated logically in the text). The desire to avoid encyclopedic proportions, and specialized emphasis, and to keep the book short explains the omission of some theorems which some teachers will miss and may want to include in the course. Exceptionally talented students can always take more advanced classes, and for them one can use the more comprehensive advanced texts which are easily available.

Berkeley, 1966   SERGE LANG

Contents

Chapter V

Vector Spaces and Modules

Chapter VI

Field Theory

Chapter VII

The Real and Complex Numbers

Chapter VIII

Sets

Appendix

CHAPTER I

The Integers

§1. Terminology of sets

A collection of objects is called a *set*. A member of this collection is also called an *element* of the set. It is useful in practice to use short symbols to denote certain sets. For instance, we denote by $\mathbf{Z}$ the set of all integers, i.e. all numbers of the type 0, ± 1, ± 2, $\ldots$. Instead of saying that x is an element of a set S, we shall also frequently say that x *lies in* S, and write $x \in S$. For instance, we have $1 \in \mathbf{Z}$, and also $-4 \in \mathbf{Z}$.

If S and S' are sets, and if every element of S' is an element of S, then we say that S' is a *subset* of S. Thus the set of positive integers $\{1, 2, 3, \ldots\}$ is a subset of the set of all integers. To say that S' is a subset of S is to say that S' is part of S. Observe that our definition of a subset does not exclude the possibility that $S' = S$. If S' is a subset of S, but $S' \neq S$, then we shall say that S' is a *proper* subset of S. Thus $\mathbf{Z}$ is a subset of $\mathbf{Z}$, and the set of positive integers is a proper subset of $\mathbf{Z}$. To denote the fact that S' is a subset of S, we write $S' \subset S$, and also say that S' is *contained* in S.

If S_1, S_2 are sets, then the *intersection* of S_1 and S_2, denoted by $S_1 \cap S_2$, is the set of elements which lie in both S_1 and S_2. For instance, if S_1 is the set of integers ≥ 1 and S_2 is the set of integers ≤ 1, then

$$S_1 \cap S_2 = \{1\}$$

(the set consisting of the number 1).

The *union* of S_1 and S_2, denoted by $S_1 \cup S_2$, is the set of elements which lie in S_1 or in S_2. For instance, if S_1 is the set of integers ≤ 0 and S_2 is the set of integers ≥ 0, then $S_1 \cup S_2 = \mathbf{Z}$ is the set of all integers.

We see that certain sets consist of elements described by certain properties. If a set has no elements, it is called the *empty* set. For instance, the set of all integers x such that $x > 0$ and $x < 0$ is empty, because there is no such integer x.

If S, S' are sets, we denote by $S \times S'$ the set of all pairs (x, x') with $x \in S$ and $x' \in S'$.

1

§2. Basic properties

The integers are so well known that it would be slightly tedious to axiomatize them immediately. Hence we shall assume that the reader is acquainted with the elementary properties of arithmetic, involving addition, multiplication, and inequalities, which are taught in all elementary schools. Later in this book, the reader will see how one can axiomatize such rules (see, for instance, the chapter on rings for the rules concerning addition and multiplication, and the chapter on ordering for the rules concerning inequalities).

We mention explicitly one property of the integers which we take as an axiom concerning them, and which is called *well-ordering*.

Every non-empty set of integers ≥ 0 has a least element.

(This means: If S is a non-empty set of integers ≥ 0, then there exists an integer $n \in S$ such that $n \leq x$ for all $x \in S$.)

Using this well-ordering, we shall prove another property of the integers, called induction. It occurs in several forms.

INDUCTION: FIRST FORM. *Suppose that for each integer $n \geq 1$ we are given an assertion $A(n)$, and that we can prove the following two properties:*

(1) *The assertion $A(1)$ is true.*
(2) *For each integer $n \geq 1$, if $A(n)$ is true, then $A(n + 1)$ is true.*

Then for all integers $n \geq 1$, the assertion $A(n)$ is true.

Proof. Let S be the set of all positive integers n for which the assertion $A(n)$ is false. We wish to prove that S is empty, i.e. that there is no element in S. Suppose there is some element in S. By well-ordering, there exists a least element n_0 in S. By assumption, $n_0 \neq 1$, and hence $n_0 > 1$. Since n_0 is least, it follows that $n_0 - 1$ is not in S, in other words the assertion $A(n_0 - 1)$ is true. But then by property (2), we conclude that $A(n_0)$ is also true because

$$n_0 = (n_0 - 1) + 1.$$

This is a contradiction, which proves what we wanted.

Example. We wish to prove that for each integer $n \geq 1$, $A(n)$:

$$1 + 2 + \cdots + n = \frac{n(n + 1)}{2}.$$

This is certainly true when $n = 1$, because

$$1 = \frac{1(1 + 1)}{2}.$$

Assume that our equation is true for an integer $n \geq 1$. Then

$$1 + \cdots + n + (n+1) = \frac{n(n+1)}{2} + (n+1)$$

$$= \frac{n(n+1) + 2(n+1)}{2}$$

$$= \frac{n^2 + n + 2n + 2}{2}$$

$$= \frac{(n+1)(n+2)}{2}.$$

Thus we have proved the two properties (1) and (2) for the statements denoted by $A(n)$, and we conclude by induction that $A(n)$ is true for all integers $n \geq 1$.

Remark. In the statement of induction, we could replace 1 by 0 everywhere, and the proof would go through just as well.

The second form is a variation on the first.

INDUCTION: SECOND FORM. *Suppose that for each integer $n \geq 0$ we are given an assertion $A(n)$, and that we can prove the following two properties:*

(1') *The assertion $A(0)$ is true.*

(2') *For each integer $n > 0$, if $A(k)$ is true for every integer k with $0 \leq k < n$, then $A(n)$ is true.*

Then the assertion $A(n)$ is true for all integers $n \geq 0$.

Proof. Again let S be the set of integers ≥ 0 for which the assertion is false. Suppose that S is not empty, and let n_0 be the least element of S. Then $n_0 \neq 0$ by assumption (1'), and since n_0 is least, for every integer k with $0 \leq k < n_0$, the assertion $A(k)$ is true. By (2') we conclude that $A(n_0)$ is true, a contradiction which proves our second form of induction.

As an example of the second form of induction, we shall prove the statement known as the *Euclidean algorithm*.

THEOREM 1. *Let m, n be integers ≥ 0, and $m > 0$. Then there exist integers q, $r \geq 0$ with $0 \leq r < m$ such that*

$$n = qm + r.$$

The integers q, r are uniquely determined by these conditions.

Proof. We prove the existence by induction, on n. If $n = 0$, we let $q = r = 0$. Suppose $n > 0$. If $n < m$, we let again $q = 0$ and $r = n$. If $n \geq m$, then $0 \leq n - m < n$. By induction, we can find integers

$q_1, r \geqq 0$ and $r < m$ such that

$$n - m = q_1 m + r.$$

Then

$$n = m + q_1 m + r = (1 + q_1)m + r.$$

This proves the existence of the integers q and r as desired.

As for uniqueness, suppose that

$$n = q_1 m + r_1, \qquad\qquad 0 \leqq r_1 < m,$$

$$n = q_2 m + r_2, \qquad\qquad 0 \leqq r_2 < m.$$

If $r_1 \neq r_2$, say $r_2 > r_1$. Subtracting, we obtain

$$(q_1 - q_2)m = r_2 - r_1.$$

But $r_2 - r_1 < m$, and $r_2 - r_1 > 0$. This is impossible because $q_1 - q_2$ is an integer, and so if $(q_1 - q_2)m > 0$ then $(q_1 - q_2)m \geqq m$. Hence we conclude that $r_1 = r_2$. But then $q_1 m = q_2 m$, and thus $q_1 = q_2$. This proves the uniqueness, and concludes the proof of our theorem.

Remark. The result of Theorem 1 is nothing but an expression of the result of long division. We call r the *remainder* of the division of n by m.

EXERCISES

1. If n, m are integers $\geqq 1$ and $n \geqq m$, define the *binomial coefficients*

$$\binom{n}{m} = \frac{n!}{m!(n-m)!}.$$

As usual, $n! = n \cdot (n-1) \cdots 1$ is the product of the first n integers. We define $0! = 1$ and

$$\binom{n}{0} = 1.$$

Prove that

$$\binom{n}{m-1} + \binom{n}{m} = \binom{n+1}{m}.$$

2. Prove by induction that for any integers x, y we have

$$(x + y)^n = \sum_{i=0}^{n} \binom{n}{i} x^i y^{n-i}.$$

The summation sign here means

$$y^n + \binom{n}{1} x y^{n-1} + \binom{n}{2} x^2 y^{n-2} + \cdots + x^n.$$

§3. *Greatest common divisor*

Let n be a non-zero integer, and d a non-zero integer. We shall say that d *divides* n if there exists an integer q such that $n = dq$. We then write $d \mid n$. If m, n are non-zero integers, by a *common divisor* of m and n we mean an integer $d \neq 0$ such that $d \mid n$ and $d \mid m$. By a *greatest common divisor* of m and n, we mean an integer $d > 0$ which is a common divisor, and such that, if e is a divisor of m, n and $e \neq 0$, then e divides d. We shall see in a moment that a greatest common divisor always exists. It is immediately verified that a greatest common divisor is uniquely determined.

Let J be a subset of the integers. We shall say that J is an *ideal* if it has the following properties:

The integer 0 is in J. If m, n are in J, then $m + n$ is in J. If m is in J, and n is an arbitrary integer, then nm is in J.

Example. Let $m_1, \ldots, m_r$ be integers. Let J be the set of all integers which can be written in the form

$$x_1 m_1 + \cdots + x_r m_r$$

with integers $x_1, \ldots, x_r$. Then it is immediately verified that J is an ideal. Indeed, if $y_1, \ldots, y_r$ are integers, then

$$(x_1 m_1 + \cdots + x_r m_r) + (y_1 m_1 + \cdots + y_r m_r)$$
$$= (x_1 + y_1) m_1 + \cdots + (x_r + y_r) m_r$$

lies in J. If n is an integer, then

$$n(x_1 m_1 + \cdots + x_r m_r) = n x_1 m_1 + \cdots + n x_r m_r$$

lies in J. Finally, $0 = 0 m_1 + \cdots + 0 m_r$ lies in J, so J is an ideal. We say that J is *generated* by $m_1, \ldots, m_r$ and that $m_1, \ldots, m_r$ are *generators*.

We note that $\{0\}$ itself is an ideal, called the *zero ideal*. Also, **Z** is an ideal, called the *unit ideal*.

THEOREM 2. *Let J be an ideal of* **Z**. *Then there exists an integer d which is a generator of J.*

Proof. If J is the zero ideal, then 0 is a generator. Suppose $J \neq \{0\}$. If $n \in J$ then $-n = (-1)n$ is also in J, so J contains some positive integer. Let d be the smallest positive integer in J. We contend that d is a generator of J. To see this, let $n \in J$, and write $n = dq + r$ with $0 \leq r < d$. Then $r = n - dq$ is in J, and since $r < d$, it follows that $r = 0$. This proves that $n = dq$, and hence that d is a generator, as was to be shown.

THEOREM 3. *Let m_1, m_2 be positive integers. Let d be a positive generator for the ideal generated by m_1, m_2. Then d is a greatest common divisor of m_1 and m_2.*

Proof. Since m_1 lies in the ideal generated by m_1, m_2 (because $m_1 = 1m_1 + 0m_2$), there exists an integer q_1 such that

$$m_1 = q_1 d,$$

whence d divides m_1. Similarly, d divides m_2. Let e be a non-zero integer dividing both m_1 and m_2, say

$$m_1 = h_1 e \quad \text{and} \quad m_2 = h_2 e$$

with integers h_1, h_2. Since d is in the ideal generated by m_1 and m_2, there are integers s_1, s_2 such that $d = s_1 m_1 + s_2 m_2$, whence

$$d = s_1 h_1 e + s_2 h_2 e = (s_1 h_1 + s_2 h_2)e.$$

Consequently, e divides d, and our theorem is proved.

Remark. Exactly the same proof applies when we have more than two integers. For instance, if $m_1, \ldots, m_r$ are non-zero integers, and d is a positive generator for the ideal generated by $m_1, \ldots, m_r$, then d is a greatest common divisor of $m_1, \ldots, m_r$.

Integers $m_1, \ldots, m_r$ whose greatest common divisor is 1 are said to be *relatively prime*. If that is the case, then there exist integers $x_1, \ldots, x_r$ such that

$$x_1 m_1 + \cdots + x_r m_r = 1,$$

because 1 lies in the ideal generated by $m_1, \ldots, m_r$.

§4. *Unique factorization*

We define a *prime number* p to be an integer ≥ 2 such that, given a factorization $p = mn$ with positive integers m, n, then $m = 1$ or $n = 1$. The first few primes are 2, 3, 5, 7, 11, $\ldots$.

THEOREM 4. *Every positive integer $n \geq 2$ can be expressed as a product of prime numbers (not necessarily distinct),*

$$n = p_1 \cdots p_r,$$

uniquely determined up to a permutation.

Proof. Suppose that there is at least one integer ≥ 2 which cannot be expressed as a product of prime numbers. Let m be the smallest such integer. Then in particular m is not prime, and we can write $m = de$ with integers $d, e > 1$. But then d and e are smaller than m, and since m was chosen smallest, we can write

$$d = p_1 \cdots p_r \quad \text{and} \quad e = p_1' \cdots p_s'$$

with prime numbers $p_1, \ldots, p_r, p_1', \ldots, p_s'$. Thus

$$m = de = p_1 \cdots p_r p_1' \cdots p_s'$$

is expressed as a product of prime numbers, a contradiction, which proves that every positive integer ≥ 2 can be expressed as a product of prime numbers.

We must now prove the uniqueness, and for this we need a lemma.

LEMMA. *Let p be a prime number, and m, n non-zero integers such that p divides mn. Then $p \mid m$ or $p \mid n$.*

Proof. Assume that p does not divide m. Then the greatest common divisor of p and m is 1, and there exist integers a, b such that

$$1 = ap + bm.$$

(We use Theorem 3.) Multiplying by n yields

$$n = nap + bmn.$$

But $mn = pc$ for some integer c, whence

$$n = (na + bc)p,$$

and p divides n, as was to be shown.

This lemma will be applied when p divides a product of prime numbers $q_1 \cdots q_s$. In that case, p divides q_1 or p divides $q_2 \cdots q_s$. If p divides q_1, then $p = q_1$. Otherwise, we can proceed inductively, and we conclude that in any case, there exists some i such that $p = q_i$.

Suppose now that we have two products of primes

$$p_1 \cdots p_r = q_1 \cdots q_s.$$

By what we have just seen, we may renumber the primes $q_1, \ldots, q_s$ and then we may assume that $p_1 = q_1$. Cancelling q_1, we obtain

$$p_2 \cdots p_r = q_2 \cdots q_s.$$

We may then proceed by induction to conclude that after a renumbering of the primes $q_1, \ldots, q_s$ we have $r = s$, and $p_i = q_i$ for all i. This proves the desired uniqueness.

In expressing an integer as a product of prime numbers, it is convenient to bunch together all equal factors. Thus let n be an integer > 1, and let $p_1, \ldots, p_r$ be the *distinct* prime numbers dividing n. Then there exist unique integers $m_1, \ldots, m_r > 0$ such that $n = p_1^{m_1} \cdots p_r^{m_r}$. We agree to the usual convention that for any non-zero integer x, $x^0 = 1$. Then given any positive integer n, we can write n as a product of prime powers with distinct primes $p_1, \ldots, p_r$:

$$n = p_1^{m_1} \cdots p_r^{m_r},$$

where the exponents $m_1, \ldots, m_r$ are integers ≥ 0, and uniquely determined.

The set of quotients of integers m/n with $n \neq 0$ is called the *rational numbers*, and denoted by $\mathbf{Q}$. We assume for the moment that the reader is familiar with $\mathbf{Q}$. We show later how to construct $\mathbf{Q}$ from $\mathbf{Z}$ and how to prove its properties.

Let $a = m/n$ be a rational number, $n \neq 0$ and assume $a \neq 0$, so $m \neq 0$. Let d be the greatest common divisor of m and n. Then we can write $m = dm'$ and $n = dn'$, and m', n' are relatively prime. Thus

$$a = \frac{m'}{n'}.$$

If we now express $m' = p_1^{i_1} \cdots p_r^{i_r}$ and $n' = q_1^{j_1} \cdots q_s^{j_s}$ as products of prime powers, we obtain a factorization of a itself, and we note that no p_ν is equal to any q_μ.

If a rational number is expressed in the form m/n where m, n are integers, $n \neq 0$, and m, n are relatively prime, then we call n the *denominator* of the rational number, and m its *numerator*. Occasionally, by abuse of language, when one writes a quotient m/n where m, n are not necessarily relatively prime, one calls n a denominator for the fraction.

§5. Equivalence relations and congruences

Let S be a set. By an *equivalence relation* in S we mean a relation, written $x \sim y$, between certain pairs of elements of S, satisfying the following conditions:

ER 1. *We have $x \sim x$ for all $x \in S$.*
ER 2. *If $x \sim y$ and $y \sim z$ then $x \sim z$.*
ER 3. *If $x \sim y$ then $y \sim x$.*

Suppose we have such an equivalence relation in S. Given an element x of S, let C_x consist of all elements of S which are equivalent to x. Then all elements of C_x are equivalent to one another, as follows at once from our three properties. (Verify this in detail.) Furthermore, you will also verify at once that if x, y are elements of S, then either $C_x = C_y$, or C_x, C_y have no element in common. Each C_x is called an *equivalence class*. We see that our equivalence relation determines a decomposition of S into disjoint equivalence classes. Each element of the class is called a *representative* of the class.

Our first example of the notion of equivalence relation will be the notion of congruence. Let n be an integer. Let x, y be integers. We shall say that x is *congruent to y modulo n* if there exists an integer m such that $x - y = mn$. This means that $x - y$ lies in the ideal generated by n. If $n \neq 0$, this also means that $x - y$ is divisible by n. We write the relation of congruence in the form

$$x \equiv y \pmod{n}.$$

It is then immediately verified that this is an equivalence relation, namely that the following properties are verified:

(a) We have $x \equiv x \pmod{n}$.
(b) If $x \equiv y$ and $y \equiv z \pmod{n}$, then $x \equiv z \pmod{n}$.
(c) If $x \equiv y \pmod{n}$ then $y \equiv x \pmod{n}$.

Congruences also satisfy further properties:

(d) If $x \equiv y \pmod{n}$ and z is an integer, then $xz \equiv yz \pmod{n}$.
(e) If $x \equiv y$ and $x' \equiv y' \pmod{n}$, then $xx' \equiv yy' \pmod{n}$. Furthermore $x + x' \equiv y + y' \pmod{n}$.

We give the proof of the first part of (e) as an example. We can write

$$x = y + mn \quad \text{and} \quad x' = y' + m'n$$

with some integers m, m'. Then

$$xx' = (y + mn)(y' + m'n) = yy' + mny' + ym'n + mm'nn,$$

and the expression on the right is immediately seen to be equal to $yy' + wn$ for some integer w, so that $xx' \equiv yy' \pmod{n}$, as desired.

We define the *even* integers to be those which are congruent to 0 mod 2. Thus n is even if and only if there exists an integer m such that $n = 2m$. We define the *odd* integers to be all the integers which are not even. It is trivially shown that an odd integer n can be written in the form $2m + 1$ for some integer m.

cancellation : $ca \equiv cb \pmod{m}$
        $\gcd(c, m) = 1$

$\Rightarrow \quad a \equiv b$

holds   if :   (1) m prime
        (2) $c \not\equiv 0 \pmod{m}$

EXERCISES

1. Let n, d be positive integers and assume $1 < d < n$. Show that n can be written in the form

$$n = c_0 + c_1 d + \cdots + c_k d^k$$

with integers c_i such that $0 \leq c_i < d$, and that these integers c_i are uniquely determined. [*Hint:* For the existence, write $m = qd + c_0$ by the Euclidean algorithm, and then use induction. For the uniqueness, use induction, assuming $c_0, \ldots, c_r$ are uniquely determined; show that c_{r+1} is then uniquely determined.]

2. Let m, n be non-zero integers written in the form

$$m = p_1^{i_1} \cdots p_r^{i_r} \quad \text{and} \quad n = p_1^{j_1} \cdots p_r^{j_r},$$

where i_ν, j_μ are integers ≥ 0 and $p_1, \ldots, p_r$ are distinct prime numbers.

(a) Show that the g.c.d. of m, n can be expressed as a product $p_1^{k_1} \cdots p_r^{k_r}$ where $k_1, \ldots, k_r$ are integers ≥ 0. Express k_ν in terms of i_ν and j_ν.

(b) Define the notion of least common multiple, and express the least common multiple of m, n as a product $p_1^{k_1} \cdots p_r^{k_r}$ with integers $k_\nu \geq 0$. Express k_ν in terms of i_ν and j_ν.

3. Give the g.c.d. and l.c.m. of the following pairs of positive integers: (a) $5^3 2^6 3$ and 225.   (b) 248 and 28.

4. Prove that there exist infinitely many prime numbers. [*Hint:* Given a prime P, let $N = 2 \cdot 3 \cdot 5 \cdots P + 1$, the product being taken over all primes $\leq P$. Show that a prime dividing N is bigger than P.]

5. Let n be an integer ≥ 2.

(a) Show that any integer x is congruent mod n to a unique integer m such that $0 \leq m < n$.

(b) Show that any integer $x \neq 0$, relatively prime to n, is congruent to a unique integer m relatively prime to n, such that $0 < m < n$.

(c) Let $\varphi(n)$ be the number of integers m relatively prime to n, such that $0 < m < n$. We call φ the *Euler phi function*. If $n = p$ is a prime number, what is $\varphi(p)$?

(d) Determine $\varphi(n)$ for each integer n with $1 \leq n \leq 10$.

6. Let n, n' be relatively prime positive integers. Let a, b be integers. Show that the congruences

$$x \equiv a \pmod{n},$$

$$x \equiv b \pmod{n'}$$

can be solved simultaneously with some $x \in \mathbf{Z}$.

7. Let a, b be non-zero relatively prime integers. Show that $1/ab$ can be written in the form

$$\frac{1}{ab} = \frac{x}{a} + \frac{y}{b}$$

with some integers x, y.

8. Show that any rational number $a \neq 0$ can be written in the form

$$a = \frac{x_1}{p_1^{r_1}} + \cdots + \frac{x_n}{p_n^{r_n}},$$

where $x_1, \ldots, x_n$ are integers, $p_1, \ldots, p_n$ are distinct prime numbers, and $r_1, \ldots, r_n$ are integers ≥ 0.

9. Let p be a prime number and n an integer, $1 \leq n \leq p - 1$. Show that the binomial coefficient $\binom{p}{n}$ is divisible by p.

10. For all integers x, y show that $(x + y)^p \equiv x^p + y^p \pmod{p}$.

CHAPTER II

Groups

§1. Groups and examples

A *group* G is a set, together with a rule (called a law of composition) which to each pair of elements x, y in G associates an element denoted by xy in G, having the following properties.

GR 1. *For all x, y, z in G we have associativity, namely*

$$(xy)z = x(yz).$$

GR 2. *There exists an element e of G such that $ex = xe = x$ for all x in G.*

GR 3. *If x is an element of G, then there exists an element y of G such that $xy = yx = e$.*

Strictly speaking, we call G a *multiplicative* group. If we denote the element of G associated with the pair (x, y) by $x + y$, then we write GR 1 in the form

$$(x + y) + z = x + (y + z),$$

GR 2 in the form that there exists an element 0 such that

$$0 + x = x + 0 = x$$

for all x in G, and GR 3 in the form that given $x \in G$, there exists an element y of G such that

$$x + y = y + x = 0.$$

With this notation, we call G an *additive* group. We shall use the $+$ notation only when the group satisfies the additional rule

$$x + y = y + x$$

for all x, y in G. With the multiplicative notation, this is written $xy = yx$ for all x, y in G, and if G has this property, we call G a *commutative*, or *abelian* group.

We shall now give examples of groups. Many of these involve notions which the reader will no doubt have encountered already in other courses.

12

Example 1.   Let **Q** denote the rational numbers, i.e. the set of all fractions m/n where m, n are integers, and $n \neq 0$. Then **Q** is a group under addition.   Furthermore, the non-zero elements of **Q** form a group under multiplication.

Example 2.   The real numbers and complex numbers are groups under addition.   The non-zero real numbers, and non-zero complex numbers are groups under multiplication.   We shall always denote the real and complex numbers by **R** and **C** respectively.

Example 3.   The complex numbers of absolute value 1 form a group under multiplication.

Example 4.   The set consisting of the numbers $1, -1$ is a group under multiplication, and this group has 2 elements.

Example 5.   The set consisting of the numbers $1, -1, i, -i$ is a group under multiplication.   This group has 4 elements.

Example 6.   *The direct product.*   Let G, G' be groups.   Let $G \times G'$ be the set consisting of all pairs (x, x') with $x \in G$ and $x' \in G'$.   If (x, x') and (y, y') are such pairs, define their product to be $(xy, x'y')$.   Then $G \times G'$ is a group.

It is a simple matter to verify that all the conditions GR 1, 2, 3 are satisfied, and we leave this to the reader.   We call $G \times G'$ the *direct product* of G and G'.

One may also take a direct product of a finite number of groups.   Thus if $G_1, \ldots, G_n$ are groups, we let

$$\prod_{i=1}^{n} G_i = G_1 \times \cdots \times G_n$$

be the set of all n-tuples $(x_1, \ldots, x_n)$ with $x_i \in G_i$. We define multiplication componentwise, and see at once that $G_1 \times \cdots \times G_n$ is a group. If e_i is the unit element of G_i, then $(e_1, \ldots, e_n)$ is the unit element of the product.

Example 7.   The Euclidean space $\mathbf{R}^n$ is nothing but the product

$$\mathbf{R}^n = \mathbf{R} \times \cdots \times \mathbf{R}$$

taken n times.   In this case, we view **R** as an additive group.

A group consisting of one element is said to be *trivial*.   A group in general may have infinitely many elements, or only a finite number.   If G has only a finite number of elements, then G is called a *finite group*, and the number of elements of G is called its *order*.   The group of Example 4 has order 2, and that of Example 5 has order 4.

In Examples 1 through 5, the groups happen to be commutative. We shall find non-commutative examples later, when we study groups of permutations.

Let G be a group. Let $x_1, \ldots, x_n$ be elements of G. We can then form their product, which we define by induction to be

$$x_1 \cdots x_n = (x_1 \cdots x_{n-1})x_n.$$

Using the associative law of GR 1, one can show that one gets the same value for this product no matter how parentheses are inserted around its elements. For instance for $n = 4$,

$$(x_1 x_2)(x_3 x_4) = x_1(x_2(x_3 x_4))$$

and also

$$(x_1 x_2)(x_3 x_4) = ((x_1 x_2)x_3)x_4.$$

We omit the proof in the general case (done by induction), because it involves slight notational complications which we don't want to go into. The above product will also be written

$$\prod_{i=1}^{n} x_i.$$

If the group is written additively, then we write the sum sign instead of the product sign, so that a sum of n terms looks like

$$\sum_{i=1}^{n} x_i = (x_1 + \cdots + x_{n-1}) + x_n = x_1 + \cdots + x_n.$$

The group G being commutative, and written additively, then it can be shown by induction that the above sum is independent of the order in which $x_1, \ldots, x_n$ are taken. We shall again omit the proof. For example, if $n = 4$,

$$\begin{aligned}
(x_1 + x_2) + (x_3 + x_4) &= x_1 + (x_2 + x_3 + x_4) \\
&= x_1 + (x_3 + x_2 + x_4) \\
&= x_3 + (x_1 + x_2 + x_4).
\end{aligned}$$

We shall now prove various simple statements which hold for all groups.

Let G be a group. *The element e of G whose existence is asserted by GR 2 is uniquely determined*, because if e, e' both satisfy this condition, then

$$e' = ee' = e.$$

We call this element the *unit element* of G. We call it the *zero* element in the additive case.

Let $x \in G$. The element y such that $yx = xy = e$ is uniquely determined, because if z satisfies $zx = xz = e$, then

$$z = ez = (yx)z = y(xz) = ye = y.$$

We call y the *inverse* of x, and denote it by x^{-1}. In the additive notation, we write $y = -x$.

Let G be a group, and H a subset of G. We shall say that H is a *subgroup* if it contains the unit element, and if, whenever x, $y \in H$, then xy and x^{-1} are also elements of H. (Additively, we write $x + y \in H$ and $-x \in H$.) Then H is itself a group in its own right, the law of composition in H being the same as that in G. The unit element of G constitutes a subgroup, and G is a subgroup of itself.

Example 8.   The additive group of rational numbers is a subgroup of the additive group of real numbers. The group of complex numbers of absolute value 1 is a subgroup of the multiplicative group of non-zero complex numbers. The group $\{1, -1\}$ is a subgroup of $\{1, -1, i, -i\}$.

There is a general way of obtaining subgroups from a group. Let S be a subset of a group G, having at least one element. Let H be the set of elements of G consisting of all products $x_1 \cdots x_n$ such that x_i or x_i^{-1} is an element of S for each i, and also containing the unit element. Then H is obviously a subgroup of G, called the subgroup *generated* by S. We also say that S is a *set of generators* of H.

Example 9.   The number 1 is a generator for the additive group of integers. Indeed, every integer can be written in the form

$$1 + 1 + \cdots + 1$$

or

$$-1 - 1 - \cdots - 1,$$

or it is the 0 integer.

Observe that in additive notation, the condition that S be a set of generators for the group is that every element of the group not 0 can be written

$$x_1 + \cdots + x_n,$$

where $x_i \in S$ or $-x_i \in S$.

Example 10.   Let G be a group, and a an element of G. If n is a positive integer, we define

$$a^n = a \cdots a,$$

the product being taken n times. We define $a^0 = e$. Then a is a generator for a subgroup of G, consisting of all the elements $(a^{-1})^n$ and a^m for all integers n, $m \geqq 0$.

EXERCISES

1. Let G be a group and a, b, c elements of G. If $ab = ac$, show that $b = c$.

2. Let G, G' be finite groups, of orders m, n respectively. What is the order of $G \times G'$?

3. Let $x_1, \ldots, x_n$ be elements of a group G. Show (by induction) that

$$(x_1 \cdots x_n)^{-1} = x_n^{-1} \cdots x_1^{-1}.$$

What does this look like in additive notation? For two elements x, $y \in G$, we have $(xy)^{-1} = y^{-1}x^{-1}$. Write this also in additive notation.

4. Let G be a group and $x \in G$. Suppose that there is an integer $n \geq 1$ such that $x^n = e$. Show that there is an integer $m \geq 1$ such that $x^{-1} = x^m$.

5. Let G be a finite group. Show that given $x \in G$, there exists an integer $n \geq 1$ such that $x^n = e$.

6. Let G be a finite group and S a set of generators. Show that every element of G can be written in the form

$$x_1 \cdots x_n,$$

where $x_i \in S$.

7. There exists a group G of order 4 having two generators x, y such that $x^2 = y^2 = e$ and $xy = yx$. Determine all subgroups of G. Show that

$$G = \{e, x, y, xy\}.$$

8. There exists a group G of order 8 having two generators x, y such that $x^4 = y^2 = e$ and $xy = yx^3$. Show that the elements

$$x^i y^j$$

with integers i, j such that $i = 0, 1, 2, 3$ and $j = 0, 1$ are distinct elements of G, and hence constitute all elements of G. Determine all subgroups of G.

9. There exists a group G of order 8 having generators denoted by i, j, k such that

$$ij = k, \qquad jk = i, \qquad ki = j,$$
$$i^2 = j^2 = k^2.$$

Denote i^2 by m. Show that the elements e, i, j, k, m, mi, mj, mk are the distinct elements of G. Determine all subgroups of G. (This group G is called the *quaternion group*.) One frequently writes -1, $-i$, $-j$, $-k$ instead of m, mi, mj, mk.

10. There exists a group G of order 12 having generators x, y such that $x^6 = y^2 = e$ and $xy = yx^5$. Show that the elements

$$x^i y^j$$

with $0 \leq i \leq 5$ and $0 \leq j \leq 1$ are the distinct elements of G. Determine all subgroups of G.

11. The groups of Exercises 8 and 10 have representations as groups of symmetries. For instance, in Exercise 8, let σ be the rotation which maps each corner of the square

on the next corner (taking, say counterclockwise rotation), and let τ be the reflection across the indicated diagonal. Show geometrically that σ and τ satisfy the relations of Exercise 8. Express in terms of powers of σ and τ the reflection across the horizontal line as indicated on the square.

12. In the case of Exercise 10, do the analogous geometric interpretation, taking a hexagon instead of a square.

(*Note:* The groups of Exercises 11 and 12 can essentially be understood as groups of permutations of the vertices. Cf. Exercises 12 and 13 of §5.)

13. Let G be a group and H a subgroup. Let $x \in G$. Let xHx^{-1} be the subset of G consisting of all elements xyx^{-1} with $y \in H$. Show that xHx^{-1} is a subgroup of G.

§2. *Mappings*

Let S, S' be sets. A *mapping* (or *map*) *from S to S'* is a rule which to every element of S associates an element of S'. Instead of saying that f is a mapping of S into S', we shall often write the symbols $f: S \to S'$.

If $f: S \to S'$ is a mapping, and x is an element of S, then we denote by $f(x)$ the element of S' associated to x by f. We call $f(x)$ the *value* of f at x, or also the *image* of x under f. The set of all elements $f(x)$, for all $x \in S$, is called the *image* of f. If T is a subset of S, then the set of elements $f(x)$ for all $x \in T$ is called the *image* of T, and denoted by $f(T)$.

If f is as above, we often write $x \mapsto f(x)$ to denote the image of x under f. Note that we distinguish two types of arrows, namely $\to$ and $\mapsto$.

Example 1. Let S and S' be both equal to **R**. Let $f: \mathbf{R} \to \mathbf{R}$ be the mapping $f(x) = x^2$, i.e. the mapping whose value at x is x^2. We can also express this by saying that f is the mapping such that $x \mapsto x^2$. The image of f is the set of real numbers ≥ 0.

Let $f: S \to S'$ be a mapping, and T a subset of S. Then we can define a map $T \to S'$ by the same rule $x \mapsto f(x)$ for $x \in T$. In other words, we can view f as defined only on T. This map is called the *restriction* of f to T and is denoted by $f \mid T: T \to S'$.

Let S, S' be sets. A map $f: S \to S'$ is said to be *injective* if whenever $x, y \in S$ and $x \neq y$ then $f(x) \neq f(y)$.

Example 2.   The mapping f of Example 1 is not injective. Indeed, we have $f(1) = f(-1)$. Let $g: \mathbf{R} \to \mathbf{R}$ be the mapping $x \mapsto x + 1$. Then g is injective, because if $x \neq y$ then $x + 1 \neq y + 1$, i.e. $g(x) \neq g(y)$.

Let S, S' be sets. A map $f: S \to S'$ is said to be *surjective* if the image $f(S)$ of S is equal to all of S'. This means that given any element $x' \in S'$, there exists an element $x \in S$ such that $f(x) = x'$. One also says that f is *onto* S'.

Example 3.   Let $f: \mathbf{R} \to \mathbf{R}$ be the mapping $f(x) = x^2$. Then f is not surjective, because no negative number is in the image of f.

Let $g: \mathbf{R} \to \mathbf{R}$ be the mapping $g(x) = x + 1$. Then g is surjective, because given a number y, we have $y = g(y - 1)$.

Remark.   Let $\mathbf{R}'$ denote the set of real numbers ≥ 0. One can view the association $x \mapsto x^2$ as a map of $\mathbf{R}$ into $\mathbf{R}'$. When so viewed, the map is then surjective. Thus it is a reasonable convention *not* to identify this map with the map $f: \mathbf{R} \to \mathbf{R}$ defined by the same formula. To be completely accurate, we should therefore denote the set of arrival and the set of departure of the map into our notation, and for instance write

$$f_{S'}^{S}: S \to S'$$

instead of our $f: S \to S'$. In practice, this notation is too clumsy, so that one omits the indices S, S'. However, the reader should keep in mind the distinction between the maps

$$f_{\mathbf{R}'}^{\mathbf{R}}: \mathbf{R} \to \mathbf{R}' \qquad \text{and} \qquad f_{\mathbf{R}}^{\mathbf{R}}: \mathbf{R} \to \mathbf{R}$$

both defined by the rule $x \mapsto x^2$. The first map is surjective whereas the second one is *not*.

Let S, S' be sets, and $f: S \to S'$ a mapping. We say that f is *bijective* if f is both injective and surjective. This means that given an element $x' \in S'$, there exists a unique element $x \in S$ such that $f(x) = x'$. (Existence because f is surjective, and uniqueness because f is injective.)

Example 4.   Let J_n be the set of integers $\{1, 2, \ldots, n\}$. A bijective map $\sigma: J_n \to J_n$ is called a *permutation* of the integers from 1 to n. Thus, in particular, a permutation σ as above is a mapping $i \mapsto \sigma(i)$. We shall study permutations in greater detail later in this chapter.

Example 5.   Let S be a non-empty set, and let

$$I: S \to S$$

be the map such that $I(x) = x$ for all $x \in S$. Then I is called the *identity* mapping, and also denoted by *id*. It is obviously bijective.

Let $f: S \to S'$ be a bijective map. We can then define its *inverse* mapping, denoted by f^{-1}, by the rule:

$$f^{-1}(x') = \text{unique element } x \in S \text{ such that } f(x) = x'.$$

Example 6. If $g: \mathbf{R} \to \mathbf{R}$ is the map such that $g(x) = x + 1$, then $g^{-1}: \mathbf{R} \to \mathbf{R}$ is the map such that $g^{-1}(x) = x - 1$.

Example 7. Let $\mathbf{R}^+$ denote the set of positive real numbers (i.e. real numbers > 0). Let $h: \mathbf{R}^+ \to \mathbf{R}^+$ be the map $h(x) = x^2$. Then h is bijective, and its inverse mapping is the square root mapping, i.e. $h^{-1}(x) = \sqrt{x}$ for all $x \in \mathbf{R}$, $x > 0$.

Remark. If $f: S \to S'$ is a mapping which is not necessarily surjective or injective, it is still convenient to introduce the notion of inverse image of an element of S'. Thus, if $y \in S'$ we define $f^{-1}(y)$ to be the set of all elements $x \in S$ such that $f(x) = y$. If y is not in the image of f, then $f^{-1}(y)$ is *empty*. If y is in the image of f, then $f^{-1}(y)$ may consist of more than one element.

Example 8. Let $f: \mathbf{R} \to \mathbf{R}$ be the mapping $f(x) = x^2$. Then

$$f^{-1}(1) = \{1, -1\},$$

and $f^{-1}(-2)$ is empty.

Let S, T, U be sets, and let

$$f: S \to T \qquad \text{and} \qquad g: T \to U$$

be mappings. Then we can form the *composite mapping*

$$g \circ f: S \to U$$

defined by the rule

$$(g \circ f)(x) = g(f(x))$$

for all $x \in S$.

Example 9. Let $f: \mathbf{R} \to \mathbf{R}$ be the map $f(x) = x^2$, and $g: \mathbf{R} \to \mathbf{R}$ the map $g(x) = x + 1$. Then $g(f(x)) = x^2 + 1$. Note that in this case, we can form also $f(g(x)) = f(x + 1) = (x + 1)^2$, and thus that

$$f \circ g \neq g \circ f.$$

Composition of mappings is associative. This means: Let S, T, U, V be sets, and let

$$f: S \to T, \quad g: T \to U, \quad h: U \to V$$

be mappings. Then

$$h \circ (g \circ f) = (h \circ g) \circ f.$$

Proof. The proof is very simple. By definition, we have, for any element $x \in S$,

$$(h \circ (g \circ f))(x) = h((g \circ f)(x)) = h(g(f(x))).$$

On the other hand,

$$((h \circ g) \circ f)(x) = (h \circ g)(f(x)) = h(g(f(x))).$$

By definition, this means that $(h \circ g) \circ f = h \circ (g \circ f)$.

Let S, T, U be sets, and $f: S \to T$, $g: T \to U$ mappings. If f and g are injective, then $g \circ f$ is injective. If f and g are surjective, then $g \circ f$ is surjective. If f and g are bijective, then so is $g \circ f$.

Proof. As to the first statement, assume that f, g are injective. Let $x, y \in S$ and $x \neq y$. Then $f(x) \neq f(y)$ because f is injective, and hence $g(f(x)) \neq g(f(y))$ because g is injective. By the definition of the composite map, we conclude that $g \circ f$ is injective. The second statement will be left as an exercise. The third is a consequence of the first two, and the definition of bijective.

Let

$$f: S \to S'$$

be a bijective mapping, and let f^{-1} be its inverse. Then we see from the definition of the inverse that

$$f \circ f^{-1} = I_{S'} \quad \text{and} \quad f^{-1} \circ f = I_S,$$

where we have indexed the identity mappings with their corresponding sets. In other words, by definition, for $x \in S$ and $x' \in S'$,

$$f(f^{-1}(x')) = x' \quad \text{and} \quad f^{-1}(f(x)) = x.$$

Example 10. *Let S be a non-empty set, and let G be the set of bijective mappings of S onto itself. Then G is a group, the law of composition being composition of mappings.*

Proof. If $f: S \to S$, $g: S \to S$ are two bijections of S onto itself, then the composite map $g \circ f$ is a map of S into itself, and is bijective. Condition GR 1 is nothing but the associativity for mappings in this case. The unit element of GR 2 is the identity mapping I. As for GR 3, it is nothing but the existence of the inverse mapping, so that all three axioms are satisfied.

We observe that the group G of Example 10 generalizes the notion of permutation, and in fact, we shall call this group G the *permutation group* of the set S. In practice, it is not always so that one wants to consider only permutations of the integers $\{1, \ldots, n\}$. One wants to consider also permutations of other sets. As a matter of notation, if σ, τ are permutations, one often writes $\sigma\tau$ instead of $\sigma \circ \tau$, to fit the abstract formalism of the law of composition of the group.

EXERCISES

1. Let $f: S \to S'$ be a mapping, and assume that there exists a map $g: S' \to S$ such that

$$g \circ f = I_S \quad \text{and} \quad f \circ g = I_{S'},$$

in other words, f has an inverse. Show that f is both injective and surjective.

2. Let $\sigma_1, \ldots, \sigma_r$ be permutations of a set S. Show that

$$(\sigma_1 \cdots \sigma_r)^{-1} = \sigma_r^{-1} \cdots \sigma_1^{-1}.$$

3. Let S be a non-empty set and G a group. Let $M(S, G)$ be the set of mappings of S into G. If f, $g \in M(S, G)$, define $fg: S \to G$ to be the map such that $(fg)(x) = f(x)g(x)$. Show that $M(S, G)$ is a group. If G is written additively, how would you write the law of composition in $M(S, G)$?

4. Give an example of two permutations of the integers $\{1, 2, 3\}$ which do not commute.

5. Let S be a set, G a group, and $f: S \to G$ a bijective mapping. For each x, $y \in S$ define the product

$$xy = f^{-1}(f(x)f(y)).$$

Show that this multiplication defines a group structure on S.

6. Let X, Y be sets and $f: X \to Y$ a mapping. Let Z be a subset of Y. Define $f^{-1}(Z)$ to be the set of all $x \in X$ such that $f(x) \in Z$. Prove that if Z, W are subsets of Y then

$$f^{-1}(Z \cup W) = f^{-1}(Z) \cup f^{-1}(W),$$
$$f^{-1}(Z \cap W) = f^{-1}(Z) \cap f^{-1}(W).$$

§3. *Homomorphisms*

Let G, G' be groups. A *homomorphism*

$$f: G \to G'$$

of G into G' is a map having the following property: For all x, $y \in G$, we have

$$f(xy) = f(x)f(y)$$

(and in additive notation, $f(x + y) = f(x) + f(y)$).

Example 1. Let G be a commutative group. The map $x \mapsto x^{-1}$ of G into itself is a homomorphism. In additive notation, this map looks like $x \mapsto -x$. The verification that it has the property defining a homomorphism is immediate.

Example 2. The map

$$z \mapsto |z|$$

is a homomorphism of the multiplicative group of non-zero complex numbers into the multiplicative group of non-zero complex numbers (in fact, into the multiplicative group of positive real numbers).

Example 3. The map

$$x \mapsto e^x$$

is a homomorphism of the additive group of real numbers into the multiplicative group of positive real numbers. Its inverse map, the logarithm, is also a homomorphism.

Example 4. Let G be a group. Let x be an element of G. If n is a positive integer, we define x^n to be

$$xx \cdots x$$

the product being taken n times. If $n = 0$, we define $x^0 = e$. If $n = -m$ where m is an integer > 0, we define

$$x^{-m} = (x^{-1})^m.$$

It is then routinely verified that the rule

$$x^{m+n} = x^m x^n$$

holds for all integers m, n. As this verification is slightly tedious, we omit it. But we note that in view of this property, the map

$$n \mapsto x^n$$

is a homomorphism of the additive group of integers $\mathbf{Z}$ into G. When G is written additively, we write nx instead of x^n.

For the sake of brevity, we sometimes say: "Let $f: G \to G'$ be a group-homomorphism" instead of saying: "Let G, G' be groups, and let f be a homomorphism of G into G'."

Let $f: G \to G'$ be a group-homomorphism, and let e, e' be the unit elements of G, G' respectively. Then $f(e) = e'$.

Proof. We have $f(e) = f(ee) = f(e)f(e)$. Multiplying by $f(e)^{-1}$ gives the desired result.

Let $f: G \to G'$ be a group-homomorphism. Let $x \in G$. Then

$$f(x^{-1}) = f(x)^{-1}.$$

Proof. We have

$$e' = f(e) = f(xx^{-1}) = f(x)f(x^{-1}).$$

Let $f: G \to G'$ and $g: G' \to G''$ be group-homomorphisms. Then the composite map $g \circ f$ is a group-homomorphism of G into G''.

Proof. We have

$$(g \circ f)(xy) = g(f(xy)) = g(f(x)f(y)) = g(f(x))g(f(y)).$$

Let $f: G \to G'$ be a group-homomorphism. We define the *kernel* of f to consist of all elements $x \in G$ such that $f(x) = e'$. *It is trivially verified that the kernel is a subgroup of G.* (It contains e because we proved that $f(e) = e'$. Prove the other properties as a trivial exercise.)

Let $f: G \to G'$ be a group-homomorphism. If the kernel of f consists of e alone, then f is injective.

Proof. Let $x, y \in G$ and suppose that $f(x) = f(y)$. Then

$$e' = f(x)f(y)^{-1} = f(x)f(y^{-1}) = f(xy^{-1}).$$

Hence $xy^{-1} = e$, and consequently $x = y$, thus showing that f is injective.

Let $f: G \to G'$ be a group-homomorphism. The image of f is a subgroup of G'.

Proof. If $x' = f(x)$ with $x \in G$, and $y' = f(y)$ with $y \in G$, then

$$x'y' = f(xy) = f(x)f(y)$$

is also in the image. Also, e' is in the image, and $x'^{-1} = f(x^{-1})$ is in the image. Hence the image is a subgroup.

Let $f: G \to G'$ be a group-homomorphism. We shall say that f is an *isomorphism* (or more precisely a group-isomorphism) if there exists a homomorphism $g: G' \to G$ such that $f \circ g$ and $g \circ f$ are the identity mappings of G' and G respectively.

Example 5. The function *exp* is an isomorphism of the additive group of the real numbers onto the multiplicative group of positive real numbers. Its inverse is the log.

Example 6.   Let G be a commutative group. The map

$$f: x \mapsto x^{-1}$$

is an isomorphism of G onto itself. What is $f \circ f$? What is f^{-1}?

A group-homomorphism $f: G \to G'$ which is injective and surjective is an isomorphism.

Proof.   We let $f^{-1}: G' \to G$ be the inverse mapping. All we need to prove is that f^{-1} is a group-homomorphism. Let x', $y' \in G'$, and let x, $y \in G$ be such that $f(x) = x'$ and $f(y) = y'$. Then $f(xy) = x'y'$. Hence by definition,

$$f^{-1}(x'y') = xy = f^{-1}(x')f^{-1}(y').$$

This proves that f^{-1} is a homomorphism, as desired.

By an *automorphism* of a group, one means an isomorphism of the group onto itself. The map of Example 6 is an automorphism of the commutative group G. What does it look like in additive notation? Examples of automorphisms will be given in the exercises. (Cf. Exercises 3, 4, 5.)

We shall now see that every group is isomorphic to a group of permutations of some set.

Example 7.   Let G be a group. For each $a \in G$, let

$$T_a: G \to G$$

be the map such that $T_a(x) = ax$. We call T the *left translation by a*. We contend that T_a is a bijection of G onto itself, i.e. a permutation of G. If $x \neq y$ then $ax \neq ay$ (multiply on the left by a^{-1} to see this), and hence T_a is injective. It is surjective, because given $x \in G$, we have

$$x = T_a(a^{-1}x).$$

The inverse mapping of T_a is obviously $T_{a^{-1}}$. Thus the map

$$a \mapsto T_a$$

is a map from G into the group of permutations of the set G. We contend that it is a *homomorphism*. Indeed, for $a, b \in G$ we have

$$T_{ab}(x) = abx = T_a(T_b(x)),$$

so that $T_{ab} = T_a T_b$. Furthermore, one sees at once that this homomorphism is injective. Thus the map

$$a \mapsto T_a \qquad\qquad (a \in G)$$

is an isomorphism of G onto a subgroup of the group of all permutations of G. Of course, not every permutation is given by a translation, i.e. the image of the map is not equal to the full group of permutations of G.

The terminology of Example 7 is taken from Euclidean geometry. Let $G = \mathbf{R}^2 = \mathbf{R} \times \mathbf{R}$. We visualize G as the plane. Elements of G are called 2-dimensional vectors. If $A \in \mathbf{R} \times \mathbf{R}$, then the translation

$$T_A : \mathbf{R} \times \mathbf{R} \to \mathbf{R} \times \mathbf{R}$$

such that $T_A(X) = X + A$ for all $X \in \mathbf{R} \times \mathbf{R}$ is visualized as the usual translation of X by means of the vector A.

Example 8. The group of homomorphisms. Let A, B be *abelian groups*, written additively. Let $\text{Hom}(A, B)$ denote the set of homomorphisms of A into B. We can make $\text{Hom}(A, B)$ into a group as follows. If f, g are homomorphisms of A into B, we define $f + g : A \to B$ to be the map such that

$$(f + g)(x) = f(x) + g(x)$$

for all $x \in A$. It is a simple matter to verify that the three group axioms are satisfied. In fact, if f, g, $h \in \text{Hom}(A, B)$, then for all $x \in A$,

$$((f + g) + h)(x) = (f + g)(x) + h(x) = f(x) + g(x) + h(x),$$

and

$$(f + (g + h))(x) = f(x) + (g + h)(x) = f(x) + g(x) + h(x).$$

Hence $f + (g + h) = (f + g) + h$. We have an additive unit element, namely the map 0 (called zero) which to each element of A assigns the zero element of B. It obviously satisfies condition **GR 2**. Furthermore, the map $-f$ such that $(-f)(x) = -f(x)$ has the property that

$$f + (-f) = 0.$$

Finally, we must of course observe that $f + g$ and $-f$ are homomorphisms. Indeed, for x, $y \in A$,

$$(f + g)(x + y) = f(x + y) + g(x + y) = f(x) + f(y) + g(x) + g(y)$$
$$= f(x) + g(x) + f(y) + g(y)$$
$$= (f + g)(x) + (f + g)(y),$$

so that $f + g$ is a homomorphism. Also,

$$(-f)(x + y) = -f(x + y) = -(f(x) + f(y)) = -f(x) - f(y),$$

and hence $-f$ is a homomorphism. This proves that $\text{Hom}(A, B)$ is a group.

EXERCISES

1. Let $\mathbf{R}^\times$ be the multiplicative group of non-zero real numbers. Describe explicitly the kernel of the homomorphism absolute value

$$x \mapsto |x|$$

of $\mathbf{R}^\times$ into itself. What is the image of this homomorphism?

2. Let $\mathbf{C}^\times$ be the multiplicative group of non-zero complex numbers. What is the kernel of the homomorphism absolute value

$$z \mapsto |z|$$

of $\mathbf{C}^\times$ into $\mathbf{R}^\times$?

3. Let G be a group. Let a be an element of G. Let

$$\sigma_a : G \to G$$

be the map such that

$$\sigma_a(x) = axa^{-1}.$$

Show that the set of all such maps σ_a with $a \in G$ is a group.

4. Show that the set of automorphisms of a group G is itself a group, denoted by $\text{Aut}(G)$.

5. Let the notation be as in Exercise 3. Show that the association $a \mapsto \sigma_a$ is a homomorphism of G into $\text{Aut}(G)$. The image of this homomorphism is called the group of *inner* automorphisms of G. Thus an inner automorphism of G is one which is equal to some σ_a for some $a \in G$.

6. Let G be a finite abelian group, of order n, and let $a_1, \ldots, a_n$ be its elements. Show that the product $a_1 \cdots a_n$ is an element whose square is the unit element.

7. (a) Let G be a subgroup of the group of permutations of a set S. If s, t are elements of S, we define s to be equivalent to t if there exists $\sigma \in G$ such that $\sigma s = t$. Show that this is an equivalence relation.

(b) Let $s \in S$, and let G_s be the set of all $\sigma \in G$ such that $\sigma s = s$. Show that G_s is a subgroup of G.

(c) If $\tau \in G$ is such that $\tau s = t$, what is the relation between G_s and G_t?

8. Show that every group of order 4 is commutative.

9. Let G be a commutative group, and n a positive integer. Show that the map $x \mapsto x^n$ is a homomorphism of G into itself.

§4. Cosets and normal subgroups

Let G be a group, and H a subgroup. Let a be an element of G. The set of all elements ax with $x \in H$ is called a *coset* of H in G. We denote it by aH.

In additive notation, a coset of H would be written $a + H$.

Since a group G may not be commutative, we shall in fact call aH a *left* coset of H. Similarly, we could define *right* cosets, but in the sequel, unless otherwise specified, *coset* will mean left coset.

THEOREM 1. *Let aH and bH be cosets of H in the group G. Either these cosets are equal, or they have no element in common.*

Proof. Suppose that aH and bH have one element in common. We shall prove that they are equal. Let x, y be elements of H such that $ax = by$. Then $a = byx^{-1}$. But yx^{-1} is an element of H. If ax' is an arbitrary element of aH, with x' in H, then

$$ax' = b(yx^{-1})x'.$$

Since $(yx^{-1})x'$ lies in H, we conclude that ax' lies in bH. Hence aH is contained in bH. Similarly, bH is contained in aH, and hence our cosets are equal.

THEOREM 2. *Let G be a group, and H a finite subgroup. Then the number of elements of a coset aH is equal to the number of elements in H.*

Proof. Let x, x' be distinct elements of H. Then ax and ax' are distinct, for if $ax = ax'$, then multiplying by a^{-1} on the left shows that $x = x'$. Hence if $x_1, \ldots, x_n$ are the distinct elements of H, then $ax_1, \ldots, ax_n$ are the distinct elements of aH, whence our assertion follows.

Let G be a group, and H a subgroup. The number of distinct cosets of H in G is called the *index* of H in G. This index may of course be infinite. If G is a finite group, then the index of any subgroup is finite. The index of a subgroup H is denoted by $(G : H)$.

COROLLARY. *Let G be a finite group and H a subgroup. Then*

$$\text{order of } G = (G : H) \text{ (order of } H).$$

Proof. Every element of G lies in some coset (namely, a lies in the coset aH since $a = ae$). By Theorem 1, every element lies in precisely one coset, and by Theorem 2, any two cosets have the same number of elements. The formula of our corollary is therefore clear.

The corollary also shows that the order of a subgroup of a finite group divides the order of the group.

Example 1. Let S_n be the group of permutations of $\{1, \ldots, n\}$. Let H be the subset of S_n consisting of all permutations σ such that $\sigma(n) = n$ (i.e. all permutations leaving n fixed). It is clear that H is a subgroup, and we may view H as the permutation group S_{n-1}. (We assume $n > 1$.) We wish to describe all the cosets of H. For each integer i with $1 \leqq i \leqq n$, let τ_i be the permutation such that $\tau_i(n) = i$, $\tau_i(i) = n$, and τ_i leaves all integers other than n and i fixed. We contend that the cosets

$$\tau_1 H, \ldots, \tau_n H$$

are distinct, and constitute all distinct cosets of H in S_n.

To see this, let $\sigma \in S_n$, and suppose $\sigma(n) = i$. Then

$$\tau_i^{-1}\sigma(n) = \tau_i^{-1}(i) = n.$$

Hence $\tau_i^{-1}\sigma$ lies in H, and therefore σ lies in $\tau_i H$. We have shown that every element of G lies in some coset $\tau_i H$, and hence $\tau_1 H, \ldots, \tau_n H$ yield all the cosets. We must still show that these cosets are distinct. If $i \neq j$, then for any $\sigma \in H$, $\tau_i \sigma(n) = \tau_i(n) = i$ and $\tau_j \sigma(n) = \tau_j(n) = n$. Hence $\tau_i H$ and $\tau_j H$ cannot have any element in common, since elements of $\tau_i H$ and $\tau_j H$ have distinct effects on n. This proves what we wanted.

From the corollary of Theorem 2, we conclude that

$$\text{order of } S_n = n \cdot \text{order of } S_{n-1}.$$

By induction, we see immediately that

$$\text{order of } S_n = n! = n(n-1) \cdots 1.$$

Let G be a group. A subgroup H is said to be *normal* if it is the kernel of some homomorphism of G into some group.

THEOREM 3. *Let $f: G \rightarrow G'$ be a homomorphism of groups. Let H be its kernel, and let a' be an element of G', which is in the image of f, say $a' = f(a)$ for $a \in G$. Then the set of elements x in G such that $f(x) = a'$ is precisely the coset aH.*

Proof. Let $x \in aH$, so that $x = ah$ with some $h \in H$. Then

$$f(x) = f(a)f(h) = f(a).$$

Conversely, suppose that $x \in G$, and $f(x) = a'$. Then

$$f(a^{-1}x) = f(a)^{-1}f(x) = a'^{-1}a' = e'.$$

Hence $a^{-1}x$ lies in the kernel H, say $a^{-1}x = h$ with some $h \in H$. Then $x = ah$, as was to be shown.

In Theorem 3, the coset aH is equal to the *right* coset Ha. This is easily shown; cf. Exercise 2(b).

Let $f: S \rightarrow S'$ be a map. If x' is an element of S', we denoted by $f^{-1}(x')$ the set of all $x \in S$ such that $f(x) = x'$, and called it the *inverse image* of x' under f. It usually consists of more than one element. In Theorem 3, we may say that the inverse image of an element a' of G' is a coset of G.

We wish now to describe a simple test for a subgroup to be normal. We need some convenient notation. Let S, S' be subsets of a group G. We define SS' to be the set of all elements xx' with $x \in S$ and $x' \in S'$.

Then it is easy to verify that if S_1, S_2, S_3 are three subsets of G, then

$$(S_1 S_2)S_3 = S_1(S_2 S_3).$$

This product simply consists of all elements xyz, with $x \in S_1$, $y \in S_2$ and $z \in S_3$.

Example 2. Show that if H is a subgroup of G, then $HH = H$.

THEOREM 4. *Let G be a group and H a subgroup having the property that $xH = Hx$ for all $x \in G$. If aH and bH are cosets of H, then the product $(aH)(bH)$ is also a coset, and the collection of cosets is a group, the product being defined as above.*

Proof. We have $(aH)(bH) = aHbH = abHH = abH$. Hence the product of two cosets is a coset. Condition GR 1 is satisfied in view of the preceding remarks on multiplication of subsets of G. Condition GR 2 is satisfied, the unit element being the coset $eH = H$ itself. (Verify this in detail.) Condition GR 3 is satisfied, the inverse of aH being $a^{-1}H$. (Again verify this in detail.) Hence Theorem 4 is proved.

The group of cosets in Theorem 4 is called the *factor group* of G by H, and denoted by G/H. We note that it is a group of left or right cosets, there being no difference between these by assumption on H. We emphasize that it is this assumption which allowed us to define multiplication of cosets. If the condition $xH = Hx$ for all $x \in G$ is not satisfied, then we cannot define a group of cosets.

COROLLARY 1. *Let G be a group and H a subgroup having the property that $xH = Hx$ for all $x \in G$. Let G/H be the factor group, and let*

$$f: G \to G/H$$

be the map which to each $a \in G$ associates the coset $f(a) = aH$. Then f is a homomorphism, and its kernel is precisely H. Hence H is normal.

Proof. The fact that f is a homomorphism is nothing but a repetition of the definition of the product of cosets. As for its kernel, it is clear that every element of H is in the kernel. Conversely, if $z \in G$, and $f(x) = xH$ is the unit element of G/H, it is the coset H itself, so $xH = H$. This means that $xe = x$ is an element of H, so H is equal to the kernel of f, as desired.

We call the homomorphism f in Corollary 1 the *canonical homomorphism* of G onto the factor group G/H.

COROLLARY 2. *Let* $f: G \to G'$ *be a group homomorphism, whose kernel is* H. *Then* G/H *is isomorphic to the image of* f, *under the map* $aH \mapsto f(aH)$, *i.e. the map which associates with each coset* aH *the element* $f(aH)$ *of* G'.

Proof. All the steps of the proof are essentially obvious, and we leave them as an exercise (cf. Exercise 11).

Example 3.   Consider the subgroup $\mathbf{Z}$ of the additive group of the real numbers $\mathbf{R}$. The factor group $\mathbf{R}/\mathbf{Z}$ is sometimes called the *circle* group. Two elements x, $y \in \mathbf{R}$ are called *congruent* mod $\mathbf{Z}$ if $x - y \in \mathbf{Z}$. This congruence is an equivalence relation, and the congruence classes are precisely the cosets of $\mathbf{Z}$ in $\mathbf{R}$. If $x \equiv y \pmod{\mathbf{Z}}$, then $e^{2\pi i x} = e^{2\pi i y}$, and conversely. Thus the map

$$x \mapsto e^{2\pi i x}$$

defines an isomorphism of $\mathbf{R}/\mathbf{Z}$ with the multiplicative group of complex numbers having absolute value 1. To prove these statements, one must of course know some facts of analysis concerning the exponential function.

Example 4.   Let $\mathbf{C}^{\times}$ be the multiplicative group of non-zero complex numbers, and $\mathbf{R}^+$ the multiplicative group of positive real numbers. Given a complex number α, we can write

$$\alpha = ru$$

where $r \in \mathbf{R}^+$ and u has absolute value 1. (Let $u = \alpha/|\alpha|$.) Such an expression is uniquely determined, and the map

$$\alpha \mapsto \frac{\alpha}{|\alpha|}$$

is a homomorphism of $\mathbf{C}^{\times}$ onto the group of complex numbers of absolute value 1. The kernel is $\mathbf{R}^+$, and it follows that $\mathbf{C}^{\times}/\mathbf{R}^+$ is isomorphic to the group of complex numbers of absolute value 1. (Cf. Exercise 11.)

For coset representatives in Examples 3 and 4, cf. Exercises 21 and 22.

EXERCISES

1. Let $f: G \to G'$ be a homomorphism with kernel H. Assume that G is finite. Show that

$$\text{order of } G = (\text{order of image of } f)(\text{order of } H).$$

2. (a) Let H be a normal subgroup of a group G. Show that if $x \in H$ and $a \in G$, then axa^{-1} also lies in H.

(b) Let H be a normal subgroup of G. Show that the left coset aH is equal to the right coset Ha.

3. Let H be a subgroup of G, and assume that $xHx^{-1} = H$ for all $x \in G$. Then $x^{-1}Hx = H$ for all $x \in G$, and $Hx = xH$ for all $x \in G$.

4. Let G be a group and H a subgroup. Show that H is normal if and only if $xHx^{-1} = H$ for all $x \in G$.

5. If G is commutative, show that every subgroup is normal.

6. Let H_1, H_2 be two normal subgroups of G. Show that $H_1 \cap H_2$ is normal.

7. Let $f: G \to G'$ be a homomorphism, and let H' be a subgroup of G'. Show that $f^{-1}(H')$ is a subgroup of G. If H' is normal in G', show that $f^{-1}(H')$ is a normal subgroup of G.

8. Let $f: G \to G'$ be a surjective homomorphism. Let H be a normal subgroup of G. Show that $f(H)$ is a normal subgroup of G'.

9. Let G be a group. Define the *center* of G to be the subset of all elements a in G such that $ax = xa$ for all $x \in G$. Show that the center is a subgroup, and that it is a normal subgroup. Show that it is the kernel of the homomorphism in Exercise 5, §3.

10. (a) Let G be a commutative group, and H a subgroup. Show that G/H is commutative. (b) Let G be a group and H a normal subgroup. Show that G/H is commutative if and only if H contains all elements $xyx^{-1}y^{-1}$ for $x, y \in G$.

11. Let $f: G \to G'$ be a group-homomorphism, and let H be its kernel. Assume that G' is the image of f. Show that G/H is isomorphic to G'.

12. Let G be a group and H a subgroup. Let N_H be the set of all $x \in G$ such that $xHx^{-1} = H$. Show that N_H is a group containing H, and H is normal in N_H.

13. Let G be a group, H a subgroup, N a normal subgroup. Show that NH is a subgroup, and $NH = HN$.

14. (a) Let G be the set of all maps of $\mathbf{R}$ into itself of type $x \mapsto ax + b$, where $a \in \mathbf{R}$, $a \neq 0$ and $b \in \mathbf{R}$. Show that G is a group. We denote such a map by $\sigma_{a,b}$. Thus $\sigma_{a,b}(x) = ax + b$.

(b) To each map $\sigma_{a,b}$ we associate the number a. Show that the association

$$\sigma_{a,b} \mapsto a$$

is a homomorphism of G into $\mathbf{R}^{\times}$. Describe the kernel.

15. Let G be a group and H a subgroup. If $x, y \in G$, define x to be equivalent to y if x is in the coset yH. Prove that this is an equivalence relation.

16. Let G be a group. Let S be the set of subgroups of G. If H, K are subgroups of G, define H to be equivalent to K if there exists an element $x \in G$ such that $xHx^{-1} = K$. Prove that this is an equivalence relation in S.

17. Let G be a group and S the set of subgroups of G. For each $x \in G$, let $f_x: S \to S$ be the map such that

$$f_x(H) = xHx^{-1}.$$

Show that f_x is a permutation of S, and that the map $x \mapsto f_x$ is a homomorphism of G into the group of permutations of S.

18. Let G be a group and H a subgroup of G. Let S be the set of cosets of H in G. For each $x \in G$, let $g_x: S \to S$ be the map which to each coset yH associates the coset xyH. Prove that g_x is a permutation of S, and that the map $x \mapsto g_x$ is a homomorphism of G into the group of permutations of S.

19. View $\mathbf{Z}$ as a subgroup of the additive group of rational numbers $\mathbf{Q}$. Show that given an element $\bar{x} \in \mathbf{Q}/\mathbf{Z}$ there exists an integer $n \geqq 1$ such that $n\bar{x} = 0$.

20. Let D be the subgroup of $\mathbf{R}$ generated by 2π. Let $\mathbf{R}^\times$ be the multiplicative group of positive real numbers, and $\mathbf{C}^\times$ the multiplicative group of non-zero complex numbers. Show that $\mathbf{C}^\times$ is isomorphic to $\mathbf{R}^+ \times \mathbf{R}/D$ under the map

$$(r, \theta) \mapsto re^{i\theta}.$$

(Of course, you must use properties of the complex exponential map.)

21. Show that every coset of $\mathbf{Z}$ in $\mathbf{R}$ has a unique coset representative x such that $0 \leqq x < 1$. [*Hint:* For each real number y, let n be the integer such that $n \leqq y < n + 1$.]

22. Show that every coset of $\mathbf{R}^+$ in $\mathbf{C}^\times$ has a unique representative complex number of absolute value 1.

23. Show that every subgroup of the quaternion group is normal. (Cf. Exercise 9 of §1.)

24. Determine all normal subgroups of the group described in Exercise 8 of §1.

§5. *Permutation groups*

In this section, we investigate more closely the permutation group S_n of n elements $\{1, \ldots, n\} = J_n$.

If $\sigma \in S_n$, then we recall that $\sigma^{-1}: J_n \to J_n$ is the permutation such that $\sigma^{-1}(k) =$ unique integer $j \in J_n$ such that $\sigma(j) = k$. A *transposition* τ is a permutation which interchanges two numbers and leaves the others fixed, i.e. there exist integers $i, j \in J_n$, $i \neq j$ such that $\tau(i) = j$, $\tau(j) = i$, and $\tau(k) = k$ if $k \neq i$ and $k \neq j$. One sees at once that if τ is a transposition, then $\tau^{-1} = \tau$ and $\tau^2 = I$. In particular, the inverse of a transposition is a transposition.

THEOREM 5. *Every permutation of J_n can be expressed as a product of transpositions.*

Proof. We shall prove our assertion by induction on n. For $n = 1$, there is nothing to prove. Let $n > 1$ and assume the assertion proved for $n - 1$. Let σ be a permutation of J_n. Let $\sigma(n) = k$. Let τ be the transposition of J_n such that $\tau(k) = n$, $\tau(n) = k$. Then $\tau\sigma$ is a permutation such that

$$\tau\sigma(n) = \tau(k) = n.$$

In other words, $\tau\sigma$ leaves n fixed. We may therefore view $\tau\sigma$ as a permutation of J_{n-1}, and by induction, there exist transpositions $\tau_1, \ldots, \tau_s$ of J_{n-1}, leaving n fixed, such that

$$\tau\sigma = \tau_1 \cdots \tau_s.$$

We can now write

$$\sigma = \tau^{-1}\tau_1 \cdots \tau_s,$$

thereby proving our proposition.

For the next theorem, we need to describe the operation of permutations on mappings. We shall consider the product

$$\mathbf{Z} \times \cdots \times \mathbf{Z} = \mathbf{Z}^n,$$

that is the set of n-tuples of integers. Let σ be a permutation of J_n. Then σ induces a mapping, which we denote by π_σ, of $\mathbf{Z}^n$ into itself, by letting

$$\pi_\sigma(x_1, \ldots, x_n) = (x_{\sigma(1)}, \ldots, x_{\sigma(n)}),$$

for all $x_1, \ldots, x_n \in \mathbf{Z}$. In other words, π_σ simply permutes the factors of $\mathbf{Z}^n$. One verifies at once that

$$\pi_\sigma \circ \pi_\tau = \pi_{\tau\sigma},$$

for all $\sigma, \tau \in S_n$. To see this, let $y_i = x_{\tau(i)}$, then

$$
\begin{aligned}
\pi_\sigma \circ \pi_\tau(x_1, \ldots, x_n) &= \pi_\sigma(x_{\tau(1)}, \ldots, x_{\tau(n)}) \\
&= \pi_\sigma(y_1, \ldots, y_n) \\
&= (y_{\sigma(1)}, \ldots, y_{\sigma(n)}) \\
&= (x_{\tau\sigma(1)}, \ldots, x_{\tau\sigma(n)}) \\
&= \pi_{\tau\sigma}(x_1, \ldots, x_n).
\end{aligned}
$$

Let

$$f : \mathbf{Z} \times \cdots \times \mathbf{Z} \to \mathbf{Z}$$

be a function. We define

$$f^\sigma = f \circ \pi_\sigma,$$

so that

$$f^\sigma(x_1, \ldots, x_n) = f(\pi_\sigma(x_1, \ldots, x_n)) = f(x_{\sigma(1)}, \ldots, x_{\sigma(n)}).$$

From the associativity of mappings, we then have

$$f^{\sigma\tau} = f \circ \pi_{\sigma\tau} = f \circ \pi_\tau \circ \pi_\sigma = (f^\tau)^\sigma.$$

If f and g are two functions of $\mathbf{Z}^n$ into $\mathbf{Z}$, then we may form their sum and product as usual. The sum $f + g$ is defined by the rule

$$(f + g)(x_1, \ldots, x_n) = f(x_1, \ldots, x_n) + g(x_1, \ldots, x_n)$$

and the product fg is defined by

$$(fg)(x_1, \ldots, x_n) = f(x_1, \ldots, x_n)g(x_1, \ldots, x_n).$$

We contend that

$$(f + g)^\sigma = f^\sigma + g^\sigma \qquad \text{and} \qquad (fg)^\sigma = f^\sigma g^\sigma.$$

To see this, we have

$$
\begin{aligned}
(f + g) \circ \pi_\sigma(x_1, \ldots, x_n) &= (f + g)(x_{\sigma(1)}, \ldots, x_{\sigma(n)}) \\
&= f(x_{\sigma(1)}, \ldots, x_{\sigma(n)}) + g(x_{\sigma(1)}, \ldots, x_{\sigma(n)}) \\
&= f \circ \pi_\sigma(x_1, \ldots, x_n) + g \circ \pi_\sigma(x_1, \ldots, x_n),
\end{aligned}
$$

thereby proving the first contention. As to the second, we have

$$
\begin{aligned}
(fg) \circ \pi_\sigma(x_1, \ldots, x_n) &= (fg)(x_{\sigma(1)}, \ldots, x_{\sigma(n)}) \\
&= f(x_{\sigma(1)}, \ldots, x_{\sigma(n)})g(x_{\sigma(1)}, \ldots, x_{\sigma(n)}) \\
&= f^\sigma(x_1, \ldots, x_n)g^\sigma(x_1, \ldots, x_n).
\end{aligned}
$$

This proves what we wanted. As an exercise, verify also that

$$(-f)^\sigma = -f^\sigma.$$

Theorem 6. *To each permutation σ of J_n it is possible to assign a sign 1 or -1, denoted by $\epsilon(\sigma)$, satisfying the following conditions:*

(a) *If τ is a transposition, then $\epsilon(\tau) = -1$.*
(b) *If σ, σ' are permutations of J_n, then*

$$\epsilon(\sigma\sigma') = \epsilon(\sigma)\epsilon(\sigma').$$

Proof. Let Δ be the function

$$\Delta(x_1, \ldots, x_n) = \prod_{i < j} (x_j - x_i),$$

the product being taken for all pairs of integers i, j satisfying

$$1 \leq i < j \leq n.$$

Let τ be a transposition, interchanging the two integers r and s. Say $r < s$. We wish to determine

$$
\begin{aligned}
\Delta^\tau(x_1, \ldots, x_n) &= \prod_{i < j} (x_{\tau(j)} - x_{\tau(i)}) \\
&= \prod_{i < j} (x_j - x_i)^\tau.
\end{aligned}
$$

For one factor, we have

$$(x_s - x_r)^\tau = (x_r - x_s) = -(x_s - x_r).$$

If a factor does not contain x_r or x_s in it, then it remains unchanged when we apply τ. All other factors can be considered in pairs as follows:

$$(x_k - x_s)(x_k - x_r) \qquad \text{if } k > s,$$
$$(x_s - x_k)(x_k - x_r) \qquad \text{if } r < k < s,$$
$$(x_s - x_k)(x_r - x_k) \qquad \text{if } k < r.$$

Each one of these pairs remains unchanged when we apply τ. Hence we see that

$$\Delta^\tau = -\Delta.$$

Now let σ be an arbitrary permutation, and express σ as a product of transpositions,

$$\sigma = \tau_m \cdots \tau_1.$$

By induction, we find that

$$\Delta^\sigma = (\Delta^{\tau_1})^{\tau_m \cdots \tau_2} = (-\Delta)^{\tau_m \cdots \tau_2} = (-1)^m \Delta.$$

Thus if we express σ as another product of transpositions,

$$\sigma = \bar\tau_1 \cdots \bar\tau_k,$$

then we see that $(-1)^m \Delta = (-1)^k \Delta$. It follows that $(-1)^m = (-1)^k$, and hence that in any such product m is either always odd or always even. We define

$$\epsilon(\sigma) = (-1)^m,$$

which we have just seen is independent of the expression of σ as a product of transpositions. If

$$\sigma = \tau_1 \cdots \tau_m \qquad \text{and} \qquad \sigma' = \tau_1' \cdots \tau_k'$$

then

$$\sigma\sigma' = \tau_1 \cdots \tau_m \tau_1' \cdots \tau_k'$$

so that

$$\epsilon(\sigma\sigma') = (-1)^{m+k} = (-1)^m(-1)^k = \epsilon(\sigma)\epsilon(\sigma').$$

This proves our theorem. We have also shown:

COROLLARY 1. *If a permutation σ of J_n is expressed as a product of transpositions,*

$$\sigma = \tau_1 \cdots \tau_s,$$

then s is even or odd according as $\epsilon(\sigma) = 1$ or -1.

COROLLARY 2. *If σ is a permutation of J_n, then*

$$\epsilon(\sigma) = \epsilon(\sigma^{-1}).$$

Proof. We have

$$1 = \epsilon(id) = \epsilon(\sigma\sigma^{-1}) = \epsilon(\sigma)\epsilon(\sigma^{-1}).$$

Hence either $\epsilon(\sigma)$ and $\epsilon(\sigma^{-1})$ are both equal to 1, or both equal to -1, as desired.

As a matter of terminology, a permutation is called *even* if its sign is 1, and it is called *odd* if its sign is -1. Thus every transposition is odd.

From Theorem 6 we see that the map

$$\epsilon: S_n \to \{1, -1\}$$

is a homomorphism of S_n onto the group consisting of the two elements 1, -1. The kernel of this homomorphism by definition consists of the even permutations, and is called the *alternating group* A_n. If τ is a transposition, then A_n and τA_n are obviously distinct cosets of A_n, and every permutation lies in A_n or τA_n. (*Proof:* If $\sigma \in S_n$ and $\sigma \notin A_n$, then $\epsilon(\sigma) = -1$, so $\epsilon(\tau\sigma) = 1$ and hence $\tau\sigma \in A_n$, whence $\sigma \in \tau^{-1}A_n = \tau A_n$.) Therefore,

$$A_n, \quad \tau A_n$$

are distinct cosets of A_n in S_n, and there is no other coset. Since A_n is the kernel of a homomorphism, it is normal in S_n. We have $\tau A_n = A_n\tau$, which can also be verified easily directly.

A permutation σ of $\{1, \ldots, n\}$ is sometimes denoted by

$$\begin{bmatrix} 1 & \cdots & n \\ \sigma(1) & \cdots & \sigma(n) \end{bmatrix}.$$

Thus

$$\begin{bmatrix} 1 & 2 & 3 \\ 2 & 1 & 3 \end{bmatrix}$$

denotes the permutation σ such that $\sigma(1) = 2$, $\sigma(2) = 1$, and $\sigma(3) = 3$. This permutation is in fact a transposition.

Let $i_1, \ldots, i_r$ be distinct integers in J_n. By the symbol

$$[i_1 \ldots i_r]$$

we shall mean the permutation σ such that

$$\sigma(i_1) = i_2, \quad \sigma(i_2) = i_3, \quad \ldots, \quad \sigma(i_r) = i_1,$$

and σ leaves all other integers fixed. For example

$$[132]$$

denotes the permutation σ such that $\sigma(1) = 3$, $\sigma(3) = 2$, $\sigma(2) = 1$, and σ leaves all other integers fixed. Such a permutation is called a *cycle*, or more precisely, an *r*-cycle.

If $\sigma = [i_1 \ldots i_r]$ is a cycle, then one verifies at once that σ^{-1} is also a cycle, and that in fact

$$\sigma^{-1} = [i_r \ldots i_1].$$

Thus if $\sigma = [132]$ then

$$\sigma^{-1} = [231].$$

Note that a 2-cycle $[ij]$ is nothing but a transposition, namely the transposition such that $i \mapsto j$ and $j \mapsto i$.

A product of cycles is easily determined. For instance,

$$[132][34] = [2134].$$

One sees this using the definition: If $\sigma = [132]$ and $\tau = [34]$, then for instance

$$\sigma\big(\tau(3)\big) = \sigma(4) = 4,$$

$$\sigma\big(\tau(4)\big) = \sigma(3) = 2,$$

$$\sigma\big(\tau(2)\big) = \sigma(2) = 1,$$

$$\sigma\big(\tau(1)\big) = \sigma(1) = 3.$$

Let G be a group. We shall say that G is *solvable* if there exists a sequence of subgroups

$$G = H_0 \supset H_1 \supset H_2 \supset \cdots \supset H_m = \{e\}$$

such that H_i is normal in H_{i-1} and such that the factor group H_i/H_{i-1} is abelian, for $i = 1, \ldots, m$. We shall prove that for $n \geq 5$, the group S_n is not solvable. We need some preliminaries.

THEOREM 7. *Let G be a group, and H a normal subgroup. Then G/H is abelian if and only if H contains all elements of the form $xyx^{-1}y^{-1}$, with $x, y \in G$.*

Proof. Let $f: G \to G/H$ be the canonical homomorphism. Assume that G/H is abelian. For any $x, y \in G$ we have

$$f(xyx^{-1}y^{-1}) = f(x)f(y)f(x)^{-1}f(y)^{-1},$$

and since G/H is abelian, the expression on the right-hand side is equal to the unit element of G/H. Hence $xyx^{-1}y^{-1} \in H$. Conversely, assume that this is the case for all x, $y \in G$. Let $\bar{x}$, $\bar{y}$ be elements of G/H. Since f is surjective, there exists x, $y \in G$ such that $\bar{x} = f(x)$ and $\bar{y} = f(y)$. Let $\bar{e}$ be the unit element of G/H, and e the unit element of G. Then

$$\bar{e} = f(e) = f(xyx^{-1}y^{-1}) = f(x)f(y)f(x)^{-1}f(y)^{-1}$$
$$= \bar{x}\,\bar{y}\,\bar{x}^{-1}\bar{y}^{-1}.$$

Multiplying by $\bar{y}$ and $\bar{x}$ on the right, we find

$$\bar{y}\,\bar{x} = \bar{x}\,\bar{y},$$

and hence G/H is abelian.

THEOREM 8. *If $n \geqq 5$, then S_n is not solvable.*

Proof. We shall first prove that if H, N are two subgroups of S_n such that $N \subset H$ and N is normal in H, if H contains every 3-cycle, and if H/N is abelian, then N contains every 3-cycle. To see this, let i, j, k, r, s be five distinct integers between 1 and n, and let

$$\sigma = [ijk] \qquad \text{and} \qquad \tau = [krs].$$

Then

$$\sigma\tau\sigma^{-1}\tau^{-1} = [ijk][krs][kji][srk]$$
$$= [rki].$$

Since the choice of i, j, k, r, s was arbitrary, we see that the cycles $[rki]$ all lie in N for all choices of distinct r, k, i thereby proving what we wanted.

Now suppose that we have a chain of subgroups

$$S_n = H_0 \supset H_1 \supset H_2 \supset \cdots \supset H_m = \{e\}$$

such that H_ν is normal in $H_{\nu-1}$ for $\nu = 1, \ldots, m$, and $H_\nu/H_{\nu-1}$ is abelian. Since S_n contains every 3-cycle, we conclude that H_1 contains every 3-cycle. By induction on m, we conclude that $H_m = \{e\}$ contains every 3-cycle, which is impossible. Hence such a chain of subgroups cannot exist, and our theorem is proved.

EXERCISES

1. Let G be a group, N a normal subgroup, and H a subgroup of G. Show that $H \cap N$ is normal in H.

2. Assumptions being as in Exercise 1, prove that if G/N is abelian, then $H/(H \cap N)$ is also abelian.

3. Let G be a solvable group, and H a subgroup. Prove that H is solvable.

4. Let G be a solvable group, and $f: G \to G'$ a surjective homomorphism. Show that G' is solvable.

5. Determine the sign of the following permutations.

(a) $\begin{bmatrix} 1 & 2 & 3 \\ 2 & 3 & 1 \end{bmatrix}$ ✦   (b) $\begin{bmatrix} 1 & 2 & 3 \\ 3 & 1 & 2 \end{bmatrix}$ (c) $\begin{bmatrix} 1 & 2 & 3 \\ 3 & 2 & 1 \end{bmatrix}$

(d) $\begin{bmatrix} 1 & 2 & 3 & 4 \\ 2 & 3 & 1 & 4 \end{bmatrix}$ (e) $\begin{bmatrix} 1 & 2 & 3 & 4 \\ 2 & 1 & 4 & 3 \end{bmatrix}$ (f) $\begin{bmatrix} 1 & 2 & 3 & 4 \\ 3 & 2 & 4 & 1 \end{bmatrix}$

6. In each one of the cases of Exercise 5, write the inverse of the permutation.

7. Show that the number of odd permutations of $\{1, \ldots, n\}$ for $n \geq 2$ is equal to the number of even permutations.

8. Show that the groups S_2, S_3, S_4 are solvable.

9. Let σ be the r-cycle $[i_1 \ldots i_r]$. Show that $\epsilon(\sigma) = (-1)^{r+1}$. *Hint:* Use induction. If $r = 2$, then σ is a transposition. If $r > 2$, then

$$[i_1 \ldots i_r] = [i_1 i_r][i_1 \ldots i_{r-1}].$$

10. Two cycles $[i_1 \ldots i_r]$ and $[j_1 \ldots j_s]$ are said to be *disjoint* if no integer i_ν is equal to any integer j_μ. Prove that a permutation is equal to a product of disjoint cycles. [*Hint:* Let σ be a permutation. Define i to be equivalent to j if there exists some power σ^k such that $\sigma^k(i) = j$, for some integer $k \geq 0$. Prove that this is an equivalence relation. Show that each equivalence class determines a cycle, e.g. $[i\sigma(i)\sigma^2(i) \ldots]$.]

11. Express the permutations of Exercise 5 as a product of disjoint cycles.

12. Show that the group of Exercise 8, §1 exists by exhibiting it as a subgroup of S_4 as follows. Let $\sigma = [1234]$ and $\tau = [24]$. Show that the subgroup generated by σ, τ has order 8, and that σ, τ satisfy the same relations as x, y in the exercise *loc. cit.*

13. Show that the group of Exercise 10, §1 exists by exhibiting it as a subgroup of S_6.

14. Let n be an even positive integer. Show that there exists a group of order $2n$, generated by two elements σ, τ such that $\sigma^n = e = \tau^2$ and $\sigma\tau = \tau\sigma^{n-1}$.

§6. *Cyclic groups*

The integers $\mathbf{Z}$ form an additive group. We shall determine its subgroups. Let H be a subgroup of $\mathbf{Z}$. If H is not trivial, let a be the smallest positive integer in H. We contend that H consists of all elements na, with $n \in \mathbf{Z}$. To prove this, let $y \in H$, and say $y > 0$. There exist integers n, r with $0 \leq r < a$ such that

$$y = na + r.$$

Since H is a subgroup and $r = y - na$, we have $r \in H$, whence $r = 0$. If $y < 0$, we apply the preceding argument to $-y$ which is in H since H is a subgroup.

Let G be a group. We shall say that G is *cyclic* if there exists an element a of G such that every element x of G can be written in the form a^n for some integer n. (This is equivalent to saying that the map $f\colon \mathbf{Z} \to G$ such that $f(n) = a^n$ is surjective.) Such an element a of G is then called a *generator* of G.

Let G be a group, and $a \in G$. The subset of all elements a^n $(n \in \mathbf{Z})$ is obviously a cyclic subgroup of G. If m is an integer such that $a^m = e$ and $m > 0$, then we shall say that m is an *exponent* of a.

Let G be a group and a an element of G. Let $f\colon \mathbf{Z} \to G$ be the homomorphism such that $f(n) = a^n$, and let H be the kernel of f. Two cases arise:

(i) The kernel is trivial. Then f is an isomorphism of $\mathbf{Z}$ onto the cyclic subgroup of G generated by a, because f is injective, and the image of f is precisely equal to this subgroup. Furthermore, this subgroup is infinite cyclic. If a generates G, then G is cyclic. We also say that a has *infinite period*.

Example 1.   The number 2 generates an infinite cyclic subgroup of the multiplicative group of complex numbers. Its elements are

$$\ldots, 2^{-5}, 2^{-4}, \tfrac{1}{8}, \tfrac{1}{4}, \tfrac{1}{2}, 1, 2, 4, 8, 2^4, 2^5, \ldots$$

(ii) The kernel is not trivial. Let d be the smallest positive integer in the kernel. Then d is called the *period* of a. If m is an integer such that $a^m = e$, then $m = ds$ for some integer s, by what we proved at the beginning of this section. We observe that the elements

$$e, a, \ldots, a^{d-1}$$

are distinct. Indeed, suppose $a^r = a^s$ with $0 \leq r \leq d - 1$ and

$$0 \leq s \leq d - 1,$$

say $r \leq s$. Then $a^{s-r} = e$. Since

$$0 \leq s - r < d,$$

we must have $s - r = 0$, whence $r = s$. We conclude that the cyclic group generated by a in this case has order d.

Example 2.   The multiplicative group $\{1, -1\}$ is cyclic of order 2.

Example 3.   The complex numbers $\{1, i, -1, -i\}$ form a cyclic group of order 4. The number i is a generator.

THEOREM 9.   *Let G be a finite group, and a an element of G. Then the period of a divides the order of G.*

Proof. The order of the subgroup generated by a is equal to the period. We can now apply the Corollary of Theorem 2, §4.

THEOREM 10. *Let G be a cyclic group. Then any subgroup of G is cyclic.*

Proof. Let a be a generator of G, so that we have a surjective homomorphism

$$f \colon \mathbf{Z} \to G$$

such that $f(n) = a^n$. Let H be a subgroup of G. Then $f^{-1}(H)$ (the set of $n \in \mathbf{Z}$ such that $f(n) \in H$) is a subgroup A of $\mathbf{Z}$, and hence is cyclic. In fact, we know that there exists a unique positive integer d such that $f^{-1}(H)$ consists of all integers which can be written in the form md with $m \in \mathbf{Z}$. Since f is surjective, it follows that f maps A on all of H, i.e. every element of H is of the form a^{md} with some integer m. It follows that H is cyclic, and in fact a^d is a generator.

EXERCISES

1. Show that a group of order 4 is isomorphic to one of the following groups:
(a) The group with two distinct elements a, b such that

$$a^2 = b^2 = e \qquad \text{and} \qquad ab = ba.$$

(b) The group G having an element a such that $G = \{e, a, a^2, a^3\}$ and $a^4 = e$.

2. Let m, n be relatively prime positive integers. Let G, G' be cyclic groups of orders m, n respectively. Show that $G \times G'$ is cyclic, of order mn.

3. Prove that every group of prime order is cyclic.

4. If G is a cyclic group of order n, show that $a^n = e$ for all $a \in G$.

5. Let G be a group of order 6, and assume that G is not commutative. Show that G is isomorphic to S_3. [*Hint:* Show that G contains elements a, b such that $a^2 = e$, $b^3 = e$, and $aba = b^2 = b^{-1}$.]

6. Let $f \colon G \to G'$ be an isomorphism of groups. Let $a \in G$. Show that the period of a is the same as the period of $f(a)$.

7. A *root of unity* in the complex numbers is a number ω such that $\omega^n = 1$ for some positive integer n. We then say that ω is an n-th root of unity. Describe the set of n-th roots of unity in $\mathbf{C}$. Show that this set is a cyclic group of order n.

8. Let G be a cyclic group, and $f \colon G \to G'$ a homomorphism. Show that the image of G is cyclic.

9. Let G be a finite cyclic group of order n. Show that for each positive integer d dividing n, there exists a subgroup of order d.

10. Let G be a finite cyclic group of order n. Let a be a generator. Let r be an integer $\neq 0$, and relatively prime to n. Show that a^r is also a generator of G. Show that every generator of G can be written in this form.

11. Let p be a prime number, and G a cyclic group of order p. How many generators does G have?

12. Let G and Z be cyclic groups of order n. Show that $\mathrm{Hom}(G, Z)$ is cyclic of order n. [*Hint:* If a is a generator of G, show that for each $z \in Z$ there exists a unique homomorphism $f: G \to Z$ such that $f(a) = z$.]

13. Let A be an abelian group, written additively, and let n be a positive integer such that $nx = 0$ for all $x \in A$. Assume that we can write $n = rs$, where r, s are positive relatively prime integers. Let A_r consist of all $x \in A$ such that $rx = 0$, and similarly A_s consist of all $x \in A$ such that $sx = 0$. Show that every element $a \in A$ can be written uniquely in the form $a = b + c$, with $b \in A_r$ and $c \in A_s$.

14. Let A be an additive abelian group, and let B, C be subgroups. Let $B + C$ consist of all sums $b + c$, with $b \in B$ and $c \in C$. Show that $B + C$ is a subgroup, called the sum of B and C. Define the sum of a finite number of subgroups similarly.

We say that A is the *direct sum* of B and C if every element $x \in A$ can be written uniquely in the form $x = b + c$ with $b \in B$ and $c \in C$, and similarly for several subgroups. We then write $A = B \oplus C$.

15. Show that the additive abelian group A is the direct sum of subgroups B and C if and only if $A = B + C$ and $B \cap C = \{0\}$.

16. Let A be a finite abelian group of order n, and let

$$n = p_1^{r_1} \ldots p_s^{r_s}$$

be its prime power factorization, the p_i being distinct. Show that A is a direct sum $A = A_1 \oplus \cdots \oplus A_s$ where every element of A_i has period dividing $p_i^{r_i}$.

17. Let G be the group of Exercise 8, §1, and let H be the subgroup generated by x. Show that G/H is cyclic of order 2.

18. Let G be the group of Exercise 10, §1, and let H be the subgroup generated by x. Show that G/H is cyclic of order 2.

CHAPTER III

Rings

In this chapter, we axiomatize the notions of addition and multiplication.

§1. Rings

A *ring* R is a set, whose objects can be added and multiplied (i.e. we are given associations $(x, y) \mapsto x + y$ and $(x, y) \mapsto xy$ from pairs of elements of R, into R), satisfying the following conditions:

RI 1. *Under addition, R is an additive (abelian) group.*

RI 2. *For all $x, y, z \in R$ we have*

$$x(y + z) = xy + xz \qquad and \qquad (y + z)x = yx + zx$$

RI 3. *For all $x, y, z \in R$, we have $(xy)z = x(yz)$.*

RI 4. *There exists an element $e \in R$ such that $ex = xe = x$ for all $x \in R$.*

Example 1.   Let R be the integers $\mathbf{Z}$. Then R is a ring.

Example 2.   The rational numbers, the real numbers, and the complex numbers all are rings.

Example 3.   Let R be the set of continuous real-valued functions on the interval $[0, 1]$. The sum and product of two functions f, g are defined as usual, namely $(f + g)(t) = f(t) + g(t)$, and $(fg)(t) = f(t)g(t)$. Then R is a ring.

More generally, let S be a non-empty set, and let R be a ring. Let $M(S, R)$ be the set of mappings of S into R. Then $M(S, R)$ is a ring, if we define the addition and product of mappings f, g by the rules

$$(f + g)(x) = f(x) + g(x) \qquad and \qquad (fg)(x) = f(x)g(x).$$

We leave the verification as a simple exercise for the reader.

Example 4.   *The ring of endomorphisms.* Let A be an abelian group. Let $\mathrm{End}(A)$ denote the set of homomorphisms of A into itself. We call $\mathrm{End}(A)$ the set of *endomorphisms* of A. Thus $\mathrm{End}(A) = \mathrm{Hom}(A, A)$ in the notation of Chapter II, §3. We know that $\mathrm{End}(A)$ is an additive

43

group. *If we let the multiplicative law of composition on* $\text{End}(A)$ *be ordinary composition of mappings, then* $\text{End}(A)$ *is a ring.* We prove this in detail. We already know RI 1. As for RI 2, let f, g, $h \in \text{End}(A)$. Then for all $x \in A$,

$$(f \circ (g + h))(x) = f((g + h)(x))$$
$$= f(g(x) + h(x)) = f(g(x)) + f(h(x))$$
$$= f \circ g(x) + f \circ h(x).$$

Hence $f \circ (g + h) = f \circ g + f \circ h$. Similarly on the other side. We observe that RI 3 is nothing but the associativity for composition of mappings in this case, and we already know it. The unit element of RI 4 is the identity mapping I. Thus we have seen that $\text{End}(A)$ is a ring.

A ring R is said to be *commutative* if $xy = yx$ for all x, $y \in R$. The rings of Examples 1, 2, 3 are commutative. In general, the ring of Example 4 is not commutative.

As with groups, the element e of a ring R satisfying RI 4 is unique, and is called the *unit element* of the ring. It is often denoted by 1. Note that if $1 = 0$ in the ring R, then R consists of 0 alone, in which case it is called the zero ring.

In a ring R, a number of ordinary rules of arithmetic can be deduced from the axioms. We shall list these.

We have $0x = 0$ for all $x \in R$. *Proof:* We have

$$0x + x = 0x + ex = (0 + e)x = ex = x.$$

Hence $0x = 0$.

We have $(-e)x = -x$ for all $x \in R$. *Proof:*

$$(-e)x + x = (-e)x + ex = (-e + e)x = 0x = 0.$$

We have $(-e)(-e) = e$. *Proof:* We multiply the equation

$$e + (-e) = 0$$

by $-e$, and find

$$-e + (-e)(-e) = 0.$$

Adding e to both sides yields $(-e)(-e) = e$, as desired.

We leave it as an exercise to prove that

$$(-x)y = -xy \qquad \text{and} \qquad (-x)(-y) = xy$$

for all x, $y \in R$.

From condition RI 2, which is called *distributivity*, we can deduce the analogous rule with several elements, namely if $x, y_1, \ldots, y_n$ are elements of the ring R, then

$$x(y_1 + \cdots + y_n) = xy_1 + \cdots + xy_n.$$

Similarly, if $x_1, \ldots, x_m$ are elements of R, then

$$(x_1 + \cdots + x_m)(y_1 + \cdots + y_m) = x_1y_1 + \cdots + x_my_m$$

$$= \sum_{i=1}^{m} \sum_{j=1}^{n} x_iy_j.$$

The sum on the right-hand side is to be taken over all indices i and j as indicated. These more general rules can be proved by induction, and we shall omit the proofs, which are tedious.

Let R be a ring. By a *subring* R' of R one means a subset of R such that the unit element of R is in R', and if $x, y \in R'$, then $-x, x + y$, and xy are also in R'. It then follows obviously that R' is a ring, the operations of addition and multiplication in R' being the same as those in R.

Example 5. The integers form a subring of the rational numbers, which form a subring of the real numbers.

Example 6. The real-valued differentiable functions on **R** form a subring of the ring of continuous functions.

Let R be a ring. It may happen that there exist elements $x, y \in R$ such that $x \neq 0$ and $y \neq 0$, but $xy = 0$. Such elements are called *divisors of zero*. A commutative ring without divisors of zero, and such that $1 \neq 0$ is called an *entire ring*. A commutative ring such that the subset of non-zero elements forms a group under multiplication is called a *field*. Observe that in a field, we have necessarily $1 \neq 0$, and that a field has no divisors of zero (proof?).

Example 7. The integers **Z** form an entire ring. Every field is an entire ring. We shall see later that the polynomials over a field form an entire ring.

EXERCISES

1. Let p be a prime number. Let R be the subset of all rational numbers m/n such that $n \neq 0$ and n is not divisible by p. Show that R is a ring.

2. Show that the ring of real-valued functions on the interval $[0, 1]$ has divisors of zero.

3. Let R be an entire ring. If $a, b, c \in R$, $a \neq 0$, and $ab = ac$, then prove that $b = c$.

4. Let R be an entire ring, and $a \in R$, $a \neq 0$. Show that the map $x \mapsto ax$ is an injective mapping of R into itself.

5. Let R be a finite entire ring. Show that R is a field. [*Hint:* Use the preceding exercise.]

6. Let R be a ring such that $x^2 = x$ for all $x \in R$. Show that R is commutative.

7. Let R be a ring, and $x \in R$. If n is a positive integer, we define

$$x^n = x \cdots x,$$

the product being taken n times. Then for positive integers m, n we have

$$x^{n+m} = x^n x^m.$$

If $x, y \in R$ and $xy = yx$, what is $(x + y)^n$? (Cf. Exercise 2 of Chapter I, §2.)

8. Let R be a commutative ring, $x \in R$. We say that x is *nilpotent* if there exists a positive integer n such that $x^n = 0$. If x, y are nilpotent, show that $x + y$ is nilpotent.

9. Let R be a ring, and let G be the subset of R consisting of all elements $x \in R$ such that there exists some $y \in R$ such that $xy = yx = e$. Show that G is a group. Elements of G are called the *units* of R.

10. How would you describe the units of the ring in Exercise 1?

11. Let R be a ring, and Z the set of all elements $a \in R$ such that $ax = xa$ for all $x \in R$. Show that Z is a subring of R.

12. Let R be the set of numbers of type $a + b\sqrt{2}$ where a, b are rational numbers. Show that R is a ring, and in fact that R is a field.

13. Let R be the set of numbers of type $a + b\sqrt{2}$ where a, b are integers. Show that R is a ring, but not a field.

14. Let R be the set of numbers of type $a + bi$ where a, b are integers and $i = \sqrt{-1}$. Show that R is a ring. List all its units.

15. Let R be the set of numbers of type $a + bi$ where a, b are rational numbers. Show that R is a field.

16. Let S be a set, R a ring, and $f: S \to R$ a bijective mapping. For each $x, y \in S$ define

$$x + y = f^{-1}(f(x) + f(y)) \qquad \text{and} \qquad xy = f^{-1}(f(x)f(y)).$$

Show that these sum and product define a ring structure on S.

§2. *Ideals*

Let R be a ring. A *left ideal* of R is a subset J of R having the following properties: If $x, y \in J$, then $x + y \in J$ also, the zero element is in J, and if $x \in J$ and $a \in R$, then $ax \in J$.

Using the negative $-e$, we see that if J is a left ideal, and $x \in J$, then $-x \in J$ also, because $-x = (-e)x$. Thus the elements of a left ideal form an additive subgroup of R and we may as well say that a left ideal is an additive subgroup J of R such that, if $x \in J$ and $a \in R$ then $ax \in J$.

We note that R is a left ideal, called the *unit ideal*, and so is the subset of R consisting of 0 alone.

Similarly, we can define a *right ideal* and a *two-sided ideal*. Thus a two-sided ideal J is by definition an additive subgroup of R such that, if $x \in J$ and $a \in R$, then ax and $xa \in J$.

Example 1.   Let R be the ring of continuous real-valued functions on the interval $[0, 1]$. Let J be the subset of functions f such that $f(\frac{1}{2}) = 0$. Then J is an ideal (two-sided, since R is commutative).

Example 2.   Let R be the ring of integers $\mathbf{Z}$. Then the even integers, i.e. the integers of type $2n$ with $n \in \mathbf{Z}$, form an ideal. Do the odd integers form an ideal?

Example 3.   Let R be a ring, and a an element of R. The set of elements xa, with $x \in R$, is a left ideal, called the *principal left ideal* generated by a. (Verify in detail that it is a left ideal.) We denote it by (a). More generally, let $a_1, \ldots, a_n$ be elements of R. The set of all elements

$$x_1 a_1 + \cdots + x_n a_n$$

with $x_i \in R$, is a left ideal, denoted by $(a_1, \ldots, a_n)$. We call $a_1, \ldots, a_n$ *generators* for this ideal.

We shall give a complete proof for this to show how easy it is, and leave the proof of further statements in the next examples as exercises. If $y_1, \ldots, y_n, x_1, \ldots, x_n \in R$ then

$$(x_1 a_1 + \cdots + x_n a_n) + (y_1 a_1 + \cdots + y_n a_n)$$
$$= x_1 a_1 + y_1 a_1 + \cdots + x_n a_n + y_n a_n$$
$$= (x_1 + y_1)a_1 + \cdots + (x_n + y_n)a_n.$$

If $z \in R$, then

$$z(x_1 a_1 + \cdots + x_n a_n) = zx_1 a_1 + \cdots + zx_n a_n.$$

Finally,

$$0 = 0a_1 + \cdots + 0a_n.$$

This proves that the set of all elements $x_1 a_1 + \cdots + x_n a_n$ with $x_i \in R$ is a left ideal.

Example 4.   Let R be a ring. Let L, M be left ideals. We denote by LM the set of all elements $x_1 y_1 + \cdots + x_n y_n$ with $x_i \in L$ and $y_i \in M$.

It is an easy exercise for the reader to verify that LM is also a left ideal. Verify also that if L, M, N are left ideals, then $(LM)N = L(MN)$.

Example 5.   Let L, M be left ideals.   We define $L + M$ to be the subset consisting of all elements $x + y$ with $x \in L$ and $y \in M$.   Then $L + M$ is a left ideal.   Besides verifying this in detail, also show that if L, M, N are left ideals, then

$$L(M + N) = LM + LN.$$

Also formulate and prove the analogues of Examples 4 and 5 for right, and two-sided ideals.

Example 6.   Let L be a left ideal, and denote by LR the set of elements $x_1y_1 + \cdots + x_ny_n$ with $x_i \in L$ and $y_i \in R$.   Then LR is a two-sided ideal.   The proof is again left as an exercise.

Exercises

1. Show that a field has no ideal other than the zero and unit ideal.

2. Let R be a commutative ring. If M is an ideal, abbreviate MM by M^2. Let M_1, M_2 be two ideals such that $M_1 + M_2 = R$. Show that $M_1^2 + M_2^2 = R$.

3. Let R be the ring of Exercise 1 in the preceding section. Show that the subset of elements m/n in R such that m is divisible by p is an ideal.

4. Let R be a ring and J_1, J_2 left ideals. Show that $J_1 \cap J_2$ is a left ideal, and similarly for right and two-sided ideals.

5. Let R be a ring and $a \in R$. Let J be the set of all $x \in R$ such that $xa = 0$. Show that J is a left ideal.

6. Let R be a ring and L a left ideal. Let M be the set of all $x \in R$ such that $xL = 0$ (i.e. $xy = 0$ for all $y \in L$). Show that M is a two-sided ideal.

7. The following example will be of interest in calculus. Let R be the ring of infinitely differentiable functions defined, say on the open interval $-1 < t < 1$. Let J_n be the set of functions $f \in R$ such that $D^k f(0) = 0$ for all integers k with $0 \leqq k \leqq n$. Here D denotes the derivative, so J_n is the set of functions all of whose derivatives up to order n vanish at 0. Show that J_n is an ideal in R.

8. Let R be the ring of real-valued functions on the interval $[0, 1]$. Let S be a subset of this interval. Show that the set of all functions $f \in R$ such that $f(x) = 0$ for all $x \in S$ is an ideal of R.

§3. *Homomorphisms*

Let R, R' be rings. By a *ring-homomorphism* $f \colon R \to R'$, we shall mean a mapping having the following properties: For all x, $y \in R$,

$$f(x + y) = f(x) + f(y), \qquad f(xy) = f(x)f(y), \qquad f(e) = e'$$

(if e, e' are the unit elements of R and R' respectively).

By the *kernel* of a ring-homomorphism $f: R \to R'$, we shall mean its kernel viewed as a homomorphism of additive groups, i.e. it is the set of all elements $x \in R$ such that $f(x) = 0$. *Exercise:* Prove that the kernel is a two-sided ideal of R.

Example 1. Let R be the ring of complex-valued functions on the interval $[0, 1]$. The map which to each function $f \in R$ associates its value $f(\frac{1}{2})$ is a ring-homomorphism of R into **C**.

Example 2. Let R be the ring of real-valued functions on the interval $[0, 1]$. Let R' be the ring of real-valued functions on the interval $[0, \frac{1}{2}]$. Each function $f \in R$ can be viewed as a function on $[0, \frac{1}{2}]$, and when we so view f, we call it the *restriction* of f to $[0, \frac{1}{2}]$. More generally, let S be a set, and S' a subset. Let R be the ring of real-valued functions on S. For each $f \in R$, we denote by $f \mid S'$ the function on S' whose value at an element $x \in S'$ is $f(x)$. Then $f \mid S'$ is called the *restriction* of f to S'. Let R' be the ring of real-valued functions on S'. Then the map

$$f \mapsto f \mid S'$$

is a ring-homomorphism of R into R'.

Since the kernel of a ring-homomorphism is defined only in terms of the additive groups involved, we know that a ring-homomorphism whose kernel is trivial is injective.

Let $f: R \to R'$ be a ring-homomorphism. If there exists a ring-homomorphism $g: R' \to R$ such that $g \circ f$ and $f \circ g$ are the respective identity mappings, then we say that f is a *ring-isomorphism*.

As with groups, *if $f: R \to R'$ is a ring-homomorphism which is a bijection, then f is a ring-isomorphism.* We shall leave the proof to the reader.

Furthermore, if $f: R \to R'$ and $g: R' \to R''$ are ring-homomorphisms, then the composite $g \circ f: R \to R''$ is also a ring-homomorphism. Again, the proof is left to the reader.

We shall now define a notion similar to that of factor group, but applied to rings.

Let R be a ring and M a two-sided ideal. If $x, y \in R$, define x *congruent to* y mod M to mean $x - y \in M$. We write this relation in the form

$$x \equiv y \pmod{M}.$$

It is then very simple to prove the following statements.

    (a) We have $x \equiv x \pmod{M}$.

    (b) If $x \equiv y$ and $y \equiv z \pmod{M}$, then $x \equiv z \pmod{M}$.

    (c) If $x \equiv y$ then $y \equiv x \pmod{M}$.

    (d) If $x \equiv y \pmod{M}$, and $z \in R$, then $xz \equiv yz \pmod{M}$, and also $zx \equiv zy \pmod{M}$.

(e) If $x \equiv y$ and $x' \equiv y'$ (mod M), then $xx' \equiv yy'$ (mod M). Furthermore, $x + x' \equiv y + y'$ (mod M).

The proofs of the preceding assertions are all trivial. As an example, we shall give the proof of (e). The hypothesis means that we can write

$$x = y + z \qquad \text{and} \qquad x' = y' + z'$$

with $z, z' \in M$. Then

$$xx' = (y + z)(y' + z') = yy' + zy' + yz' + zz'.$$

Since M is a two-sided ideal, each one of zy', yz', zz' lies in M, and consequently their sum lies in M. Hence $xx' \equiv yy'$ (mod M), as was to be shown.

Remark. The present notion of congruence generalizes that defined for the integers in Chapter I. Indeed, if $R = \mathbf{Z}$, then the congruence

$$x \equiv y \quad (\text{mod } n)$$

in Chapter I, meaning that $x - y$ is divisible by n, is equivalent to the property that $x - y$ lies in the ideal generated by n.

If $x \in R$, we let $\bar{x}$ be the set of all elements of R which are congruent to x (mod M). Recalling the definition of a factor group, we see that $\bar{x}$ is none other than the additive coset $x + M$ of x, relative to M. Any element of that coset (also called *congruence class* of x mod M) is called a *representative* of the coset.

We let $\bar{R}$ be the set of all congruence classes of R mod M. In other words, we let $\bar{R} = R/M$ be the additive factor group of R modulo M. Then we already know that $\bar{R}$ is an additive group. We shall now define a multiplication which will make $\bar{R}$ into a ring.

If $\bar{x}$ and $\bar{y}$ are additive cosets of M, we define their product to be the coset of xy, i.e. to be $\overline{xy}$. Using condition (e) above, we see that this coset is independent of the selected representatives x in $\bar{x}$ and y in $\bar{y}$. Thus our multiplication is well defined by the rule

$$(x + M)(y + M) = (xy + M).$$

It is now a simple matter to verify that the axioms of a ring are satisfied. RI 1 is already known since R/M is taken as the factor group. For RI 2, let $\bar{x}$, $\bar{y}$, $\bar{z}$ be congruence classes, with representatives x, y, z respectively in R. Then $y + z$ is a representative of $\bar{y} + \bar{z}$ by definition, and $x(y + z)$ is a representative of $\bar{x}(\bar{y} + \bar{z})$. But $x(y + z) = xy + xz$. Furthermore, xy is a representative of $\bar{x}\,\bar{y}$ and xz is a representative of $\bar{x}\,\bar{z}$. Hence by definition,

$$\bar{x}(\bar{y} + \bar{z}) = \bar{x}\,\bar{y} + \bar{x}\,\bar{z}.$$

Similarly, one proves RI 3. As for RI 4, if e denotes the unit element of R, then $\bar{e}$ is a unit element in $\bar{R}$, because $ex = x$ is a representative of $\bar{e}\,\bar{x}$. This proves all the axioms.

We call $\bar{R} = R/M$ the *factor ring* of R modulo M.

We observe that the map $f: R \to R/M$ such that $f(x) = \bar{x}$ is a ring-homomorphism of R onto R/M, whose kernel is M. The verification is immediate, and essentially amounts to the definition of the addition and multiplication of cosets of M.

THEOREM 1. *Let $f: R \to S$ be a ring-homomorphism and let M be its kernel. For each coset C of M the image $f(C)$ is an element of S, and the association*

$$\bar{f}: C \mapsto f(C)$$

is a ring-isomorphism of R/M onto the image of f.

Proof. The fact that the image of f is a subring of S is left as an exercise (Exercise 1). Each coset C consists of all elements $x + z$ with some x and all $z \in M$. Thus

$$f(x + z) = f(x) + f(z) = f(x)$$

implies that $f(C)$ consists of one element. Thus we get a map $\bar{f}: C \mapsto f(C)$ as asserted. If x, y represent cosets of M, then the relations

$$f(xy) = f(x)f(y),$$

$$f(x + y) = f(x) + f(y),$$

$$f(e_R) = e_S$$

show that $\bar{f}$ is a homomorphism of R/M into S. If $\bar{x} \in R/M$ is such that $\bar{f}(\bar{x}) = 0$, this means that for any representative x of $\bar{x}$ we have $f(x) = 0$, whence $x \in M$ and $\bar{x} = 0$ (in R/M). Thus $\bar{f}$ is injective. This proves what we wanted.

Example 3. If $R = \mathbf{Z}$, and n is a non-zero integer, then $R/(n) = \mathbf{Z}/(n)$ is called the ring of integers modulo n. We note that this is a finite ring, having exactly n elements. (Proof?) We also write $\mathbf{Z}/n\mathbf{Z}$ instead of $\mathbf{Z}/(n)$.

Example 4. Let R be any ring, with unit element e. It is easy to prove by induction that the map $f: \mathbf{Z} \to R$ such that $f(n) = ne$ is a ring homomorphism. Since any ring-homomorphism of $\mathbf{Z}$ into R must be such that $f(1) = e$, it follows by induction that any such map f is uniquely determined, and that the only possible value for $f(n)$ is ne. Assume $R \neq \{0\}$ so that $1 \neq 0$. Then the kernel of f is not all of R, and hence is the ideal $n\mathbf{Z}$ for some positive integer n. It follows from Theorem 1 that $\mathbf{Z}/n\mathbf{Z}$ is isomorphic to the image of f.

EXERCISES

1. Let $f: R \to R'$ be a ring-homomorphism. Show that the image of f is a subring of R'.

2. Show that a ring-homomorphism of a field K is either the zero map, or is an isomorphism of K onto its image.

3. Let n be a positive integer, and let $\mathbf{Z}_n = \mathbf{Z}/n\mathbf{Z}$ be the factor ring of $\mathbf{Z}$ modulo n. Show that the units of $\mathbf{Z}_n$ are precisely those residue classes $\bar{x}$ having a representative integer $x \neq 0$ and relatively prime to n. (For the definition of unit, see Exercise 9 of §1.)

4. Let x be an integer relatively prime to n. Let φ be the Euler function. Show that $x^{\varphi(n)} \equiv 1 \pmod{n}$.

5. (a) Let p be a prime number. Show that in the ring $\mathbf{Z}/(p)$, every non-zero element has a multiplicative inverse, and that the non-zero elements form a multiplicative group.

   (b) If a is an integer, $a \not\equiv 0 \pmod{p}$, show that $a^{p-1} \equiv 1 \pmod{p}$.

6. Let F be a finite field having q elements. Prove that $x^{q-1} = 1$ for every non-zero element $x \in F$. Show that $x^q = x$ for every element x of F.

7. Let n, n' be relatively prime positive integers. Let a, b be integers. Show that the congruences

$$x \equiv a \pmod{n}, \qquad x \equiv b \pmod{n'}$$

can be solved simultaneously with some $x \in \mathbf{Z}$.

8. If p is a prime number, and r an integer ≥ 1, show that

$$\varphi(p^r) = (p - 1)p^{r-1}.$$

9. Let R be a ring, and M, M' two-sided ideals. Assume that M contains M'. If $x \in R$, denote its residue class mod M by $x(M)$. Show that there is a (unique) ring-homomorphism $R/M' \to R/M$ which maps $x(M')$ on $x(M)$.

10. If n, m are integers $\neq 0$, such that n divides m, apply Exercise 9 to get a ring-homomorphism $\mathbf{Z}/(m) \to \mathbf{Z}/(n)$.

11. Let R, R' be rings. Let $R \times R'$ be the set of all pairs (x, x') with $x \in R$ and $x' \in R'$. Show how one can make $R \times R'$ into a ring, by defining addition and multiplication componentwise. In particular, what is the unit element of $R \times R'$?

12. (a) Let m, n be relatively prime positive integers. Show that $\mathbf{Z}/(mn)$ is ring-isomorphic to $\mathbf{Z}/(n) \times \mathbf{Z}/(m)$ under the map

$$x \pmod{mn} \mapsto (x \bmod n, x \bmod m).$$

   (b). Prove that if m, n are positive relatively prime integers, then

$$\varphi(mn) = \varphi(m)\varphi(n).$$

13. Let P be the set of positive integers and R the set of functions defined on P, with values in a commutative ring K. Define the sum in R to be the ordinary

addition of functions, and define the product by the formula

$$(f*g)(m) = \sum_{xy=m} f(x)g(y),$$

where the sum is taken over all pairs (x, y) of positive integers such that $xy = m$.

(a) Show that R is a commutative ring, whose unit element is the function δ such that $\delta(1) = 1$ and $\delta(x) = 0$ if $x \neq 1$.

(b) A function f is said to be *multiplicative* if $f(mn) = f(m)f(n)$ whenever m, n are relatively prime. If f, g are multiplicative, show that $f*g$ is multiplicative.

(c) Let μ be the function such that $\mu(1) = 1$, $\mu(p_1 \cdots p_r) = (-1)^r$ if $p_1, \ldots, p_r$ are distinct primes, and $\mu(m) = 0$ if m is divisible by p^2 for some prime p. Show that $\mu*\varphi_1 = \delta$ (where φ_1 denotes the constant function having value 1). [*Hint:* Show first that μ is multiplicative and then prove the assertion for prime powers.] The *Möbius inversion formula* of elementary number theory is then nothing else but the relation $\mu*\varphi_1*f = f$.

14. Let $f: R \to R'$ be a ring-homomorphism. Let J' be a two-sided ideal of R', and let J be the set of elements x of R such that $f(x)$ lies in J. Show that J is a two-sided ideal of R.

15. Let R be a commutative ring, and N the set of elements $x \in R$ such that $x^n = 0$ for some positive integer n. Show that N is an ideal.

16. In Exercise 15, if $\bar{x}$ is an element of R/N, and if there exists an integer $n \geq 1$ such that $\bar{x}^n = 0$, show that $\bar{x} = 0$.

17. Let R be a commutative ring. An ideal P is said to be a *prime* ideal if $P \neq R$, and whenever $a, b \in R$ and $ab \in P$ then $a \in P$ or $b \in P$. Show that a non-zero ideal of $\mathbf{Z}$ is prime if and only if it is generated by a prime number.

18. Let R be a commutative ring. An ideal M of R is said to be a *maximal* ideal if $M \neq R$, and if there is no ideal J such that $R \supset J \supset M$, and $R \neq J$, $J \neq M$. Show that every maximal ideal is prime.

19. Let R be a commutative ring. (a) Show that an ideal P is prime if and only if R/P is entire. (b) Show that an ideal M is maximal if and only if R/M is a field.

20. Let S be a set, X a subset, and assume neither S nor X is empty. Let R be a ring. Let $F(S, R)$ be the ring of all mappings of S into R, and let

$$\rho: F(S, R) \to F(X, R)$$

be the restriction, i.e. if $f \in F(S, R)$, then $\rho(f)$ is just f viewed as a map of X into R. Show that ρ is surjective. Describe the kernel of ρ.

21. Let K be a field and S a set. Let x_0 be an element of S. Let $F(S, K)$ be the ring of mappings of S into K, and let J be the set of maps $f \in F(S, K)$ such that $f(x_0) = 0$. Show that J is a maximal ideal. Show that $F(S, K)/J$ is isomorphic to K.

§4. Quotient fields

In the preceding sections, we have assumed that the reader is acquainted with the rational numbers, in order to give examples for more abstract concepts. We shall now study how one can define the rationals from the integers. Furthermore, in the next chapter, we shall study polynomials over a field. One is accustomed to form quotients f/g $(g \neq 0)$ of polynomials, and such quotients are called rational functions. Our discussion will apply to this situation also.

Before giving the abstract discussion, we analyse the case of the rational numbers more closely. In elementary school, what is done (or what should be done), is to give rules for determining when two quotients of rational numbers are equal. This is needed, because, for instance, $\frac{3}{4} = \frac{6}{8}$. The point is that a fraction is determined by a pair of numbers, in this special example $(3, 4)$, but also by other pairs, e.g. $(6, 8)$. If we view all pairs giving rise to the same quotient as equivalent, then we get our cue how to define the fraction, namely as a certain equivalence class of pairs. Next, one must give rules for adding fractions, and the rules we shall give in general are precisely the same as those which are (or should be) given in elementary school.

Our discussion will apply to an arbitrary entire ring R. (Recall that entire means that $1 \neq 0$, that R is commutative and without divisors of 0.)

Let (a, b) and (c, d) be pairs of elements in R, with $b \neq 0$ and $d \neq 0$. We shall say that these pairs are equivalent if $ad = bc$. We contend that this is an equivalence relation. Going back to the definition of Chapter I, §5, we see that ER 1 and ER 3 are obvious. As for ER 2, suppose that (a, b) is equivalent to (c, d) and (c, d) is equivalent to (e, f). By definition,

$$ad = bc \quad \text{and} \quad cf = de.$$

Multiplying the first equality by f and the second by b, we obtain

$$adf = bcf \quad \text{and} \quad bcf = bde,$$

whence $adf = bde$, and $daf - dbe = 0$. Then $d(af - be) = 0$. Since R has no divisors of 0, it follows that $af - be = 0$, i.e. $af = be$. This means that (a, b) is equivalent to (e, f), and proves ER 2.

We denote the equivalence class of (a, b) by a/b. We must now define how to add and multiply such classes.

If a/b and c/d are such classes, we define their sum to be

$$\frac{a}{b} + \frac{c}{d} = \frac{ad + bc}{bd}$$

and their product to be

$$\frac{a}{b}\frac{c}{d} = \frac{ac}{bd}.$$

We must show of course that in defining the sum and product as above, the result is independent of the choice of pairs (a, b) and (c, d) representing the given classes. We shall do this for the sum. Suppose that

$$a/b = a'/b' \quad \text{and} \quad c/d = c'/d'.$$

We must show that

$$\frac{ad + bc}{bd} = \frac{a'd' + b'c'}{b'd'}.$$

This is true if and only if

$$b'd'(ad + bc) = bd(a'd' + b'c'),$$

or in other words

(1) $$b'd'ad + b'd'bc = bda'd' + bdb'c'.$$

But $ab' = a'b$ and $cd' = c'd$ by assumption. Using this, we see at once that (1) holds. We leave the analogous statement for the product as an exercise.

We now contend that the set of all quotients a/b with $b \neq 0$ is a ring, the operations of addition and multiplication being defined as above. Note first that there is a unit element, namely $1/1$, where 1 is the unit element of R. One must now verify all the other axioms of a ring. This is tedious, but obvious at each step. As an example, we shall prove the associativity of addition. For three quotients a/b, c/d, and e/f we have

$$\left(\frac{a}{b} + \frac{c}{d}\right) + \frac{e}{f} = \frac{ad + bc}{bd} + \frac{e}{f} = \frac{fad + fbc + bde}{bdf}.$$

On the other hand,

$$\frac{a}{b} + \left(\frac{c}{d} + \frac{e}{f}\right) = \frac{a}{b} + \frac{cf + de}{df} = \frac{adf + bcf + bde}{bdf}.$$

It is then clear that the expressions on the right-hand sides of these equations are equal, thereby proving associativity of addition. The other axioms are equally easy to prove, and we shall omit this tedious routine. We note that our ring of quotients is commutative.

Let us denote the ring of all quotients a/b by K. We contend that K is a field. To see this, all we need to do is prove that every non-zero element has a multiplicative inverse. But the zero element of K is $0/1$, and if

$a/b = 0/1$ then $a = 0$. Hence any non-zero element can be written in the form a/b with $b \neq 0$ and $a \neq 0$. Its inverse is then b/a, as one sees directly from the definition of multiplication of quotients.

Finally, observe that we have a natural map of R into K, namely the map

$$a \mapsto a/1.$$

It is again routine to verify that this map is an injective ring-homomorphism. Any injective ring-homomorphism will be called an *embedding*. We see that R is embedded in K in a natural way.

We call K the *quotient field of R*. When $R = \mathbf{Z}$, then K is by definition the field of rational numbers. When R is the ring of polynomials defined in the next chapter, its quotient field is called the field of *rational functions*.

Suppose that R is a subring of a field F. The set of all elements ab^{-1} with $a, b \in R$ and $b \neq 0$ is easily seen to form a field, which is a subfield of F. We also call this field the quotient field of R in F. There can be no confusion with this terminology, because the quotient field of R as defined previously is isomorphic to this subfield, under the map

$$a/b \mapsto ab^{-1}.$$

The verification is trivial, and in view of this, the element ab^{-1} of F is also denoted by a/b.

Example. Let K be a field and as usual, $\mathbf{Q}$ the rational numbers. There does not necessarily exist an embedding of $\mathbf{Q}$ into K (for instance, K may be finite). However, if an embedding of $\mathbf{Q}$ into K exists, there is only one. This is easily seen, because any homomorphism

$$f \colon \mathbf{Q} \to K$$

must be such that $f(1) = e$ (unit element of K). Then for any integer $n > 0$ one sees by induction that $f(n) = ne$, and consequently

$$f(-n) = -ne.$$

Furthermore,

$$e = f(1) = f(nn^{-1}) = f(n)f(n^{-1})$$

so that $f(n^{-1}) = f(n)^{-1} = (ne)^{-1}$. Thus for any quotient $m/n = mn^{-1}$ with integers m, n and $n > 0$ we must have

$$f(m/n) = (me)/(ne)^{-1}$$

thus showing that f is uniquely determined. It is then customary to identify $\mathbf{Q}$ inside K and view every rational number as an element of K.

Finally, we make some remarks on the extension of an embedding of a ring into a field. *Let R be an entire ring, and*

$$f: R \to E$$

an embedding of R into some field E. Let K be the quotient field of R. Then f admits a unique extension to an embedding of K into E, that is an embedding $f^*: K \to E$ whose restriction to R is equal to f.

To see the uniqueness, observe that if f^* is an extension of f, and

$$f^*: K \to E$$

is an embedding, then for all $a, b \in R$ we must have

$$f^*(a/b) = f^*(a)/f^*(b) = f(a)/f(b),$$

so the effect of f^* on K is determined by the effect of f on R. Conversely, one can *define* f^* by the formula

$$f^*(a/b) = f(a)/f(b),$$

and it is seen at once that the value of f^* is independent of the choice of the representation of the quotient a/b, that is if $a/b = c/d$ with

$$a, b, c, d \in R \qquad \text{and} \qquad bd \neq 0,$$

then

$$f(a)/f(b) = f(c)/f(d).$$

One also verifies routinely that f^* so defined is a homomorphism, thereby proving the existence.

Exercises

1. Put in all details in the proof of the existence of the extension f^* at the end of this section.

2. A (ring-) isomorphism of a ring onto itself is also called an *automorphism*. Let R be an entire ring, and $\sigma: R \to R$ an automorphism of R. Show that σ admits a unique extension to an automorphism of the quotient field.

3. Let K be a field and $f: \mathbf{Z} \to K$ the homomorphism of the integers into K. (a) Show that the kernel of f is a prime ideal. If f is an embedding then we say that K has *characteristic* 0. (b) If $\operatorname{Ker} f \neq \{0\}$, show that $\operatorname{Ker} f$ is generated by a prime number p. In this case we say that K has *characteristic p*.

4. Let K be a field of characteristic p. Show that $(x + y)^p = x^p + y^p$ for all $x, y \in K$.

5. Let K be a finite field of characteristic p. Show that the map $x \mapsto x^p$ is an automorphism of K.

CHAPTER IV

Polynomials

Throughout this chapter, unless otherwise specified, by a field we shall mean a field containing an infinite number of elements.

§1. Euclidean algorithm

If K is a field, a map of a set into K will also be called a function.

Let K be a field. By a *polynomial* over K *or in* K we shall mean a function f of K into itself such that there exist elements $a_0, \ldots, a_n \in K$ such that

$$f(t) = a_n t^n + \cdots + a_0$$

for all $t \in K$. Let

$$g(t) = b_m t^m + \cdots + b_0$$

be another polynomial with $b_j \in K$, then we can form the sum $f + g$. If, say, $n \geq m$ we can write $b_j = 0$ if $j > m$,

$$g(t) = 0t^n + \cdots + b_m t^m + \cdots + b_0,$$

and then we can write the values of the sum $f + g$ as

$$(f + g)(t) = (a_n + b_n)t^n + \cdots + (a_0 + b_0).$$

Thus $f + g$ is again a polynomial. If $c \in K$, then

$$(cf)(t) = ca_n t^n + \cdots + ca_0,$$

and hence cf is a polynomial.

We can also take the product of the two polynomials, fg, and

$$(fg)(t) = (a_n b_m)t^{n+m} + \cdots + a_0 b_0,$$

so that fg is again a polynomial. In fact, if we write

$$(fg)(t) = c_{n+m} t^{n+m} + \cdots + c_0,$$

then

$$c_k = \sum_{i=0}^{k} a_i b_{k-i} = a_0 b_k + a_1 b_{k-1} + \cdots + a_k b_0.$$

This expression for c_k simply comes from collecting all the terms

$$a_i t^i b_{k-i} t^{k-i} = a_i b_{k-i} t^k$$

in the product which will give rise to the term involving t^k. Since the sum and product of two polynomials are again polynomials, and since the constant function 1 is a polynomial, we see that the set of polynomials is a subring of the ring of all functions of K into itself. This ring of polynomials will be denoted by $K[t]$.

Let α be an element of K. We shall say that α is a *root* of f if $f(\alpha) = 0$.

THEOREM 1. *Let f be a polynomial in K, written in the form*

$$f(t) = a_n t^n + \cdots + a_0.$$

If not all $a_0, \ldots, a_n$ are equal to 0, then f has at most n roots in K. If

$$g(t) = b_n t^n + \cdots + b_0$$

is another polynomial such that $f(t) = g(t)$ for all $t \in K$, then $a_i = b_i$ for all i.

Proof. We shall need a lemma.

LEMMA. *Let f be a polynomial over K, and let $\alpha \in K$. Then there exist elements $c_0, \ldots, c_n \in K$ such that*

$$f(t) = c_0 + c_1(t - \alpha) + \cdots + c_n(t - \alpha)^n.$$

Proof. We write $t = \alpha + (t - \alpha)$, and substitute this value for t in the expression of f. For each integer k with $1 \leq k \leq n$, we have

$$t^k = (\alpha + (t - \alpha))^k = \alpha^k + \cdots + (t - \alpha)^k$$

(the expansion being that obtained with the binomial coefficients), and therefore

$$a_k t^k = a_k \alpha^k + \cdots + a_k(t - \alpha)^k$$

can be written as a sum of powers of $(t - \alpha)$, multiplied by elements of K. Taking the sum of $a_k t^k$ for $k = 0, \ldots, n$ we find the desired expression for f, and prove the lemma.

Observe that in the lemma, we have $f(\alpha) = c_0$. Hence, if $f(\alpha) = 0$, then $c_0 = 0$, and we can write

$$f(t) = (t - \alpha)h(t),$$

where we can write

$$h(t) = d_1 + d_2(t - \alpha) + \cdots + d_n(t - \alpha)^{n-1}$$

for some elements $d_1, d_2, \ldots, d_n$ in K. Suppose that f has more than n roots in K, and say $\alpha_1, \ldots, \alpha_{n+1}$ are $n+1$ distinct roots in K. Let $\alpha = \alpha_1$. Then $\alpha_i - \alpha_1 \neq 0$ for $i = 2, \ldots, n+1$. Since

$$0 = f(\alpha_i) = (\alpha_i - \alpha_1)h(\alpha_i),$$

we conclude that $h(\alpha_i) = 0$ for $i = 2, \ldots, n+1$. By induction on n we now see that this is impossible, thereby proving that f has at most n roots in K.

Finally, suppose $f(t) = g(t)$ for all $t \in K$. Consider the polynomial

$$f(t) - g(t) = (a_n - b_n)t^n + \cdots + (a_0 - b_0).$$

Every element of K is a root of this polynomial. Hence by what we have just proved, we must have $a_i - b_i = 0$ for $i = 0, \ldots, n$, in other words, $a_i = b_i$, thereby proving the theorem.

Theorem 1 shows that when we write a polynomial f in the form

$$f(t) = a_n t^n + \cdots + a_0$$

with $a_i \in K$, then the numbers $a_0, \ldots, a_n$ are uniquely determined. They are called the *coefficients* of the polynomial. If n is the largest integer such that $a_n \neq 0$, then we say that n is the *degree* of f and write $n = \deg f$. We also say that a_n is the *leading coefficient* of f. We say that a_0 is the *constant term* of f. If f is the zero polynomial then we shall use the convention that $\deg f = -\infty$. We agree to the convention that

$$-\infty + -\infty = -\infty,$$
$$-\infty + a = -\infty, \qquad -\infty < a$$

for every integer a, and *no other operation with $-\infty$ is defined.*

The reason for our convention is that it makes the following theorem true without exception.

THEOREM 2. *Let f, g be polynomials with coefficients in K. Then*

$$\deg(fg) = \deg f + \deg g.$$

Proof. Let

$$f(t) = a_n t^n + \cdots + a_0 \qquad \text{and} \qquad g(t) = b_m t^m + \cdots + b_0$$

with $a_n \neq 0$ and $b_m \neq 0$. Then from the multiplication rule for fg, we see that

$$f(t)g(t) = a_n b_m t^{n+m} + \text{terms of lower degree},$$

and $a_n b_m \neq 0$. Hence $\deg fg = n + m = \deg f + \deg g$. If f or g is 0, then our convention about $-\infty$ makes our assertion also come out.

A polynomial of degree 1 is also called a *linear* polynomial.

COROLLARY. *The ring $K[t]$ has no divisors of zero, and is therefore an entire ring.*

Proof. If f, g are non-zero polynomials, then $\deg f$ and $\deg g$ are ≥ 0, whence $\deg(fg) \geq 0$, and $fg \neq 0$, as was to be shown.

The next theorem is the Euclidean algorithm, or long division, taught in elementary school. It is the analogue of the Euclidean algorithm for integers.

THEOREM 3. *Let f, g be polynomials over the field K, i.e. polynomials in $K[t]$, and assume $\deg g \geq 0$. Then there exist polynomials q, r in $K[t]$ such that*

$$f(t) = q(t)g(t) + r(t),$$

and $\deg r < \deg g$. The polynomials q, r are uniquely determined by these conditions.

Proof. Let $m = \deg g \geq 0$. Write

$$f(t) = a_n t^n + \cdots + a_0,$$
$$g(t) = b_m t^m + \cdots + b_0,$$

with $b_m \neq 0$. If $n < m$, let $q = 0$, $r = f$. If $n \geq m$, let

$$f_1(t) = f(t) - a_n b_m^{-1} t^{n-m} g(t).$$

(This is the first step in the process of long division.) Then $\deg f_1 < \deg f$. Continuing in this way, or more formally by induction on n, we can find polynomials q_1, r such that

$$f_1 = q_1 g + r,$$

with $\deg r < \deg g$. Then

$$\begin{aligned} f(t) &= a_n b_m^{-1} t^{n-m} g(t) + f_1(t) \\ &= a_n b_m^{-1} t^{n-m} g(t) + q_1(t)g(t) + r(t) \\ &= (a_n b_m^{-1} t^{n-m} + q_1)g(t) + r(t), \end{aligned}$$

and we have consequently expressed our polynomial in the desired form. To prove the uniqueness, suppose that

$$f = q_1 g + r_1 = q_2 g + r_2,$$

with $\deg r_1 < \deg g$ and $\deg r_2 < \deg g$. Then

$$(q_1 - q_2)g = r_2 - r_1.$$

The degree of the left-hand side is either $\geq \deg g$, or the left-hand side is equal to 0. The degree of the right-hand side is either $< \deg g$, or the right-hand side is equal to 0. Hence the only possibility is that they are both 0, whence

$$q_1 = q_2 \quad \text{and} \quad r_1 = r_2,$$

as was to be shown.

From the Euclidean algorithm, we can re-prove a fact already proved by other means.

COROLLARY 1. *Let f be a non-zero polynomial in $K[t]$. Let $\alpha \in K$ be such that $f(\alpha) = 0$. Then there exists a polynomial $q(t)$ in $K[t]$ such that*

$$f(t) = (t - \alpha)q(t).$$

Proof. We can write

$$f(t) = q(t)(t - \alpha) + r(t),$$

where $\deg r < \deg(t - \alpha)$. But $\deg(t - \alpha) = 1$. Hence r is constant. Since

$$0 = f(\alpha) = q(\alpha)(\alpha - \alpha) + r(\alpha) = r(\alpha),$$

it follows that $r = 0$, as desired.

COROLLARY 2. *Let K be a field such that every non-constant polynomial in $K[t]$ has a root in K. Let f be such a polynomial. Then there exist elements $\alpha_1, \ldots, \alpha_n \in K$ and $c \in K$ such that*

$$f(t) = c(t - \alpha_1) \cdots (t - \alpha_n).$$

Proof. In Corollary 1, observe that $\deg q = \deg f - 1$. Let $\alpha = \alpha_1$ in Corollary 1. By assumption, if q is not constant, we can find a root α_2 of q, and thus write

$$f(t) = q_2(t)(t - \alpha_1)(t - \alpha_2).$$

Proceeding inductively, we keep on going until q_{n+1} is constant.

A field K having the property stated in Corollary 2, that every non-constant polynomial over K has a root in K, is called *algebraically closed*. We shall prove later in the book that the complex numbers are algebraically closed.

EXERCISES

1. In each of the following cases, write $f = qg + r$ with $\deg r < \deg g$.

(a) $f(t) = t^2 - 2g + 1$, $g(t) = t - 1$
(b) $f(t) = t^3 + t - 1$, $g(t) = t^2 + 1$
(c) $f(t) = t^3 + t$, $g(t) = t$
(d) $f(t) = t^3 - 1$, $g(t) = t - 1$

2. If $f(t)$ has integer coefficients and if $g(t)$ has integer coefficients and leading coefficient 1, show that when we express $f = qg + r$ with $\deg r < \deg g$, the polynomials q and r also have integer coefficients.

3. Using the intermediate value theorem of calculus, show that every polynomial of odd degree over the real numbers has a root in the real numbers.

4. Let $f(t) = t^n + \cdots + a_0$ be a polynomial with complex coefficients, of degree n, and let α be a root. Show that $|\alpha| \leq n \cdot \max_i |a_i|$. [*Hint:* Write

$$-\alpha^n = a_{n-1}\,\alpha^{n-1} + \cdots + a_0.$$

If $|\alpha| > n \cdot \max_i |a_i|$, divide by α^n and take the absolute value, together with a simple estimate, to get a contradiction.]

§2. *Greatest common divisor*

Having the Euclidean algorithm, we may now develop the theory of divisibility exactly as for the integers, in Chapter I.

THEOREM 4. *Let J be an ideal of $K[t]$. Then there exists a polynomial g which is a generator of J.*

Proof. Suppose that J is not the zero ideal. Let g be a polynomial in J which is not 0, and is of smallest degree. We assert that g is a generator for J. Let f be any element of J. By the Euclidean algorithm, we can find polynomials q, r such that

$$f = qg + r$$

with $\deg r < \deg g$. Then $r = f - qg$, and by the definition of an ideal, it follows that r also lies in J. Since $\deg r < \deg g$, we must have $r = 0$. Hence $f = qg$, and g is a generator for J, as desired.

Remark. Let g_1 be a non-zero generator for an ideal J, and let g_2 also be a generator. Then there exists a polynomial q such that $g_1 = qg_2$. Since

$$\deg g_1 = \deg q + \deg g_2,$$

it follows that $\deg g_2 \leq \deg g_1$. By symmetry, we must have

$$\deg g_2 = \deg g_1.$$

Hence q is constant. We can write

$$g_1 = cg_2$$

with some constant c. Write

$$g_2(t) = a_n t^n + \cdots + a_0$$

with $a_n \neq 0$. Take $b = a_n^{-1}$. Then bg_2 is also a generator of J, and its leading coefficient is equal to 1. Thus we can always find a generator for an ideal ($\neq 0$) whose leading coefficient is 1. It is furthermore clear that this generator is uniquely determined.

Let f, g be non-zero polynomials. We shall say that g *divides* f, and write $g \mid f$, if there exists a polynomial q such that $f = gq$. Let f_1, f_2 be polynomials $\neq 0$. By a *greatest common divisor* of f_1, f_2 we shall mean a polynomial g such that g divides f_1 and f_2, and furthermore, if h divides f_1 and f_2, then h divides g.

THEOREM 5. *Let f_1, f_2 be non-zero polynomials in $K[t]$. Let g be a generator for the ideal generated by f_1, f_2. Then g is a greatest common divisor of f_1 and f_2.*

Proof. Since f_1 lies in the ideal generated by f_1, f_2, there exists a polynomial q_1 such that

$$f_1 = q_1 g,$$

whence g divides f_1. Similarly, g divides f_2. Let h be a polynomial dividing both f_1 and f_2. Write

$$f_1 = h_1 h \quad \text{and} \quad f_2 = h_2 h$$

with some polynomials h_1 and h_2. Since g is in the ideal generated by f_1, f_2, there are polynomials g_1, g_2 such that $g = g_1 f_1 + g_2 f_2$, whence

$$g = g_1 h_1 h + g_2 h_2 h = (g_1 h_1 + g_2 h_2)h.$$

Consequently h divides g, and our theorem is proved.

Remark 1. The greatest common divisor is determined up to a non-zero constant multiple. If we select a greatest common divisor with leading coefficient 1, then it is uniquely determined.

Remark 2. Exactly the same proof applies when we have more than two polynomials. For instance, if $f_1, \ldots, f_n$ are non-zero polynomials, and if g is a generator for the ideal generated by $f_1, \ldots, f_n$, then g is a greatest common divisor of $f_1, \ldots, f_n$.

Polynomials $f_1, \ldots, f_n$ whose greatest common divisor is 1 are said to be *relatively prime*.

1. Show that $t^n - 1$ is divisible by $t - 1$.

2. Show that $t^4 + 4$ can be factored as a product of polynomials of degree 2 with integer coefficients.

3. If n is odd, find the quotient of $t^n + 1$ by $t + 1$.

§3. *Unique factorization*

A polynomial p in $K[t]$ will be said to be *irreducible* (over K) if it is of degree ≥ 1, and if, given a factorization $p = fg$ with f, $g \in K[t]$, then $\deg f$ or $\deg g = 0$ (i.e. one of f, g is constant). Thus, up to a non-zero constant factor, the only divisors of p are p itself, and 1.

Example 1. The only irreducible polynomials over the complex numbers are the polynomials of degree 1, i.e. non-zero constant multiples of polynomials of type $t - \alpha$, with $\alpha \in \mathbf{C}$.

Example 2. The polynomial $t^2 + 1$ is irreducible over $\mathbf{R}$.

THEOREM 6. *Every polynomial in $K[t]$ of degree ≥ 1 can be expressed as a product $p_1 \cdots p_m$ of irreducible polynomials. In such a product, the polynomials $p_1, \ldots, p_m$ are uniquely determined, up to a rearrangement, and up to non-zero constant factors.*

Proof. We first prove the existence of the factorization into a product of irreducible polynomials. Let f be in $K[t]$, of degree ≥ 1. If f is irreducible, we are done. Otherwise, we can write

$$f = gh$$

where $\deg g < \deg f$ and $\deg h < \deg f$. By induction we can express g and h as products of irreducible polynomials, and hence $f = gh$ can also be expressed as such a product.

We must now prove uniqueness. We need a lemma.

LEMMA. *Let p be irreducible in $K[t]$. Let f, $g \in K[t]$ be non-zero polynomials, and assume p divides fg. Then p divides f or p divides g.*

Proof. Assume that p does not divide f. Then the greatest common divisor of p and f is 1, and there exist polynomials h_1, h_2 in $K[t]$ such that

$$1 = h_1 p + h_2 f.$$

(We use Theorem 5.) Multiplying by g yields

$$g = gh_1 p + h_2 fg.$$

But $fg = ph_3$ for some h_3, whence

$$g = (gh_1 + h_2h_3)p,$$

and p divides g, as was to be shown.

The lemma will be applied when p divides a product of irreducible polynomials $q_1 \cdots q_s$. In that case, p divides q_1 or p divides $q_2 \cdots q_s$. Hence there exists a constant c such that $p = cq_1$, or p divides $q_2 \cdots q_s$. In the latter case, we can proceed inductively, and we conclude that in any case, there exists some i such that p and q_i differ by a constant factor.

Suppose now that we have two products of irreducible polynomials

$$p_1 \cdots p_r = q_1 \cdots q_s.$$

After renumbering the q_i, we may assume that $p_1 = c_1q_1$ for some constant c_1. Cancelling q_1, we obtain

$$c_1p_2 \cdots p_r = q_2 \cdots q_s.$$

Repeating our argument inductively, we conclude that there exist constants c_i such that $p_i = c_iq_i$ for all i, after making a possible permutation of $q_1, \ldots, q_s$. This proves the desired uniqueness.

COROLLARY 1. *Let f be a polynomial in $K[t]$ of degree ≥ 1. Then f has a factorization $f = cp_1 \cdots p_s$, where $p_1, \ldots, p_s$ are irreducible polynomials with leading coefficient 1, uniquely determined up to a permutation.*

COROLLARY 2. *Let K be algebraically closed. Let f be a polynomial in $K[t]$, of degree ≥ 1. Then f has a factorization*

$$f(t) = c(t - \alpha_1) \cdots (t - \alpha_n),$$

with $\alpha_i \in K$ and $c \in K$. The factors $t - \alpha_i$ are uniquely determined up to a permutation.

We shall deal mostly with polynomials having leading coefficient 1. Let f be such a polynomial of degree ≥ 1. Let $p_1, \ldots, p_r$ be the *distinct* irreducible polynomials (with leading coefficient 1) occurring in its factorization. Then we can express f as a product

$$f = p_1^{i_1} \cdots p_r^{i_r}$$

where $i_1, \ldots, i_r$ are positive integers, uniquely determined by $p_1, \ldots, p_r$. This factorization will be called a normalized factorization for f. In particular, over an algebraically closed field, we can write

$$f(t) = (t - \alpha_1)^{i_1} \cdots (t - \alpha_r)^{i_r}.$$

A polynomial with leading coefficient 1 is sometimes called *monic*.

If p is irreducible, and $f = p^m g$, where p does not divide g, and m is an integer ≥ 0, then we say that m is the *multiplicity* of p in f. (We define p^0 to be 1.) We denote this multiplicity by $\text{ord}_p f$, and also call it the *order* of f at p.

If α is a root of f, and

$$f(t) = (t - \alpha)^m g(t),$$

with $g(\alpha) \neq 0$, then $t - \alpha$ does not divide $g(t)$, and m is the multiplicity of $t - \alpha$ in f. We also say that m is the multiplicity of α in f.

There is an easy test for $m > 1$ in terms of the derivative.

Let $f(t) = a_n t^n + \cdots + a_0$ be a polynomial. Define its (formal) derivative to be

$$Df(t) = f'(t) = na_n t^{n-1} + (n - 1)a_{n-1}t^{n-2} + \cdots + a_1.$$

Then we have the following statements, whose proofs are left as exercises. If f, g are polynomials, then

$$(f + g)' = f' + g'.$$

Also

$$(fg)' = f'g + fg'.$$

If c is constant, then $(cf)' = cf'$.

If $f(t) = h(t)^m$ for some integer $m \geq 1$, then

$$f'(t) = mh(t)^{m-1}h'(t).$$

(Prove this last statement by induction.)

THEOREM 7. *Let K be a field. Let f be a polynomial over K, of degree ≥ 1, and let α be a root of f in K. Then the multiplicity of α in f is > 1 if and only if $f'(\alpha) = 0$.*

Proof. Suppose that

$$f(t) = (t - \alpha)^m g(t)$$

with $m > 1$. Taking the derivative, we find

$$f'(t) = m(t - \alpha)^{m-1}g(t) + (t - \alpha)^m g'(t).$$

Substituting α shows that $f'(\alpha) = 0$ because $m - 1 \geq 1$. Conversely, suppose

$$f(t) = (t - \alpha)^m g(t),$$

and $g(\alpha) \neq 0$, so that m is the multiplicity of α in f. If $m = 1$ then

$$f'(t) = g(t) + (t - \alpha)g'(t),$$

so that $f'(\alpha) = g(\alpha) \neq 0$. This proves our theorem.

EXERCISES

1. Let f be a polynomial of degree 2 over a field K. Show that either f is irreducible over K, or f has a factorization into linear factors over K.

2. Let f be a polynomial of degree 3 over a field K. If f is not irreducible over K, show that f has a root in K.

3. Let $f(t)$ be an irreducible polynomial with leading coefficient 1 over the real numbers. Assume $\deg f = 2$. Show that $f(t)$ can be written in the form

$$f(t) = (t - a)^2 + b^2$$

with some $a, b \in \mathbf{R}$ and $b \neq 0$. Conversely, prove that any such polynomial is irreducible over $\mathbf{R}$.

4. Let f be a polynomial with complex coefficients, say

$$f(t) = \alpha_n t^n + \cdots + \alpha_0.$$

Define its complex conjugate,

$$\bar{f}(t) = \bar{\alpha}_n t^n + \cdots + \bar{\alpha}_0$$

by taking the complex conjugate of each coefficient. Show that if f, g are in $\mathbf{C}[t]$, then

$$\overline{(f + g)} = \bar{f} + \bar{g}, \qquad \overline{(fg)} = \bar{f}\,\bar{g},$$

and if $\beta \in \mathbf{C}$, then $\overline{(\beta f)} = \bar{\beta}\bar{f}$.

5. Let $f(t)$ be a polynomial with real coefficients. Let α be a root of f, which is complex but not real. Show that $\bar{\alpha}$ is also a root of f.

6. Terminology being as in Exercise 5, show that the multiplicity of α in f is the same as that of $\bar{\alpha}$.

7. Show that the following polynomials have no multiple roots in $\mathbf{C}$.
(a) $t^4 + t$ (b) $t^5 - 5t + 1$
(c) any polynomial $t^2 + bt + c$ if b, c are numbers such that $b^2 - 4c$ is not 0.

8. Show that the polynomial $t^n - 1$ has no multiple roots in $\mathbf{C}$. Can you determine all the roots and give its factorization into factors of degree 1?

9. Let K be a subfield of $\mathbf{C}$, and $\alpha \in \mathbf{C}$. Let J be the set of all polynomials $f(t)$ in $K[t]$ such that $f(\alpha) = 0$. Show that J is an ideal. If J is not the zero ideal, show that the monic generator of J is irreducible.

10. Let f, g be two polynomials, written in the form

$$f = p_1^{i_1} \cdots p_r^{i_r}$$

and

$$g = p_1^{j_1} \cdots p_r^{j_r}$$

where i_ν, j_ν are integers ≥ 0, and $p_1, \ldots, p_r$ are distinct irreducible polynomials.

(a) Show that the greatest common divisor of f and g can be expressed as a product $p_1^{k_1} \cdots p_r^{k_r}$ where $k_1, \ldots, k_r$ are integers ≥ 0. Express k_ν in terms of i_ν and j_ν.

(b) Define the least common multiple of polynomials, and express the least common multiple of f and g as a product $p_1^{k_1} \cdots p_r^{k_r}$ with integers $k_\nu \geq 0$. Express k_ν in terms of i_ν and j_ν.

11. Give the greatest common divisor and least common multiple of the following pairs of polynomials:

(a) $(t - 2)^3(t - 3)^4(t - i)$ and $(t - 1)(t - 2)(t - 3)^3$
(b) $(t^2 + 1)(t^2 - 1)$ and $(t + i)^3(t^3 - 1)$

12. Let K be a field, $R = K[t]$ the ring of polynomials, and F the quotient field of R, i.e. the field of rational functions. Let $\alpha \in K$. Let R_α be the set of rational functions which can be written as a quotient f/g of polynomials such that $g(\alpha) \neq 0$. Show that R_α is a ring. If φ is a rational function, and $\varphi = f/g$ such that $g(\alpha) \neq 0$, define $\varphi(\alpha) = f(\alpha)/g(\alpha)$. Show that this value $\varphi(\alpha)$ is independent of the choice of representation of φ as a quotient f/g. Show that the map $\varphi \mapsto \varphi(\alpha)$ is a ring-homomorphism of R_α into K. Show that the kernel of this ring-homomorphism consists of all rational functions f/g such that $g(\alpha) \neq 0$ and $f(\alpha) = 0$. If M_α denotes this kernel, show that M_α is a prime ideal of R_α.

13. Let R be a commutative ring, and K a subfield (i.e. a subring which is also a field). Let $f \in K[t]$ be a polynomial with coefficients in K, say

$$f(t) = a_n t^n + \cdots + a_0.$$

Let $b \in R$. Define

$$f(b) = a_n b^n + \cdots + a_0.$$

Show that the map $f \mapsto f(b)$ is a ring-homomorphism of $K[t]$ into R.

14. Let R be a rational function over the field K, and express R as a quotient of polynomials, $R = g/f$. Define the derivative

$$R' = \frac{fg' - gf'}{f^2},$$

where the prime means the formal derivative of polynomials as in the text.

(a) Show that this derivative is independent of the expression of R as a quotient of polynomials, i.e. if $R = g_1/f_1$ then

$$\frac{fg' - gf'}{f^2} = \frac{f_1 g_1' - g_1 f_1'}{f_1^2}.$$

(b) Show that this derivative of rational functions satisfies the same rules as before, namely for rational functions R_1 and R_2 we have

$$(R_1 + R_2)' = R_1' + R_2' \quad \text{and} \quad (R_1 R_2)' = R_1 R_2' + R_1' R_2.$$

(c) Let $\alpha_1, \ldots, \alpha_n$ and $a_1, \ldots, a_n$ be elements of K such that

$$\frac{1}{(t - \alpha_1) \cdots (t - \alpha_n)} = \frac{a_1}{t - \alpha_1} + \cdots + \frac{a_n}{t - \alpha_n}.$$

Let $f(t) = (t - \alpha_1) \cdots (t - \alpha_n)$ and assume that $\alpha_1, \ldots, \alpha_n$ are distinct. Show that

$$a_1 = \frac{1}{(\alpha_1 - \alpha_2) \cdots (\alpha_1 - \alpha_n)} = \frac{1}{f'(\alpha_1)}.$$

§4. Partial fractions

In the preceding section, we proved that a polynomial can be expressed as a product of powers of irreducible polynomials in a unique way (up to a permutation of the factors). The same is true of a rational function, if we allow negative exponents. Let $R = g/f$ be a rational function, expressed as a quotient of polynomials g, f with $f \neq 0$. Suppose $R \neq 0$. If g, f are not relatively prime, we may cancel their greatest common divisor and thus obtain an expression of R as a quotient of relatively prime polynomials. Factoring out their constant leading coefficients, we can write

$$R = c \frac{g_1}{f_1}$$

where f_1, g_1 have leading coefficient 1. Then f_1, g_1, and c are uniquely determined, for suppose

$$c g_1 / f_1 = c_2 g_2 / f_2$$

for constants c, c_2 and pairs of relatively prime polynomials f_1, g_1 and f_2, g_2 with leading coefficient 1. Then

$$c g_1 f_2 = c_2 g_2 f_1.$$

From the unique factorization of polynomials, we conclude that $g_1 = g_2$ and $f_1 = f_2$ so that $c = c_2$.

If we now factorize f_1 and g_1 into products of powers of irreducible polynomials, we obtain the unique factorization of R. This is entirely analogous to the factorization of a rational number obtained in Chapter I, §4.

We wish to decompose a rational function into a sum of rational functions, such that the denominator of each term is equal to a power of an irreducible polynomial. Such a decomposition is called a partial fraction decomposition. We begin by a lemma which allows us to apply induction.

LEMMA. *Let f_1, f_2 be non-zero, relatively prime polynomials over a field K. Then there exist polynomials h_1, h_2 over K such that*

$$\frac{1}{f_1 f_2} = \frac{h_1}{f_1} + \frac{h_2}{f_2}.$$

Proof. Since f_1, f_2 are relatively prime, there exist polynomials h_1, h_2 such that

$$h_2 f_1 + h_1 f_2 = 1.$$

Dividing both sides by $f_1 f_2$, we obtain what we want.

THEOREM 8. *Every rational function R can be written in the form*

$$R = \frac{h_1}{p_1^{i_1}} + \cdots + \frac{h_n}{p_n^{i_n}} + h,$$

where $p_1, \ldots, p_n$ are distinct irreducible polynomials with leading coefficient 1; $i_1, \ldots, i_n$ are integers ≥ 0; $h_1, \ldots, h_n$, h are polynomials, satisfying

$$\deg h_\nu < \deg p_\nu^{i_\nu} \qquad and \qquad p_\nu \nmid h_\nu$$

for $\nu = 1, \ldots, n$. In such an expression, the integers i_ν and the polynomials h_ν, h ($\nu = 1, \ldots, n$) are uniquely determined.

Proof. We first prove the existence of the expression described in our theorem. Let $R = g/f$ where f is a non-zero polynomial, and write

$$f = p_1^{i_1} \cdots p_n^{i_n}$$

where $p_1, \ldots, p_n$ are distinct irreducible polynomials, and $i_1, \ldots, i_n$ are integers ≥ 0. By the lemma, there exist polynomials g_1, g_1^* such that

$$\frac{1}{f} = \frac{g_1}{p_1^{i_1}} + \frac{g_1^*}{p_2^{i_2} \cdots p_n^{i_n}},$$

and by induction, there exist polynomials $g_2, \ldots, g_n$ such that

$$\frac{g_1^*}{p_2^{i_2} \cdots p_n^{i_n}} = \frac{g_2}{p_2^{i_2}} + \cdots + \frac{g_n}{p_n^{i_n}}.$$

Multiplying by g, we obtain

$$\frac{g}{f} = \frac{g g_1}{p_1^{i_1}} + \cdots + \frac{g g_n}{p_n^{i_n}}.$$

By the Euclidean algorithm, we can divide gg_ν by $p_\nu^{i_\nu}$ for $\nu = 1, \ldots, n$ letting

$$gg_\nu = q_\nu p_\nu^{i_\nu} + h_\nu, \qquad\qquad \deg h_\nu < \deg p_\nu^{i_\nu}.$$

In this way obtain the desired expression for g/f, with $h = q_1 + \cdots + q_n$.

Next we prove the uniqueness. Suppose we have expressions

$$\frac{h_1}{p_1^{i_1}} + \cdots + \frac{h_n}{p_n^{i_n}} + h = \frac{\overline{h}_1}{p_1^{j_1}} + \cdots + \frac{\overline{h}_n}{p_n^{j_n}} + \overline{h},$$

satisfying the conditions stated in the theorem. (We can assume that the irreducible polynomials $p_1, \ldots, p_n$ are the same on both sides, letting some i_ν be equal to 0 if necessary.) Then there exist polynomials φ, ψ such that $\psi \neq 0$ and $p_1 \nmid \psi$, for which we can write

$$\frac{h_1}{p_1^{i_1}} - \frac{\overline{h}_1}{p_1^{j_1}} = \frac{\varphi}{\psi}.$$

Say $i_1 \leqq j_1$. Then

$$\frac{h_1 p_1^{j_1 - i_1} - \overline{h}_1}{p_1^{j_1}} = \frac{\varphi}{\psi}.$$

Since ψ is not divisible by p_1, it follows from unique factorization that $p_1^{j_1}$ divides $h_1 p_1^{j_1 - i_1} - \overline{h}_1$. If $j_1 \neq i_1$ then $p_1 | \overline{h}_1$, contrary to the conditions stated in the theorem. Hence $j_1 = i_1$. Again since ψ is not divisible by p_1, it follows now that $p_1^{j_1}$ divides $h_1 - \overline{h}_1$. By hypothesis,

$$\deg(h_1 - \overline{h}_1) < \deg p_1^{j_1}.$$

Hence $h_1 - \overline{h}_1 = 0$, whence $h_1 = \overline{h}_1$. We therefore conclude that

$$\frac{h_2}{p_2^{i_2}} + \cdots + \frac{h_n}{p_n^{i_n}} + h = \frac{\overline{h}_2}{p_2^{j_2}} + \cdots + \frac{\overline{h}_n}{p_n^{j_n}} + \overline{h},$$

and we can conclude the proof by induction.

The expression of Theorem 8 is called the *partial fraction decomposition* of R.

The irreducible polynomials $p_1, \ldots, p_n$ in Theorem 8 can be described somewhat more precisely, and the next theorem gives additional information on them, and also on h.

THEOREM 9. *Let the notation be as in Theorem 8, and let the rational function R be expressed in the form $R = g/f$ where g, f are relatively prime* *polynomials, $f \neq 0$. Assume that all integers $i_1, \ldots, i_n$ are > 0. Then*

$$f = p_1^{i_1} \cdots p_n^{i_n}$$

is the prime power factorization of f. Furthermore, if $\deg g < \deg f$, then $h = 0$.

Proof. If we put the partial fraction expression for R in Theorem 8 over a common denominator, we obtain

$$(*) \qquad R = \frac{h_1 p_2^{i_2} \cdots p_n^{i_n} + \cdots + h_n p_1^{i_1} \cdots p_{n-1}^{i_{n-1}} + h p_1^{i_1} \cdots p_n^{i_n}}{p_1^{i_1} \cdots p_n^{i_n}}.$$

Then p_ν does not divide the numerator on the right in (*), for any index $\nu = 1, \ldots, n$. Indeed, p_ν divides every term in this numerator *except* the term

$$h_\nu p_1^{i_1} \cdots \widehat{p_\nu^{i_\nu}} \cdots p_n^{i_n}$$

(where the roof over $p_\nu^{i_\nu}$ means that we omit this factor). This comes from the hypothesis that p_ν does not divide h_ν. Hence the numerator and denominator on the right in (*) are relatively prime, thereby proving our first assertion.

As to the second, letting g be the numerator of R and f its denominator, we have $f = p_1^{i_1} \cdots p_n^{i_n}$, and

$$g = Rf = h_1 p_2^{i_2} \cdots p_n^{i_n} + \cdots + h_n p_1^{i_1} \cdots p_{n-1}^{i_{n-1}} + h p_1^{i_1} \cdots p_n^{i_n}.$$

Assume that $\deg g < \deg f$. Then every term in the preceding sum has degree $< \deg f$, except possibly the last term

$$hf = h p_1^{i_1} \cdots p_n^{i_n}.$$

If $h \neq 0$, then this last term has degree $\geq \deg f$, and we then get

$$hf = g - h_1 p_2^{i_2} \cdots p_n^{i_n} - \cdots - h_n p_1^{i_1} \cdots p_{n-1}^{i_{n-1}}$$

where the left-hand side has degree $\geq \deg f$ and the right-hand side has degree $< \deg f$. This is impossible. Hence $h = 0$, as was to be shown.

Remark. Given a rational function $R = g/f$ where g, f are relatively prime polynomials, we can use the Euclidean algorithm and write

$$g = g_1 f + g_2$$

where g_1, g_2 are polynomials and $\deg g_2 < \deg f$. Then

$$\frac{g}{f} = \frac{g_2}{f} + g_1,$$

and we can apply Theorem 9 to the rational function g_2/f. In studying rational functions, it is always useful to perform first this long division to reduce the study of the rational function to the case when the degree of the numerator is smaller than the degree of its denominator.

Example 1. Let $\alpha_1, \ldots, \alpha_n$ be distinct elements of K. Then there exist elements $a_1, \ldots, a_n \in K$ such that

$$\frac{1}{(t - \alpha_1) \cdots (t - \alpha_n)} = \frac{a_1}{t - \alpha_1} + \cdots + \frac{a_n}{t - \alpha_n}.$$

Indeed, in the present case we can apply Theorems 8 and 9, with $g = 1$, and hence deg $g <$ deg f. In Exercise 14 of the preceding section, we showed how to determine a_i in a special way.

Each expression $h_\nu/p_\nu^{i_\nu}$ in the partial fraction decomposition can be further analyzed, by writing h_ν in a special way, which we now describe.

THEOREM 10. *Let φ be a non-zero polynomial over the field K. Let h be any polynomial over K. Then there exist polynomials $\psi_0, \ldots, \psi_m$ such that*

$$h = \psi_0 + \psi_1\varphi + \cdots + \psi_m\varphi^m$$

and deg $\psi_i <$ deg φ *for all* $i = 0, \ldots, m$. *The polynomials* $\psi_0, \ldots, \psi_m$ *are uniquely determined by these conditions.*

Proof. We prove the existence of $\psi_0, \ldots, \psi_m$ by induction on the degree of h. By the Euclidean algorithm, we can write

$$h = q\psi + \psi_0$$

with polynomials q, ψ_0, and deg $\psi_0 <$ deg φ. Then deg $q <$ deg h, so that by induction we can write

$$\dot{q} = \psi_1 + \psi_2\varphi + \cdots + \psi_m\varphi^{m-1}$$

with polynomials ψ_i such that deg $\psi_i <$ deg φ. Substituting, we obtain

$$h = (\psi_1 + \psi_2\varphi + \cdots + \psi_m\varphi^{m-1})\varphi + \psi_0,$$

which yields the desired expression.

As for uniqueness, we observe first that in the expression given in the theorem, namely

$$h = \psi_0 + \psi_1\varphi + \cdots + \psi_m\varphi^m = \psi_0 + \varphi(\psi_1 + \cdots + \psi_m\varphi^{m-1})$$

the polynomial ψ_0 is necessarily the remainder of the division of h by φ, so that its uniqueness is given by the Euclidean algorithm. Then, writing

$h = q\varphi + \psi_0$, we conclude that

$$q = \psi_1 + \cdots + \psi_m\varphi^{m-1} ,$$

and q is uniquely determined. Thus $\psi_1, \ldots, \psi_m$ are uniquely determined by induction, as was to be proved.

The expression of h in terms of powers of φ as given in Theorem 10 is called its φ-*adic expansion*. We can apply this to the case where φ is an irreducible polynomial p, in which case this expression is the p-adic expansion of h. Suppose that

$$h = \psi_0 + \psi_1 p + \cdots + \psi_m p^m$$

is its p-adic expansion. Then dividing by p^i for some integer $i > 0$, we obtain the following theorem.

THEOREM 11. *Let h be a polynomial and p an irreducible polynomial over the field K. Let i be an integer > 0. Then there exists a unique expression*

$$\frac{h}{p^i} = \frac{g_{-i}}{p^i} + \frac{g_{-i+1}}{p^{i-1}} + \cdots + g_0 + g_1 p + \cdots + g_s p^s$$

where g_μ are polynomials of degree $< \deg p$.

In Theorem 11, we have adjusted the numbering of $g_{-i}, g_{-i+1}, \ldots$ so that it would fit the exponent of p occurring in the denominator. Otherwise, except for this numbering, these polynomials g are nothing but $\psi_0, \psi_1, \ldots$ found in the p-adic expansion of h.

COROLLARY. *Let $\alpha \in K$, and let h be a polynomial over K. Then*

$$\frac{h(t)}{(t - \alpha)^i} = \frac{a_{-i}}{(t - \alpha)^i} + \frac{a_{-i+1}}{(t - \alpha)^{i+1}} + \cdots + a_0 + a_1(t - \alpha) + \cdots$$

where a_μ are elements of K, uniquely determined.

Proof. In this case, $p(t) = t - \alpha$ has degree 1, so that the coefficients in the p-adic expansion must be constants.

Example 2. To determine the partial fraction decomposition of a given rational function, one can solve a system of linear equations. We give an example. We wish to write

$$\frac{1}{(t - 1)(t - 2)} = \frac{a}{t - 1} + \frac{b}{t - 2}$$

with constants a and b. Putting the right-hand side over a common denominator, we have

$$\frac{1}{(t-1)(t-2)} = \frac{a(t-2) + b(t-1)}{(t-1)(t-2)}.$$

Setting the numerators equal to each other, we must have

$$a + b = 0,$$
$$-2a - b = 1.$$

We then solve for a and b to get $a = -1$ and $b = 1$. The general case can be handled similarly.

EXERCISES

1. Determine the partial fraction decomposition of the following rational functions.

(a) $\dfrac{t+1}{(t-1)(t+2)}$ (b) $\dfrac{1}{(t+1)(t^2+2)}$

2. Let $R = g/f$ be a rational function with $\deg g < \deg f$. Let

$$g/f = \frac{h_1}{p_1^{i_1}} + \cdots + \frac{h_n}{p_n^{i_n}}$$

be its partial fraction decomposition. Let $d_\nu = \deg p_\nu$. Show that the coefficients of $h_1, \ldots, h_n$ are the solutions of a system of linear equations, such that the number of variables is equal to the number of equations, namely

$$\deg f = i_1 d_1 + \cdots + i_n d_n.$$

Theorem 9 shows that this system has a unique solution.

3. Find the $(t-2)$-adic expansion of the following polynomials.
(a) $t^2 - 1$ (b) $t^3 + t - 1$ (c) $t^2 + 3$ (d) $t^4 + 2t^3 - t + 5$

4. Find the $(t-3)$-adic expansion of the polynomials in Exercise 3.

§5. *Polynomials over the integers*

Polynomials with coefficients in the integers $\mathbf{Z}$ form a particularly interesting ring. We shall prove some special properties of such polynomials, leading to an important criterion for irreducibility of polynomials over the rational numbers. If R is a ring, contained in a field, we denote by $R[t]$ the set of polynomials with coefficients in R. It is then clearly a ring, called the polynomial ring over R.

LEMMA 1. *Let f be a polynomial $\neq 0$ over the rational numbers. Then there exists a rational number $r \neq 0$ such that rf has integer coefficients, which are relatively prime.*

Proof. Write

$$f(t) = a_n t^n + \cdots + a_0$$

where $a_0, \ldots, a_n$ are rational numbers, and $a_n \neq 0$. Let d be a common denominator for $a_0, \ldots, a_n$. Then df has integral coefficients, namely $da_n, \ldots, da_0$. Let b be a greatest common divisor for $da_n, \ldots, da_0$. Then

$$\frac{d}{b} f(t) = \frac{da_n}{b} t^n + \cdots + \frac{da_0}{b}$$

has relatively prime integral coefficients, as was to be shown.

LEMMA 2. *Let f, g be non-zero polynomials over the integers, and assume that f has relatively prime coefficients, and so does g. Then fg has relatively prime coefficients.*

Proof. Write

$$f(t) = a_n t^n + \cdots + a_0, \qquad\qquad a_n \neq 0,$$

$$g(t) = b_m t^m + \cdots + b_0, \qquad\qquad b_m \neq 0,$$

with relatively prime $(a_n, \ldots, a_0)$ and relatively prime $(b_m, \ldots, b_0)$. Let p be a prime number. It will suffice to prove that p does not divide any coefficient of fg. Let r be the largest integer such that $0 \leq r \leq n$, $a_r \neq 0$, and p does not divide a_r. Similarly, let b_s be the coefficient of g farthest to the left, $b_s \neq 0$, such that p does not divide b_s. Consider the coefficient of t^{r+s} in $f(t)g(t)$. This coefficient is equal to

$$c = a_r b_s + a_{r+1} b_{s-1} + \cdots$$
$$+ a_{r-1} b_{s+1} + \cdots$$

and p does not divide $a_r b_s$. However, p divides every other non-zero term in this sum since each term will be of the form

$$a_i b_{r+s-i}$$

with a_i to the left of a_r, that is $i > r$, or of the form

$$a_{r+s-j} b_j$$

with $j > s$, that is b_j to the left of b_s. Hence p does not divide c, and our lemma is proved.

THEOREM 12 (Gauss). *Let f be a polynomial with relatively prime integer coefficients and $\deg f \geq 1$. If f is reducible over $\mathbf{Q}$, that is if we can write $f = gh$ with g, $h \in \mathbf{Q}[t]$, and $\deg g \geq 1$, $\deg h \geq 1$, then there exist rational numbers r, s such that, if we let $g_1 = rg$ and $h_1 = sh$, then g_1, h_1 have integer coefficients, and $f = g_1 h_1$.*

Proof. By Lemma 1, let r, s be non-zero rational numbers such that rg and sh have integer coefficients, relatively prime. Let $g_1 = rg$ and $h_1 = sh$. Then

$$f = \frac{1}{r} g_1 \frac{1}{s} h_1,$$

whence $rsf = g_1 h_1$. By Lemma 2, $g_1 h_1$ has relatively prime integer coefficients. Since the coefficients of f are assumed to be relatively prime integers, it follows at once that rs itself must be an integer, and cannot be divisible by any prime. Hence $rs = \pm 1$, and dividing say g_1 by rs we obtain what we want.

THEOREM 13 (Eisenstein's criterion). *Let*

$$f(t) = a_n t^n + \cdots + a_0$$

be a polynomial of degree $n \geq 1$ with integer coefficients. Let p be a prime, and assume

$$a_n \not\equiv 0 \pmod{p}, \qquad a_i \equiv 0 \pmod{p} \quad \textit{for all } i < n,$$

$$a_0 \not\equiv 0 \pmod{p^2}.$$

Then f is irreducible over the rationals.

Proof. We first divide f by the greatest common divisor of its coefficients, and we may then assume that f has relatively prime coefficients. By Theorem 5, we must show that f cannot be written as a product $f = gh$ with g, h having integral coefficients, and deg g, deg $h \geq 1$. Suppose this can be done, and write

$$g(t) = b_d t^d + \cdots + b_0,$$

$$h(t) = c_m t^m + \cdots + c_0,$$

with d, $m \geq 1$ and $b_d c_m \neq 0$. Since $b_0 c_0 = a_0$ is divisible by p but not p^2, it follows that one of the numbers b_0, c_0 is not divisible by p, say b_0. Then $p \mid c_0$. Since $c_m b_d = a_n$ is not divisible by p, it follows that p does not divide c_m. Let c_r be the coefficient of h farthest to the right such that $c_r \not\equiv 0 \pmod{p}$. Then $r \neq n$ and

$$a_r = b_0 c_r + b_1 c_{r-1} + \cdots.$$

Since $p \nmid b_0 c_r$ but p divides every other term in this sum, we conclude that $p \nmid a_r$, a contradiction which proves our theorem.

Example. The polynomial $t^5 - 2$ is irreducible over the rational numbers, as a direct application of Theorem 13.

Remark. The proofs of the unique factorization of polynomials and of integers (given in Chapter I) are very similar. We first used the Euclidean algorithm in both cases to prove that every ideal can be generated by one element. There are very few examples of rings in which such a Euclidean algorithm is valid. However, the subsequent arguments depended only on this consequence. Thus it is useful to give a name to such rings: A ring R is called a *principal ring* if it is entire, and if every ideal can be generated by one element. One can then prove a unique factorization theorem for elements of principal rings, and also prove the analogues of Theorems 12 and 13 over such rings. There exist many examples of such rings, and thus it is worth while to carry out such axiomatizations. We refer the reader to more advanced texts for a systematic exposition.

EXERCISES

1. Let $f(t) = t^n + \cdots + a_0$ be a polynomial of degree $n \geq 1$ with integer coefficients, and leading coefficient 1. Show that if f has a root in the rational numbers, then this root is in fact an integer, and that this integer divides a_0.

2. Determine which of the following polynomials are irreducible over the rational numbers: (a) $t^3 - t + 1$,   (b) $t^3 + 2t + 10$,   (c) $t^3 - t - 1$, (d) $t^3 - 2t^2 + t + 15$.

3. Determine which of the following polynomials are irreducible over the rational numbers: (a) $t^4 + 2$,   (b) $t^4 - 2$,   (c) $t^4 + 4$,   (d) $t^4 - t + 1$.

4. Let $f(t) = a_n t^n + \cdots + a_0$ be a polynomial of degree $n \geq 1$ with integer coefficients, assumed relatively prime, and $a_0 \neq 0$. If b/c is a rational number expressed as a quotient of relatively prime integers, $b, c \neq 0$, and if $f(b/c) = 0$, show that c divides a_n and b divides a_0. (This result allows us to determine effectively all possible rational roots of f since there is only a finite number of divisors of a_n and a_0.)

5. Determine all rational roots of the following polynomials: (a) $t^7 - 1$, (b) $t^8 - 1$,   (c) $2t^2 - 3t + 4$,   (d) $3t^3 + t - 5$,   (e) $2t^4 - 4t + 3$.

§6. *Transcendental elements*

Let K be a field, and assume that K is a subring of a commutative ring E. Let $x \in E$. We use the symbols $K[x]$ to denote the set of all elements

$$a_0 + a_1 x + \cdots + a_n x^n$$

with all $a_i \in K$ and all integers $n \geq 0$. It is then clear that $K[x]$ is a ring, which is said to be *generated over* K by x. Let

$$f(t) = a_0 + a_1 t + \cdots + a_n t^n$$

be a polynomial with coefficients in K. Then we *define*

$$f(x) = a_0 + a_1 x + \cdots + a_n x^n.$$

(Since the coefficients of f are uniquely determined by f, this map is well defined.) We now contend that the map

$$f \mapsto f(x)$$

is a ring-homomorphism of $K[t]$ into E. This is easily verified. For instance, let

$$g(t) = b_0 + b_1 t + \cdots + b_m t^m$$

be another polynomial over K. Then

$$f(x)g(x) = (a_0 + a_1 x + \cdots + a_n x^n)(b_0 + \cdots + b_m x^m)$$

$$= \sum_{i=0}^{n} \sum_{j=0}^{m} a_i x^i b_j x^j = \sum_{i=0}^{n} \sum_{j=0}^{m} a_i b_j x^{i+j}$$

$$= \sum_{k=0}^{m+n} \left(\sum_{i+j=k} a_i b_j \right) x^k$$

$$= (fg)(x).$$

This shows that $(fg)(x) = f(x)g(x)$. Even more trivially, one sees that $(f + g)(x) = f(x) + g(x)$, and the constant polynomial 1 maps on the element 1 of E. Thus we have a ring-homomorphism, which is said to be obtained by *substitution of x in the polynomials*.

If this ring homomorphism is an isomorphism, then we say that x is *transcendental over K*, and we then obtain an isomorphism

$$K[t] \rightarrow K[x].$$

The function I of K into itself such that $I(t) = t$ is transcendental over K, and essentially when we write a polynomial $f(t)$, the symbol t is merely a notation for this function I. The essential thing is that we were able to prove the existence of transcendental elements over K by exhibiting these as polynomial functions.

If x, y are transcendental over K, then $K[x]$ and $K[y]$ are isomorphic, since they are both isomorphic to the polynomial ring $K[t]$. Thus our definition of polynomials was merely a concrete way of dealing with a ring generated over K by a transcendental element.

When K is a *finite* field, one can no longer use the functions to do this. Indeed, if K has q elements, the map $t \mapsto t^q$ is the identity map of K onto itself (because the multiplicative group of non-zero elements of K has

$q - 1$ elements, so that if $x \in K$, $x \neq 0$, then $x^{q-1} = 1$ and $x^q = x$). It is still possible to prove the existence of transcendental elements, by various technical devices. We shall now describe one of them.

We start with a symbol X, and by X^n denote a new symbol for each integer $n \geqq 0$.

We wish to define sums. First, we ask: What do we require of a polynomial

$$a_0 X^0 + \cdots + a_n X^n?$$

We require that it be a sum (in some sense) of terms $a_i X^i$. Thus we must first give a definition for each term $a_i X^i$. If $a \in K$, we wish $a X^n$ to be completely determined by a and n, and see that this should be nothing more than an association of a with X^n, and 0 with X^i for all $i \neq n$. But an association is nothing but a function. This tells us how to define $a X^n$:

We *define* $a X^n$ to be the function, defined on the set $\{X^0, X^1, \ldots\}$ which associates a with X^n and 0 with any X^i for $i \neq n$. We call $a X^n$ a *monomial* with coefficients in K.

We denote by $K[X]$ the set of all sums of such monomials

$$a_0 X^0 + \cdots + a_n X^n$$

with $a_i \in K$, that is the set of all functions of the set $\{X^0, X^1, \ldots\}$ into K which can be written as finite sums of monomials. We call $K[X]$ the set of *formal polynomials* over K, and call X a *variable*, or *indeterminate*, over K. If two sums

$$\sum a_i X^i \qquad \text{and} \qquad \sum b_i X^i$$

are equal, then by definition, we have $a_i = b_i$ for all i. We then call $a_0, a_1, \ldots$ the coefficients of the polynomial $\sum a_i X^i$. Having defined sums, we now define the product of two polynomials in a natural way, that is the product

$$(a_0 X^0 + \cdots + a_n X^n)(b_0 X^0 + \cdots + b_m X^m)$$

is defined to be the polynomial

$$c_0 X^0 + \cdots + c_{m+n} X^{m+n}$$

where

$$c_r = \sum_{i+j=r} a_i b_j = a_0 b_r + a_1 b_{r-1} + \cdots + a_r b_0.$$

It is then a routine matter to prove that $K[X]$ is a ring, that is our addition and multiplication satisfy all the axioms of a ring. We shall prove associativity of multiplication, and leave the other axioms as exercises.

Let

$$f(X) = \sum a_i X^i, \qquad g(X) = \sum b_i X^i, \qquad h(X) = \sum d_i X^i$$

be polynomials. Then

$$f(X)g(X) = \sum c_i X^i$$

with

$$c_r = \sum_{i+j=r} a_i b_j$$

and

$$(f(X)g(X))h(X) = \sum e_i X^i,$$

where by definition

$$e_s = \sum_{r+k=s} c_r d_k = \sum_{r+k=s} \left(\sum_{i+j=r} a_i b_j \right) d_k$$

$$= \sum_{i+j+k=s} a_i b_j d_k.$$

This last sum is taken over all triples (i, j, k) of integers ≥ 0 such that $i + j + k = s$. If we now compute $f(X)(g(X)h(X))$ in a similar way, we find exactly the same coefficients as for $(f(X)g(X))h(X)$, thereby proving associativity.

It is also nothing more than a routine exercise to prove that the map

$$a \mapsto aX^0$$

is an embedding of K into the ring $K[X]$. As a matter of notation, we usually write X instead of $1X$, so $X^n X^m = X^{n+m}$.

From here on, it is possible to prove all the theorems of §1 through §4 without any change in the proofs, the only exception being the last statement in Theorem 1: If f, g are two formal polynomials over a *finite* field K, it is *not true in general* that if $f(t) = g(t)$ for all $t \in K$, then $f = g$. For example, if K has q elements, then the two polynomials

$$X \qquad \text{and} \qquad X^q$$

give rise to the same function of K into itself, but are not equal as formal polynomials. The first has degree 1, whereas the second has degree q.

The only role that the last statement of Theorem 1 played previously was in showing that a polynomial function determines its coefficients uniquely, and for this we needed an infinite field. Using the present approach of formal polynomials, this comes directly from the definition.

In mathematics, by a polynomial, one usually means a formal polynomial unless otherwise specified. When one wishes to deal with a polynomial *function* one says so explicitly.

Let K be a field, which we may assume to be finite, and let K be a subfield of a field E. Let $x \in E$. The set of all elements $f(x)$, where f is a (formal) polynomial over K and $x \in E$ is obviously a subring of E, denoted by $K[x]$. The set of all quotients

$$\frac{f(x)}{g(x)}$$

where f, g are polynomials over K, and $g(x) \neq 0$, is obviously a subfield of E, which we denote by $K(x)$.

Let X be an indeterminate over K, as above. The map

$$f(X) \mapsto f(x)$$

is a homomorphism of $K[X]$ onto the ring $K[x]$. If this homomorphism is an isomorphism, i.e. if x is transcendental over K, then we may extend this map to the quotient field of $K[X]$, which is denoted by $K(X)$, and thus $K(X)$ and $K(x)$ are also isomorphic.

In Chapter VI, we shall study the case when the map

$$f(X) \mapsto f(x)$$

is *not* an isomorphism.

Exercises

1. Let K be a finite field with q elements. If f, g are polynomials over K of degrees $< q$, and if $f(x) = g(x)$ for all $x \in K$, prove that $f = g$ (as formal polynomials).

2. Let K be a finite field with q elements. Let f be a polynomial over K. Show that there exists a polynomial f^* over K of degree $< q$ such that

$$f^*(x) = f(x)$$

for all $x \in K$.

3. Let K be a finite field with q elements. Let $a \in K$. Show that there exists a polynomial f over K such that $f(a) = 0$ and $f(x) = 1$ for $x \in K$, $x \neq a$. [*Hint:* $(X - a)^{q-1}$.]

4. Let K be a finite field with q elements. Let $a \in K$. Show that there exists a polynomial f over K such that $f(a) = 1$ and $f(x) = 0$ for all $x \in K$, $x \neq a$.

5. Let K be a finite field with q elements. Let $\varphi \colon K \to K$ be any function of K into itself. Show that there exists a polynomial f over K such that $\varphi(x) = f(x)$ for all $x \in K$.

§7. *Polynomials in several variables*

Let n be an integer ≥ 1. Let K be a field (*assumed infinite* according to our conventions). We define a *polynomial in n variables over K* to be a function

$$f \colon K^n \to K$$

which can be written in the form

$$f(t_1, \ldots, t_n) = \text{finite sum of terms of type } a_{i_1 \cdots i_n} t_1^{i_1} \cdots t_n^{i_n}$$

with $a_{i_1 \cdots i_n} \in K$, and $i_1, \ldots, i_n$ integers ≥ 0. We shall abbreviate such a sum in the form

$$f(t_1, \ldots, t_n) = \sum_{(i)} a_{(i)} M_{(i)}(t_1, \ldots, t_n),$$

where

$$M_{(i)}(t_1, \ldots, t_n) = t_1^{i_1} \cdots t_n^{i_n}.$$

If we collect all terms having the same exponent i_n for t_n, we can write f in the form

$$f(t_1, \ldots, t_n) = \sum_{i_n=0}^{d_n} \left(\sum_{i_1, \ldots, i_{n-1}} a_{(i)} t_1^{i_1} \cdots t_{n-1}^{i_{n-1}} \right) t_n^{i_n}$$

and thus see that f can be written

$$f(t_1, \ldots, t_n) = \sum_{j=0}^{d_n} f_j(t_1, \ldots, t_{n-1}) t_n^{j},$$

where f_j are polynomials in $n - 1$ variables.

THEOREM 14. *Let $f(t_1, \ldots, t_n)$ be a polynomial over the field K as above. Let $S_1, \ldots, S_n$ be infinite subsets of K, and assume that $f(t_1, \ldots, t_n) = 0$ for all $t_i \in S_i$. Then $a_{(i)} = 0$ for all n-tuples (i) of integers ≥ 0.*

Proof. By induction on n. If $n = 1$, this is a special case of Theorem 1, §1. Let $n > 1$, and assume the theorem proved for $n - 1$. Let $t_1, \ldots, t_{n-1}$ be elements of $S_1, \ldots, S_{n-1}$ respectively. Then we obtain a polynomial in one variable

$$g(t) = \sum_{j=0}^{d_n} b_j t^j,$$

where $b_j = f_j(t_1, \ldots, t_{n-1})$. Furthermore, $g(t) = 0$ for all $t \in S_n$. Hence $b_j = 0$ for all j. By induction, it follows that $a_{(i)} = 0$ for all (i), as desired.

From Theorem 14, we conclude that if f admits expressions

$$\sum_{(i)} a_{(i)} M_{(i)}(t_1, \ldots, t_n) = \sum_{(i)} b_{(i)} M_{(i)}(t_1, \ldots, t_n)$$

then $a_{(i)} = b_{(i)}$ for all (i). (Subtract, and apply Theorem 14.) Thus the elements $a_{(i)}$ of K are uniquely determined by f, and are again called the *coefficients* of f.

It will be convenient to abbreviate $f(t_1, \ldots, t_n)$ by $f(t)$. It is clear that the product of polynomials in several variables is again a polynomial, and so is the sum. Hence polynomials in n variables form a subring of the ring of all functions of K^n into K, denoted by $K[t_1, \ldots, t_n]$, and also abbreviated sometimes by $K[t]$.

Just as with polynomials in one variable, suppose that K is a subring of a commutative ring E. Let $x_1, \ldots, x_n$ be elements of E. Let f be a polynomial in n variables over K, written as previously, with coefficients $a_{(i)}$, and define

$$f(x_1, \ldots, x_n) = \sum_{(i)} a_{(i)} x_1^{i_1} \cdots x_n^{i_n}.$$

Then the map

$$f \mapsto f(x_1, \ldots, x_n)$$

is a ring-homomorphism of $K[t_1, \ldots, t_n]$ into E. Its image is denoted by $K[x_1, \ldots, x_n]$. If our map is an isomorphism of $K[t_1, \ldots, t_n]$ onto its image, then we say that $x_1, \ldots, x_n$ are *algebraically independent over K*. One can make for several variables the same comments that we made in the preceding section concerning the construction of polynomials over fields which are not infinite.

In a way similar to the case of one element, we can define $K(x_1, \ldots, x_n)$ to be the set of all quotients

$$\frac{f(x_1, \ldots, x_n)}{g(x_1, \ldots, x_n)}$$

where f, g are polynomials in several variables over K, and

$$g(x_1, \ldots, x_n) \neq 0.$$

It is clear that $K(x_1, \ldots, x_n)$ is a subfield of E. (Give the proof in all details.)

THEOREM 15. *Let K be a subfield of a field E, and let $x_1, \ldots, x_n \in E$. Let $K_r = K(x_1, \ldots, x_r)$ for $1 \leq r \leq n$. If x_{r+1} is transcendental over K_r for each $r = 1, \ldots, n - 1$, then $x_1, \ldots, x_n$ are algebraically independent over K, and conversely.*

Proof. We leave it as an exercise to the reader.

CHAPTER V

Vector Spaces and Modules

§1. Vector spaces and bases

Let K be a field. A *vector space V over the field K* is an additive (abelian) group, together with a multiplication of elements of V by elements of K, i.e. an association

$$(x, v) \mapsto xv$$

of $K \times V$ into V, satisfying the following conditions:

VS 1. *If 1 is the unit element of K, then $1v = v$ for all $v \in V$.*
VS 2. *If $c \in K$ and v, $w \in V$, then $c(v + w) = cv + cw$.*
VS 3. *If $x, y \in K$ and $v \in V$, then $(x + y)v = xv + yv$.*
VS 4. *If $x, y \in K$ and $v \in V$, then $(xy)v = x(yv)$.*

Example 1. Let V be the set of continuous real-valued functions on the interval $[0, 1]$. Then V is a vector space over **R**. The addition of functions is defined as usual: If f, g are functions, we define

$$(f + g)(t) = f(t) + g(t).$$

If $c \in \mathbf{R}$, we define $(cf)(t) = cf(t)$. It is then a simple routine matter to verify that all four conditions are satisfied.

Example 2. Let S be a non-empty set, and V the set of all maps of S into K. Then V is a vector space over K, the addition of maps and the multiplication of maps by elements of K being defined as for functions in the preceding example.

Example 3. Let K^n denote the product $K \times \cdots \times K$, i.e. the set of n-tuples of elements of K. (If $K = \mathbf{R}$, this is the usual Euclidean space.) We define addition of n-tuples componentwise, that is if

$$X = (x_1, \ldots, x_n) \qquad \text{and} \qquad Y = (y_1, \ldots, y_n)$$

are elements of K^n with x_i, $y_i \in K$, then we define

$$X + Y = (x_1 + y_1, \ldots, x_n + y_n).$$

If $c \in K$, we define

$$cX = (cx_1, \ldots, cx_n).$$

It is routine to verify that all four conditions of a vector space are satisfied by these operations.

Example 4.   Taking $n = 1$ in Example 3, we see that K is a vector space over itself.

Let V be a vector space over the field K. Let $v \in V$. Then $0v = 0$. Proof: $0v + v = 0v + 1v = (0 + 1)v = 1v = v$.   Hence adding $-v$ to both sides shows that $0v = 0$.

If $c \in K$ and $cv = 0$, but $c \neq 0$, then $v = 0$. To see this, multiply by c^{-1} to find $c^{-1}cv = 0$ whence $v = 0$.

We have $(-1)v = -v$. Proof:

$$(-1)v + v = (-1)v + 1v = (-1 + 1)v = 0v = 0.$$

Hence $(-1)v = -v$.

Let V be a vector space, and W a subset of V. We shall say that W is a *subspace* if W is a subgroup (of the additive group of V), and if given $c \in K$ and $v \in W$ then cv is also an element of W. In other words, a subspace W of V is a subset satisfying the following conditions:

(i)   If v, w are elements of W, their sum $v + w$ is also an element of W.
(ii)   The element 0 of V is also an element of W.
(iii)   If $v \in W$ and $c \in K$ then $cv \in W$.

Then W itself is a vector space. Indeed, properties VS 1 through VS 4, being satisfied for all elements of V, are satisfied *a fortiori* for the elements of W.

Let V be a vector space, and $w_1, \ldots, w_n$ elements of V. Let W be the set of all elements

$$x_1 w_1 + \cdots + x_n w_n$$

with $x_i \in K$. Then W is a subspace of V, as one verifies without difficulty. It is called the subspace *generated* by $w_1, \ldots, w_n$, and we call $w_1, \ldots, w_n$ *generators* for this subspace.

Let V be a vector space over the field K, and let $v_1, \ldots, v_n$ be elements of V. We shall say that $v_1, \ldots, v_n$ are *linearly dependent* over K if there exist elements $a_1, \ldots, a_n$ in K not all equal to 0 such that

$$a_1 v_1 + \cdots + a_n v_n = 0.$$

If there do not exist such elements, then we say that $v_1, \ldots, v_n$ are *linearly independent over K*. We often omit the words "over K".

Example 5.   Let $V = K^n$ and consider the vectors

$$v_1 = (1, 0, \ldots, 0)$$
$$\vdots$$
$$v_n = (0, 0, \ldots, 1).$$

Then $v_1, \ldots, v_n$ are linearly independent.   Indeed, let $a_1, \ldots, a_n$ be elements of K such that $a_1 v_1 + \cdots + a_n v_n = 0$.   Since

$$a_1 v_1 + \cdots + a_n v_n = (a_1, \ldots, a_n),$$

it follows that all $a_i = 0$.

Example 6.   Let V be the vector space of all functions of a real variable t.   Let $f_1(t), \ldots, f_n(t)$ be n functions.   To say that they are linearly dependent is to say that there exist n real numbers $a_1, \ldots, a_n$ not all equal to 0 such that

$$a_1 f_1(t) + \cdots + a_n f_n(t) = 0$$

for *all* values of t.

The two functions e^t, e^{2t} are linearly independent.   To prove this, suppose that there are numbers a, b such that

$$ae^t + be^{2t} = 0$$

(for all values of t).   Differentiate this relation.   We obtain

$$ae^t + 2be^{2t} = 0.$$

Subtract the first from the second relation.   We obtain $be^t = 0$, and hence $b = 0$.   From the first relation, it follows that $ae^t = 0$, and hence $a = 0$. Hence e^t, e^{2t} are linearly independent.

Consider again an arbitrary vector space V over a field K.   Let $v_1, \ldots, v_n$ be linearly independent elements of V.   Let $x_1, \ldots, x_n$ and $y_1, \ldots, y_n$ be numbers.   Suppose that we have

$$x_1 v_1 + \cdots + x_n v_n = y_1 v_1 + \cdots + y_n v_n.$$

In other words, two linear combinations of $v_1, \ldots, v_n$ are equal.   Then we must have $x_i = y_i$ for each $i = 1, \ldots, n$.   Indeed, subtracting the right-hand side from the left-hand side, we get

$$x_1 v_1 - y_1 v_1 + \cdots + x_n v_n - y_n v_n = 0.$$

We can write this relation also in the form

$$(x_1 - y_1)v_1 + \cdots + (x_n - y_n)v_n = 0.$$

By definition, we must have $x_i - y_i = 0$ for all $i = 1, \ldots, n$, thereby proving our assertion.

We define a *basis* of V over K to be a sequence of elements $\{v_1, \ldots, v_n\}$ of V which generate V and are linearly independent.

The vectors $v_1, \ldots, v_n$ of Example 5 form a basis of K^n over K.

Let W be the vector space of functions generated over $\mathbf{R}$ by the two functions e^t, e^{2t}. Then $\{e^t, e^{2t}\}$ is a basis of W over $\mathbf{R}$.

Let V be a vector space, and let $\{v_1, \ldots, v_n\}$ be a basis of V. The elements of V can be represented by n-tuples relative to this basis, as follows. If an element v of V is written as a linear combination

$$v = x_1 v_1 + \cdots + x_n v_n$$

of the basis elements, then we call $(x_1, \ldots, x_n)$ the *coordinates* of v with respect to our basis, and we call x_i the i-th coordinate. We say that the n-tuple $X = (x_1, \ldots, x_n)$ is the *coordinate vector* of v with respect to the basis $\{v_1, \ldots, v_n\}$.

For example, let V be the vector space of functions generated by the two functions e^t, e^{2t}. Then the coordinates of the function

$$3e^t + 5e^{2t}$$

with respect to the basis $\{e^t, e^{2t}\}$ are $(3, 5)$.

Example 7.   Show that the vectors $(1, 1)$ and $(-3, 2)$ are linearly independent over $\mathbf{R}$.

Let a, b be two real numbers such that

$$a(1, 1) + b(-3, 2) = 0.$$

Writing this equation in terms of components, we find

$$a - 3b = 0,$$
$$a + 2b = 0.$$

This is a system of two equations which we solve for a and b. Subtracting the second from the first, we get $-5b = 0$, whence $b = 0$. Substituting in either equation, we find $a = 0$. Hence a, b are both 0, and our vectors are linearly independent.

Example 8.   Find the coordinates of $(1, 0)$ with respect to the two vectors $(1, 1)$ and $(-1, 2)$.

We must find numbers a, b such that

$$a(1, 1) + b(-1, 2) = (1, 0).$$

Writing this equation in terms of coordinates, we find

$$a - b = 1,$$

$$a + 2b = 0.$$

Solving for a and b in the usual manner yields $b = -\frac{1}{3}$ and $a = \frac{2}{3}$. Hence the coordinates of $(1, 0)$ with respect to $(1, 1)$ and $(-1, 2)$ are $(\frac{2}{3}, -\frac{1}{3})$.

Let $\{v_1, \ldots, v_n\}$ be a set of elements of a vector space V over a field K. Let r be a positive integer $\leqq n$. We shall say that $\{v_1, \ldots, v_r\}$ is a *maximal* subset of linearly independent elements if $v_1, \ldots, v_r$ are linearly independent, and if in addition, given any v_i with $i > r$, the elements $v_1, \ldots, v_r, v_i$ are linearly dependent.

The next theorem gives us a useful criterion to determine when a set of elements of a vector space is a basis.

THEOREM 1. *Let $\{v_1, \ldots, v_n\}$ be a set of generators of a vector space V. Let $\{v_1, \ldots, v_r\}$ be a maximal subset of linearly independent elements. Then $\{v_1, \ldots, v_r\}$ is a basis of V.*

Proof. We must prove that $v_1, \ldots, v_r$ generate V. We shall first prove that each v_i (for $i > r$) is a linear combination of $v_1, \ldots, v_r$. By hypothesis, given v_i, there exist $x_1, \ldots, x_r, y \in K$, not all 0, such that

$$x_1 v_1 + \cdots + x_r v_r + y v_i = 0.$$

Furthermore, $y \neq 0$, because otherwise, we would have a relation of linear dependence for $v_1, \ldots, v_r$. Hence we can solve for v_i, namely

$$v_i = \frac{x_1}{-y} v_1 + \cdots + \frac{x_r}{-y} v_r,$$

thereby showing that v_i is a linear combination of $v_1, \ldots, v_r$.

Next, let v be any element of V. There exist $c_1, \ldots, c_n \in K$ such that

$$v = c_1 v_1 + \cdots + c_n v_n.$$

In this relation, we can replace each v_i $(i > r)$ by a linear combination of $v_1, \ldots, v_r$. If we do this, and then collect terms, we find that we have expressed v as a linear combination of $v_1, \ldots, v_r$. This proves that $v_1, \ldots, v_r$ generate V, and hence form a basis of V.

Let V, W be vector spaces over K. A map

$$f: V \to W$$

is called a *K-linear map,* or a *homomorphism of vector spaces,* if f satisfies the following conditions.

For all $x \in K$ and $v, v' \in V$ we have

$$f(v + v') = f(v) + f(v'), \qquad f(xv) = xf(v).$$

Thus f is a homomorphism of V into W viewed as additive groups, satisfying the additional condition $f(xv) = xf(v)$. We usually say "linear map" instead of "K-linear map".

THEOREM 2. *Let V, W be vector spaces, and $\{v_1, \ldots, v_n\}$ a basis of V. Let $w_1, \ldots, w_n$ be elements of W. Then there exists a unique linear map $f: V \to W$ such that $f(v_i) = w_i$ for all i.*

Proof. The K-linear map f is uniquely determined, because if

$$v = x_1 v_1 + \cdots + x_n v_n$$

is an element of V, with $x_i \in K$, then we must necessarily have

$$f(v) = x_1 f(v_1) + \cdots + x_n f(v_n)$$
$$= x_1 w_1 + \cdots + x_n w_n.$$

The map f exists, for given an element v as above, we *define* $f(v)$ to be $x_1 w_1 + \cdots + x_n w_n$. We must then see that f is a linear map. Let

$$w = y_1 v_1 + \cdots + y_n v_n$$

be an element of V with $y_i \in K$. Then

$$v + w = (x_1 + y_1)v_1 + \cdots + (x_n + y_n)v_n.$$

Hence

$$f(v + w) = (x_1 + y_1)w_1 + \cdots + (x_n + y_n)w_n$$
$$= x_1 w_1 + y_1 w_1 + \cdots + x_n w_n + y_n w_n$$
$$= f(v) + f(w).$$

If $c \in K$, then $cv = cx_1 v_1 + \cdots + cx_n v_n$, and hence

$$f(cv) = cx_1 w_1 + \cdots + cx_n w_n = cf(v).$$

This proves that f is linear, and concludes the proof of the theorem.

As with groups, we say that a linear map $f: V \to W$ is an *isomorphism* (i.e. a vector space isomorphism) if there exists a linear map $g: W \to V$ such that $g \circ f$ is the identity of V, and $f \circ g$ is the identity of W. The *kernel* of a linear map is defined to be the kernel of the map viewed as an additive group-homomorphism. Again as an exercise, prove that the kernel and image of a linear map are subspaces.

EXERCISES

1. Show that the following vectors are linearly independent, over **R** and over **C**.

(a) $(1, 1, 1)$ and $(0, 1, -1)$ (b) $(1, 0)$ and $(1, 1)$

(c) $(-1, 1, 0)$ and $(0, 1, 2)$ (d) $(2, -1)$ and $(1, 0)$

(e) $(\pi, 0)$ and $(0, 1)$ (f) $(1, 2)$ and $(1, 3)$

(g) $(1, 1, 0)$, $(1, 1, 1)$ and $(0, 1, -1)$ (h) $(0, 1, 1)$, $(0, 2, 1)$ and $(1, 5, 3)$

2. Express the given vector X as a linear combination of the given vectors A, B and find the coordinates of X with respect to A, B.

(a) $X = (1, 0)$, $A = (1, 1)$, $B = (0, 1)$

(b) $X = (2, 1)$, $A = (1, -1)$, $B = (1, 1)$

(c) $X = (1, 1)$, $A = (2, 1)$, $B = (-1, 0)$

(d) $X = (4, 3)$, $A = (2, 1)$, $B = (-1, 0)$

(You may view the above vectors as elements of $\mathbf{R}^2$ or $\mathbf{C}^2$. The coordinates will be the same.)

3. Find the coordinates of the vector X with respect to the vectors A, B, C.

(a) $X = (1, 0, 0)$, $A = (1, 1, 1)$, $B = (-1, 1, 0)$, $C = (1, 0, -1)$

(b) $X = (1, 1, 1)$, $A = (0, 1, -1)$, $B = (1, 1, 0)$, $C = (1, 0, 2)$

(c) $X = (0, 0, 1)$, $A = (1, 1, 1)$, $B = (-1, 1, 0)$, $C = (1, 0, -1)$

4. Let (a, b) and (c, d) be two vectors in the plane. If $ad - bc = 0$, show that they are linearly dependent. If $ad - bc \neq 0$, show that they are linearly independent.

5. Prove that 1, $\sqrt{2}$ are linearly independent over the rational numbers.

6. Prove that 1, $\sqrt{3}$ are linearly independent over the rational numbers.

7. Let α be a complex number. Show that α is rational if and only if 1, α are linearly dependent over the rational numbers.

8. Let V, W be vector spaces over the field K, and denote by $\mathrm{Hom}_K(V, W)$ the set of all linear maps of V into W. Show that $\mathrm{Hom}_K(V, W)$ is a subgroup of the (additive) group of all maps of V into W. If $f\colon V \to W$ is a linear map, $c \in K$, define cf to be the map such that $(cf)(v) = cf(v)$. Show that $\mathrm{Hom}_K(V, W)$ is then a vector space over K.

§2. *Dimension of a vector space*

The main result of this section is that any two bases of a vector space have the same number of elements. To prove this, we first have an intermediate result.

THEOREM 3. *Let V be a vector space over the field K. Let $\{v_1, \ldots, v_m\}$ be a basis of V over K. Let $w_1, \ldots, w_n$ be elements of V, and assume that $n > m$. Then $w_1, \ldots, w_n$ are linearly dependent.*

Proof. Assume that $w_1, \ldots, w_n$ are linearly independent. Since $\{v_1, \ldots, v_m\}$ is a basis, there exist elements $a_1, \ldots, a_m \in K$ such that

$$w_1 = a_1 v_1 + \cdots + a_m v_m.$$

By assumption, we know that $w_1 \neq 0$, and hence some $a_i \neq 0$. After renumbering $v_1, \ldots, v_m$ if necessary, we may assume without loss of generality that say $a_1 \neq 0$. We can then solve for v_1, and get

$$a_1 v_1 = w_1 - a_2 v_2 - \cdots - a_m v_m,$$

$$v_1 = a_1^{-1} w_1 - a_1^{-1} a_2 v_2 - \cdots - a_1^{-1} a_m v_m.$$

The subspace of V generated by $w_1, v_2, \ldots, v_m$ contains v_1, and hence must be all of V since $v_1, v_2, \ldots, v_m$ generate V. The idea is now to continue our procedure stepwise, and to replace successively $v_2, v_3, \ldots$ by $w_2, w_3, \ldots$ until all the elements $v_1, \ldots, v_m$ are exhausted, and $w_1, \ldots, w_m$ generate V. Let us now assume by induction that there is an integer r with $1 \leq r < m$ such that, after a suitable renumbering of $v_1, \ldots, v_m$, the elements $w_1, \ldots, w_r, v_{r+1}, \ldots, v_m$ generate V. There exist elements $b_1, \ldots, b_r, c_{r+1}, \ldots, c_m$ in K such that

$$w_{r+1} = b_1 w_1 + \cdots + b_r w_r + c_{r+1} v_{r+1} + \cdots + c_m v_m.$$

We cannot have $c_j = 0$ for $j = r + 1, \ldots, m$, for otherwise, we get a relation of linear dependence between $w_1, \ldots, w_{r+1}$, contradicting our assumption. After renumbering $v_{r+1}, \ldots, v_m$ if necessary, we may assume without loss of generality that say $c_{r+1} \neq 0$. We then obtain

$$c_{r+1} v_{r+1} = w_{r+1} - b_1 w_1 - \cdots - b_r w_r - c_{r+2} v_{r+2} - \cdots - c_m v_m.$$

Dividing by c_{r+1}, we conclude that v_{r+1} is in the subspace generated by $w_1, \ldots, w_{r+1}, v_{r+2}, \ldots, v_m$. By our induction assumption, it follows that $w_1, \ldots, w_{r+1}, v_{r+2}, \ldots, v_m$ generate V. Thus by induction, we have proved that $w_1, \ldots, w_m$ generate V. If we write

$$w_{m+1} = x_1 w_1 + \cdots + x_m w_m$$

with $x_i \in K$, we obtain a relation of linear dependence

$$w_{m+1} - x_1 w_1 - \cdots - x_m w_m = 0,$$

as was to be shown.

THEOREM 4. *Let V be a vector space over K, and let $\{v_1, \ldots, v_n\}$ and $\{w_1, \ldots, w_m\}$ be two bases of V. Then $m = n$.*

Proof. By Theorem 3, we must have $n \leq m$ and $m \leq n$, so $m = n$.

If a vector space has one basis, then every other basis has the same number of elements. This number is called the *dimension* of V (over K). If V is the zero vector space, we define V to have dimension 0.

COROLLARY. *Let V be a vector space of dimension n, and let W be a subspace containing n linearly independent elements. Then $W = V$.*

Proof. Let $v \in V$ and let $w_1, \ldots, w_n$ be linearly independent elements of W. Then $w_1, \ldots, w_n, v$ are linearly dependent, so there exist $a, b_1, \ldots, b_n \in K$ not all zero such that

$$av + b_1 w_1 + \cdots + b_n w_n = 0.$$

We cannot have $a = 0$, otherwise $w_1, \ldots, w_n$ are linearly dependent. Then

$$v = -a^{-1} b_1 w_1 - \cdots - a^{-1} b_n w_n$$

is an element of W. This proves $V \subset W$, so $V = W$.

§3. *Modules*

We may consider a generalization of the notion of vector space over a field, namely module over a ring. Let R be a ring. By a (left) *module* over R, or an *R-module*, one means an additive group M, together with a map $R \times M \to M$, which to each pair (x, v) with $x \in R$ and $v \in M$ associates an element xv of M, satisfying the four conditions:

MOD 1. *If e is the unit element of R, then $ev = v$ for all $v \in M$.*

MOD 2. *If $x \in R$ and $v, w \in M$, then $x(v + w) = xv + xw$.*

MOD 3. *If $x, y \in R$ and $v \in M$, then $(x + y)v = xv + yv$.*

MOD 4. *If $x, y \in R$ and $v \in M$, then $(xy)v = x(yv)$.*

Example 1. Every left ideal of R is a module. The additive group consisting of 0 alone is an R-module for every ring R.

As with vector spaces, we have $0v = 0$ for every $v \in M$. (Note that the 0 in $0v$ is the zero element of R, while the 0 on the other side of the equation is the zero element of the additive group M. However, there will be no confusion in using the same symbol 0 for all zero elements everywhere.) Also, we have $(-e)v = -v$, with the same proof as for vector spaces.

Let M be a module over R and let N be a subgroup of M. We say that N is a *submodule* of M if whenever $v \in N$ and $x \in R$ then $xv \in N$. It follows that N is then itself a module.

Example 2. Let M be a module and $v_1, \ldots, v_n$ elements of M. Let N be the subset of M consisting of all elements

$$x_1 v_1 + \cdots + x_n v_n$$

with $x_i \in R$. Then M is a submodule of M. Indeed,

$$0 = 0v_1 + \cdots + 0v_n$$

so $0 \in N$. If $y_1, \ldots, y_n \in R$, then

$$x_1 v_1 + \cdots + x_n v_n + y_1 v_1 + \cdots + y_n v_n$$
$$= (x_1 + y_1)v_1 + \cdots + (x_n + y_n)v_n$$

is in N. Finally, if $c \in R$, then

$$c(x_1 v_1 + \cdots + x_n v_n) = c x_1 v_1 + \cdots + c x_n v_n$$

is in N, so we have proved that N is a submodule. It is called the submodule *generated* by $v_1, \ldots, v_n$, and we call $v_1, \ldots, v_n$ *generators* for N.

Example 3. Let M be an (abelian) additive group, and let R be a subring of $\mathrm{End}(M)$. (We defined $\mathrm{End}(M)$ in Chapter III, §1 as the ring of homomorphisms of M into itself.) Then M is an R-module, if to each $f \in R$ and $v \in M$ we associate the element $fv = f(v) \in M$. The verification of the four conditions for a module is trivially carried out.

Conversely, given a ring R and an R-module M, to each $x \in R$ we associate the mapping $\lambda_x: M \to M$ such that $\lambda_x(v) = xv$ for $v \in M$. Then the association

$$x \mapsto \lambda_x$$

is a ring-homomorphism of R into $\mathrm{End}(M)$, where $\mathrm{End}(M)$ is the ring of endomorphisms of M viewed as additive group. This is but another way of formulating the four conditions MOD 1 through MOD 4. For instance, MOD 4 in the present notation can be written

$$\lambda_{xy} = \lambda_x \lambda_y \qquad \text{or} \qquad \lambda_{xy} = \lambda_x \circ \lambda_y$$

since the multiplication in $\mathrm{End}(M)$ is composition of mappings.

Warning: It may be that the ring-homomorphism $x \mapsto \lambda_x$ is not injective, so that in general, when dealing with a module, we cannot view R as a subring of $\mathrm{End}(M)$.

Let R be a ring, and let M, M' be R-modules. By an R-*linear* map (or R-*homomorphism*) $f: M \to M'$ one means a map such that for all $x \in R$ and $v, w \in M$ we have

$$f(xv) = xf(v), \qquad f(v + w) = f(v) + f(w).$$

Thus an R-*linear* map is the generalization of a K-linear map when the module is a vector space over a field.

The set of all R-linear maps of M into M' will be denoted by $\mathrm{Hom}_R(M, M')$.

Example 4.   Let M, M', M'' be R-modules. If

$$f\colon M \to M' \qquad \text{and} \qquad g\colon M' \to M''$$

are R-linear maps, then the composite map $g \circ f$ is R-linear.

In analogy with previous definitions, we say that an R-homomorphism $f\colon M \to M'$ is an *isomorphism* if there exists an R-homomorphism $g\colon M' \to M$ such that $g \circ f$ and $f \circ g$ are the identity mappings of M and M', respectively. We leave it to the reader to verify that *an R-homomorphism which is injective and bijective is an isomorphism, and conversely.*

As with vector spaces and additive groups, we have to consider very frequently the set of R-linear maps of a module M into itself, and it is convenient to have a name for these maps. They are called *R-endomorphisms* of M. The set of R-endomorphisms of M is denoted by $\operatorname{End}_R(M)$. We often suppress the prefix R- when the reference to the ring R is clear.

Let $f\colon M \to M'$ be a homomorphism of modules over R. We define the *kernel* of f to be its kernel viewed as a homomorphism of additive groups.

In analogy with previous results, we have:

Let $f\colon M \to M'$ be a homomorphism of R-modules. Then the kernel of f and the image of f are submodules of M and M' respectively.

Proof.   Let E be the kernel of f. Then we already know that E is an additive subgroup of M. Let $v \in E$ and $x \in R$. Then

$$f(xv) = xf(v) = x0 = 0,$$

so $xv \in E$, and this proves that the kernel of f is a submodule of M. We already know that the image of f is a subgroup of M'. Let v' be in the image of f, and $x \in R$. Let v be an element of M such that

$$f(v) = v'.$$

Then $f(xv) = xf(v) = xv'$ also lies in the image of M, which is therefore a submodule of M', thereby proving our assertion.

Example 5.   Let R be a ring, and M a left ideal. Let $y \in M$. The map

$$r_y\colon M \to M$$

such that

$$r_y(x) = xy$$

is an R-linear map of M into itself. Indeed, if $x \in M$ then $xy \in M$ since M is a left ideal, and the conditions for R-linearity are reformulations of definitions. For instance,

$$r_y(x_1 + x_2) = (x_1 + x_2)y = x_1y + x_2y$$
$$= r_y(x_1) + r_y(x_2).$$

Furthermore, for $z \in R$, $x \in M$,

$$r_y(zx) = zxy = zr_y(x).$$

We call r_y *right multiplication* by y. Thus r_y is an R-endomorphism of M.

Observe that any abelian group can be viewed as a module over the integers. Thus an R-module M is also a $\mathbf{Z}$-module, and any R-endomorphism of M is also an endomorphism of M viewed as abelian group. Thus $\operatorname{End}_R(M)$ is a subset of $\operatorname{End}(M) = \operatorname{End}_{\mathbf{Z}}(M)$.

In fact, $\operatorname{End}_R(M)$ *is a subring of* $\operatorname{End}(M)$, *so that* $\operatorname{End}_R(M)$ *is itself a ring.* The proof is routine. For instance, if f, $g \in \operatorname{End}_R(M)$, and $x \in R$, $v \in M$, then

$$\begin{aligned}(f + g)(xv) &= f(xv) + g(xv)\\ &= xf(v) + xg(v)\\ &= x\big(f(v) + g(v)\big)\\ &= x(f + g)(v).\end{aligned}$$

So $f + g \in \operatorname{End}_R(M)$. Equally easily,

$$(f \circ g)(xv) = f(g(xv)) = f(xg(v)) = xf(g(v)).$$

The identity is in $\operatorname{End}_R(M)$. This proves that $\operatorname{End}_R(M)$ is a subring of $\operatorname{End}_{\mathbf{Z}}(M)$.

We now also see that M can be viewed as a module over $\operatorname{End}_R(M)$ since M is a module over $\operatorname{End}_{\mathbf{Z}}(M) = \operatorname{End}(M)$.

Let us denote $\operatorname{End}_R(M)$ by $R'(M)$ or simply R' for clarity of notation. Let $f \in R'$ and $x \in R$. Then by definition,

$$f(xv) = xf(v),$$

and consequently

$$f \circ \lambda_x(v) = \lambda_x \circ f(v).$$

Hence λ_x is an R'-linear map of M into itself, i.e. an element of $\operatorname{End}_{R'}(M)$. The association

$$\lambda \colon x \mapsto \lambda_x$$

is therefore a ring-homomorphism of R into $\operatorname{End}_{R'}(M)$, not only into $\operatorname{End}(M)$.

THEOREM 5. *Let R be a ring, and M an R-module. Let J be the set of elements $x \in R$ such that $xv = 0$ for all $v \in M$. Then J is a two-sided ideal of R.*

Proof. If $x, y \in J$, then $(x + y)v = xv + yv = 0$ for all $v \in M$. If $a \in R$, then

$$(ax)v = a(xv) = 0 \qquad \text{and} \qquad (xa)v = x(av) = 0$$

for all $v \in M$. This proves the theorem.

We observe that the two-sided ideal of Theorem 5 is none other than the kernel of the ring-homomorphism

$$x \mapsto \lambda_x$$

described in the preceding discussion.

THEOREM 6 (Wedderburn-Rieffel). *Let R be a ring, and L a non-zero left ideal, viewed as R-module. Let $R' = \mathrm{End}_R(L)$, and $R'' = \mathrm{End}_{R'}(L)$. Let*

$$\lambda \colon R \to R''$$

be the ring-homomorphism such that $\lambda_x(y) = xy$ for $x \in R$ and $y \in L$. Assume that R has no two-sided ideals other than 0 and R itself. Then λ is a ring-isomorphism.

Proof. (Rieffel) The fact that λ is injective follows from Theorem 5, and the hypothesis that L is non-zero. Therefore, the only thing to prove is that λ is surjective. By Example 6 of Chapter III, §2, we know that LR is a two-sided ideal, non-zero since R has a unit, and hence equal to R by hypothesis. Then

$$\lambda(LR) = \lambda(L)\lambda(R) = \lambda(R).$$

We now contend that $\lambda(L)$ is a left ideal of R''. To prove this, let $f \in R''$, and let $x \in L$. For all $y \in L$, we know from Example 5 that r_y is in R', and hence that

$$f \circ r_y = r_y \circ f.$$

This means that $f(xy) = f(x)y$. We may rewrite this relation in the form

$$f \circ \lambda_x(y) = \lambda_{f(x)}(y).$$

Hence $f \circ \lambda_x$ is an element of $\lambda(L)$, namely $\lambda_{f(x)}$. This proves that $\lambda(L)$ is a left ideal of R''. But then

$$R''\lambda(R) = R''\lambda(L)\lambda(R) = \lambda(L)\lambda(R) = \lambda(R).$$

Since $\lambda(R)$ contains the identity map, say e, it follows that for every $f \in R''$, the map $f \circ e = f$ is contained in $\lambda(R)$, i.e. R'' is contained in $\lambda(R)$, and therefore $R'' = \lambda(R)$, as was to be proved.

The whole point of Theorem 6 is that it represents R as a ring of endomorphisms of some module, namely the left ideal L. This is important in the following case.

Let D be a ring. We shall say that D is a *division ring* if the set of non-zero elements of D is a multiplicative group (and so in particular, $1 \neq 0$ in the ring). Note that a commutative division ring is what we called a field.

Let R be a ring, and M a module over R. We shall say that M is a *simple module* if $M \neq \{0\}$, and if M has no submodules other than $\{0\}$ and M itself.

THEOREM 7 (Schur's Lemma). *Let M be a simple module over the ring R. Then $\mathrm{End}_R(M)$ is a division ring.*

Proof. We know it is a ring, and we must prove that every non-zero element f has an inverse. Since $f \neq 0$, the image of f is a submodule of $M \neq 0$ and hence is equal to all of M, so that f is surjective. The kernel of f is a submodule of M and is not equal to M, so that the kernel of f is 0, and f is therefore injective. Hence f has an inverse as a group-homomorphism, and it is verified at once that this inverse is an R-homomorphism, thereby proving our theorem.

Example 6. Let R be a ring, and L a left ideal which is simple as an R-module (we say then that L is a simple left ideal). Then $\mathrm{End}_R(L) = D$ is a division ring. If it happens that D is commutative, then by Theorem 6, we conclude that $R = \mathrm{End}_D(L)$ is the ring of all D-linear maps of L into itself, and L is a vector space over the field D. Thus we have a concrete picture concerning the ring R.

EXERCISES

1. Let R be a ring. Show that R can be viewed as a module over itself, and has one generator.

2. Let R be a ring and M an R-module. Show that $\mathrm{Hom}_R(R, M)$ and M are isomorphic as additive groups, under the mapping $f \mapsto f(1)$.

3. Let E, F be R-modules. Show that $\mathrm{Hom}_R(E, F)$ is a module over $\mathrm{End}_R(F)$, the operation of the ring $\mathrm{End}_R(F)$ on the additive group $\mathrm{Hom}_R(E, F)$ being composition of mappings.

4. Let E be a module over the ring R, and let L be a left ideal of R. Let LE be the set of all elements $x_1 v_1 + \cdots + x_n v_n$ with $x_i \in R$ and $v_i \in E$. Show that LE is a submodule of E.

5. (a) Let R be a ring, E a module, and L a left ideal. Assume that L and E are simple. Show that $LE = E$ or $LE = \{0\}$.

(b) Assume that $LE = E$. Define the notion of isomorphisms of modules. Prove that L is isomorphic to E as R-module. [*Hint:* Let $v_0 \in E$ be an element such that $Lv_0 \neq \{0\}$. Show that the map $x \mapsto xv_0$ establishes an R-isomorphism between L and E.]

6. Let R be a ring and let E, F be R-modules. Let $\sigma : E \to F$ be an isomorphism. Show that $\mathrm{End}_R(E)$ and $\mathrm{End}_R(F)$ are ring-isomorphic, under the map

$$f \mapsto \sigma \circ f \circ \sigma^{-1}$$

for $f \in \mathrm{End}_R(E)$.

7. Let E, F be simple modules over the ring R. Let $f : E \to F$ be a homomorphism. Show that f is 0 or f is an isomorphism.

8. Verify in detail the last assertion made in the proof of Theorem 7.

9. Let R be a ring, and E a module. We say that E is a *free* module if there exist elements $v_1, \ldots, v_n$ in E such that every element $v \in E$ has a unique expression of the form

$$v = x_1 v_1 + \cdots + x_n v_n$$

with $x_i \in R$. If this is the case, then $\{v_1, \ldots, v_n\}$ is called a *basis* of E (over R).

10. Let E be a free module over the ring R, with basis $\{v_1, \ldots, v_n\}$. Let F be a module, and $w_1, \ldots, w_n$ elements of F. Show that there exists a unique homomorphism $f : E \to F$ such that $f(v_i) = w_i$ for $i = 1, \ldots, n$.

11. Let R be a ring, and S a set consisting of n elements, say $s_1, \ldots, s_n$. Let F be the set of mappings from S into R. (a) Show that F is a module. (b) If $x \in R$, denote by xs_i the function of S into R which associates x to s_i and 0 to s_j for $j \neq i$. Show that F is a free module, that $\{1s_1, \ldots, 1s_n\}$ is a basis for F over R, and that every element $v \in F$ has a unique expression of the form $x_1 s_1 + \cdots + x_n s_n$ with $x_i \in R$.

12. Let R be a ring, E a module, and F a submodule. Describe how to make the factor group E/F into an R-module.

13. Let K be a field, and $R = K[X]$ the polynomial ring over K. Let J be the ideal generated by X^2. Show that R/J is a K-space. What is its dimension?

14. Let K be a field and $R = K[X]$ the polynomial ring over K. Let $f(X)$ be a polynomial of degree $d > 0$ in $K[X]$. Let J be the ideal generated by $f(X)$. What is the dimension of R/J over K? Exhibit a basis of R/J over K. Show that R/J is an entire ring if and only if f is irreducible.

15. If R is a *commutative* ring, and E, F are modules, show that $\mathrm{Hom}_R(E, F)$ is an R-module in a natural way. Is this still true if R is not commutative?

16. Let K be a field, and R a vector space over K of dimension 2. Let $\{e, u\}$ be a basis of R over K. If a, b, c, d are elements of K, define the product

$$(ae + bu)(ce + du) = ace + (bc + ad)u.$$

Show that this product makes R into a ring. What is the unit element? Show that this ring is isomorphic to the ring $K[X]/(X^2)$ of Exercise 13.

17. Let the notation be as in the preceding exercise. Let $f(X)$ be a polynomial in $K[X]$. Show that

$$f(ae + u) = f(a)e + f'(a)u$$

where f' is the formal derivative of f.

18. Let R be a ring, and let E', E, F be R-modules. If $f: E' \to E$ is an R-homomorphism, show that the map $\varphi \mapsto f \circ \varphi$ is a $\mathbf{Z}$-homomorphism $\mathrm{Hom}_R(F, E') \to \mathrm{Hom}_R(F, E)$, and is an R-homomorphism if R is commutative.

19. A sequence of homomorphisms of abelian groups

$$A \xrightarrow{f} B \xrightarrow{g} C$$

is said to be *exact* if $\mathrm{Im}\, f = \mathrm{Ker}\, g$. Thus to say that $0 \to A \xrightarrow{f} B$ is exact means that f is injective. Let R be a ring. If

$$0 \to E' \xrightarrow{f} E \xrightarrow{g} E''$$

is an exact sequence of R-modules, show that

$$0 \to \mathrm{Hom}_R(F, E') \to \mathrm{Hom}_R(F, E) \to \mathrm{Hom}_R(F, E'')$$

is an exact sequence.

CHAPTER VI

Field Theory

In this chapter, we assume for concreteness that all fields are subfields of the complex numbers. The results actually hold if instead of $\mathbf{C}$ we take any field which is algebraically closed and contains the rationals as a subfield.

§1. Algebraic extensions

Let F be a field. A number α is said to be *algebraic* over F if there exists a non-zero polynomial $f \in F[t]$ such that $f(\alpha) = 0$, i.e. if α satisfies a polynomial equation

$$a_n \alpha^n + \cdots + a_0 = 0$$

with coefficients in F, not all 0. If F is a subfield of E, and every element of E is algebraic over F, we say that E is *algebraic* over F.

Example 1. If $\alpha^2 = 2$, i.e. if α is one of the two possible square roots of 2, then α is algebraic over the rational numbers $\mathbf{Q}$. Similarly, a cube root of 2 is algebraic. Any one of the numbers $e^{2\pi i/n}$ (with n integer ≥ 1) is algebraic over $\mathbf{Q}$, since it is a root of $t^n - 1$. It is known (but hard to prove) that neither e nor π is algebraic over $\mathbf{Q}$.

Let F be a subfield of a field E. We may view E as a vector space over F. We also say that E is an *extension* of F. We shall say that E is a *finite* extension if E is a finite dimensional vector space over F. For instance, $\mathbf{C}$ is a finite extension of $\mathbf{R}$, and $\{1, i\}$ is a basis of $\mathbf{C}$ over $\mathbf{R}$. The real numbers are not a finite extension of $\mathbf{Q}$.

THEOREM 1. *If E is a finite extension of F, then every element of E is algebraic over F.*

Proof. The powers of an element α of E, namely $1, \alpha, \alpha^2, \ldots, \alpha^n$ cannot be linearly independent over F, if $n > \dim E$. Hence there exist elements $a_0, \ldots, a_n \in F$ not all 0 such that $a_n \alpha^n + \cdots + a_0 = 0$. This means that α is algebraic over F.

Let α be algebraic over F. Let J be the ideal of polynomials in $F[t]$ of which α is a root, i.e. polynomials f such that $f(\alpha) = 0$. Let $p(t)$ be a generator of J,

102

with leading coefficient 1. *Then p is irreducible.* Proof: Suppose that $p = gh$ with $\deg g < \deg p$ and $\deg h < \deg p$. Since $p(\alpha) = 0$, we have $g(\alpha) = 0$ or $h(\alpha) = 0$. Say $g(\alpha) = 0$. Since $\deg g < \deg p$, this is impossible, by the assumption on p.

The irreducible polynomial p (with leading coefficient 1) is uniquely determined by α in $F[t]$, and will be called *the irreducible polynomial of α over F*. Its degree will be called the *degree* of α over F. We shall immediately give another interpretation for this degree.

THEOREM 2. *Let α be algebraic over F. Let n be the degree of its irreducible polynomial over F. Then the vector space generated over F by* $1, \alpha, \ldots, \alpha^{n-1}$ *is a field, and the dimension of that vector space is n.*

Proof. Let f be any polynomial in $F[t]$. We can find $q, r \in F[t]$ such that $f = qp + r$, and $\deg r < \deg p$. Then

$$f(\alpha) = q(\alpha)p(\alpha) + r(\alpha) = r(\alpha).$$

Hence if we denote the vector space generated by $1, \alpha, \ldots, \alpha^{n-1}$ by E, we find that the product of two elements of E is again in E. Suppose that $f(\alpha) \neq 0$. Then f is not divisible by p. Hence there exist polynomials $g, h \in F[t]$ such that

$$gf + hp = 1.$$

We obtain $g(\alpha)f(\alpha) + h(\alpha)p(\alpha) = 1$, whence $g(\alpha)f(\alpha) = 1$. Thus every non-zero element of E is invertible, and hence E is a field.

The field generated by the powers of α over F as in Theorem 2 will be denoted by $F(\alpha)$.

If E is a finite extension of F, we denote by

$$[E : F]$$

the dimension of E viewed as vector space over F, and call it the *degree* of E over F.

THEOREM 3. *Let E_1 be a finite extension of F, and let E_2 be a finite extension of E_1. Then E_2 is a finite extension of F, and*

$$[E_2 : F] = [E_2 : E_1][E_1 : F].$$

Proof. Let $\{\alpha_1, \ldots, \alpha_n\}$ be a basis of E_1 over F, and $\{\beta_1, \ldots, \beta_m\}$ a basis of E_2 over E_1. We prove that the elements $\{\alpha_i \beta_j\}$ form a basis of E_2 over F. Let v be an element of E_2. We can write

$$v = \sum_j w_j \beta_j = w_1 \beta_1 + \cdots + w_m \beta_m$$

with some elements $w_j \in E_1$. We write each w_j as a linear combination of $\alpha_1, \ldots, \alpha_n$ with coefficients in F, say

$$w_j = \sum_i c_{ij}\alpha_i.$$

Substituting, we find

$$v = \sum_j \sum_i c_{ij}\alpha_i\beta_j.$$

Hence the elements $\alpha_i\beta_j$ generate E_2 over F. Assume that we have a relation

$$0 = \sum_j \sum_i x_{ij}\alpha_i\beta_j$$

with $x_{ij} \in F$. Thus

$$\sum_j \left(\sum_i x_{ij}\alpha_i \right) \beta_j = 0.$$

From the linear independence of $\beta_1, \ldots, \beta_m$ over E_1, we conclude that

$$\sum_i x_{ij}\alpha_i = 0$$

for each j, and from the linear independence of $\alpha_1, \ldots, \alpha_n$ over F we conclude that $x_{ij} = 0$ for all i, j as was to be shown.

Let α, β be algebraic over F. Then *a fortiori*, β is algebraic over $F(\alpha)$. We can form the field $F(\alpha)(\beta)$. Any field which contains F and α, β will contain $F(\alpha)(\beta)$. Hence $F(\alpha)(\beta)$ is the smallest field containing F and both α, β. Furthermore, by Theorem 3, $F(\alpha)(\beta)$ is finite over F, being decomposed in the tower

$$F \subset F(\alpha) \subset F(\alpha)(\beta).$$

Hence by Theorem 1, the field $F(\alpha)(\beta)$ is algebraic over F. Furthermore, it does not matter whether we write $F(\alpha)(\beta)$ or $F(\beta)(\alpha)$. Thus we shall denote this field by $F(\alpha, \beta)$.

Inductively, if $\alpha_1, \ldots, \alpha_r$ are algebraic over F, we let $F(\alpha_1, \ldots, \alpha_r)$ be the smallest field containing F and $\alpha_1, \ldots, \alpha_r$. It can be expressed as $F(\alpha_1)(\alpha_2) \cdots (\alpha_r)$. It is algebraic over F by repeated applications of Theorem 3. We call it the field obtained by *adjoining* $\alpha_1, \ldots, \alpha_r$ to F.

THEOREM 4. *Let p be an irreducible polynomial over the field F. Let $n = \deg p$. Then p has n distinct roots in the complex numbers.*

Proof. We can write

$$p(t) = (t - \alpha_1) \cdots (t - \alpha_n)$$

with $\alpha_i \in \mathbf{C}$. Let α be a root of p. It will suffice to prove that α has multiplicity 1. We note that p is the irreducible polynomial of α over F. We also note that the formal derivative p' has degree $< p$. (Cf. Chapter IV, §3.) Hence we cannot have $p'(\alpha) = 0$, because p' is not the zero polynomial (immediate from the definition of the formal derivative—the leading coefficient of p' is $na_n \neq 0$). Hence α has multiplicity 1.

EXERCISES

1. Let $\alpha^2 = 2$. Show that the field $\mathbf{Q}(\alpha)$ is of degree 2 over $\mathbf{Q}$.

2. Show that a polynomial $(t - a)^2 + b^2$ with a, b rational, $b \neq 0$, is irreducible over the rational numbers.

3. Show that the polynomial $t^3 - p$ is irreducible over the rational numbers for each prime number p.

4. What is the degree of the following fields over $\mathbf{Q}$?

(a) $\mathbf{Q}(\alpha)$ where $\alpha^3 = 2$
(b) $\mathbf{Q}(\alpha)$ where $\alpha^3 = p$ (prime)
(c) $\mathbf{Q}(\alpha)$ where α is a root of $t^3 - t - 1$
(d) $\mathbf{Q}(\alpha, \beta)$ where α is a root of $t^2 - 2$ and β is a root of $t^2 - 3$

5. Show that the cube root of unity $\omega = e^{2\pi i/3}$ is the root of a polynomial of degree 2 over $\mathbf{Q}$. Show that $\mathbf{Q}(\omega) = \mathbf{Q}(\sqrt{-3})$.

6. What is the degree over $\mathbf{Q}$ of the number $\cos(2\pi/3)$?

7. What is the degree over $\mathbf{Q}$ of the field $\mathbf{Q}(i, \sqrt{3})$?

8. Let E be an extension of degree 2 of a field F. Show that E can be written $F(\alpha)$ for some root α of a polynomial $t^2 - a$, with $a \in F$. [*Hint:* Use the elementary school formula for the solution of a quadratic equation.]

9. Let $t^2 + bt + c$ be a polynomial of degree 2 with b, c in F. Let α be a root. Show that $F(\alpha)$ has degree 2 over F if $b^2 - 4c$ is not a square in F, and otherwise, that $F(\alpha)$ has degree 1 over F, i.e. $\alpha \in F$.

10. Let $a \in \mathbf{C}$, and $a \neq 0$. Let α be a root of $t^n - a$. Show that all roots of $t^n - a$ are of type $\omega\alpha$, where ω is an n-th root of unity, i.e.

$$\omega = e^{2\pi i k/n}, \qquad\qquad k = 0, \dots, n - 1.$$

§2. *Embeddings*

Let F be a field, and L another field. By an *embedding* of F in L, we shall mean a mapping

$$\sigma : F \to L$$

such that, for all x, $y \in F$ we have

$$\sigma(x + y) = \sigma(x) + \sigma(y) \qquad \text{and} \qquad \sigma(xy) = \sigma(x)\sigma(y),$$

and such that $\sigma(1) = 1$. Then if $x \neq 0$, it follows that $\sigma(x) \neq 0$ (because $1 = \sigma(xx^{-1}) = \sigma(x)\sigma(x^{-1})$). Consequently σ is a homomorphism for both the additive group of F and the multiplicative group of non-zero elements of F. Furthermore, since the kernel of σ, viewed as additive homomorphism, is 0, it follows that σ is injective, i.e. $\sigma(x) \neq \sigma(y)$ if $x \neq y$. This is the reason for calling σ an embedding. We shall often write σx instead of $\sigma(x)$, and σF instead of $\sigma(F)$.

An embedding $\sigma \colon F \to F'$ is said to be an *isomorphism* if the image of σ is F'. (One should specify an isomorphism of *fields*, or a *field-isomorphism* but the context will always make our meaning clear.) If $\sigma \colon F \to L$ is an embedding, then the image σF of F under σ is obviously a subfield of L, and thus σ gives rise to an isomorphism of F with σF. If $\sigma \colon F \to F'$ is an isomorphism, then one can define an inverse isomorphism $\sigma^{-1} \colon F' \to F$ in the usual way.

Let $f(t)$ be a polynomial in $F[t]$. Let $\sigma \colon F \to L$ be an embedding. Write

$$f(t) = a_n t^n + \cdots + a_0.$$

We define σf to be the polynomial

$$\sigma f(t) = \sigma(a_n)t^n + \cdots + \sigma(a_0).$$

Then it is trivially verified that for two polynomials f, g in $F[t]$, we have $\sigma(f + g) = \sigma f + \sigma g$ and $\sigma(fg) = (\sigma f)(\sigma g)$.

If $p(t)$ is an irreducible polynomial in $F[t]$, then σp is irreducible over σF. This is an important fact. Its proof is easy, for if we have a factorization

$$\sigma p = gh$$

over σF, then

$$p = \sigma^{-1}\sigma p = (\sigma^{-1}g)(\sigma^{-1}h)$$

has a factorization over F.

Let $f(t) \in F[t]$, and let α be algebraic over F. Let $\sigma \colon F(\alpha) \to L$ be an embedding into some field L. Then

$$(\sigma f)(\sigma \alpha) = \sigma(f(\alpha)).$$

This is immediate from the definition of an embedding, for if $f(t)$ is as above, then

$$f(\alpha) = a_n \alpha^n + \cdots + a_0,$$

whence

(*) $$\sigma(f(\alpha)) = \sigma(a_n)\sigma(\alpha)^n + \cdots + \sigma(a_0).$$

In particular, if α is a root of f, then $\sigma(\alpha)$ is a root of σf. We also observe that if σ is an embedding of $F(\alpha)$ whose effect is known on F, and on α, then the effect of σ is uniquely determined on $F(\alpha)$, by (*).

Let $\sigma: F \to L$ be an embedding. Let E be an extension of F. An embedding $\tau: E \to L$ is said to be an *extension* of σ if $\tau(x) = \sigma(x)$ for all $x \in F$. We then also say that σ is a restriction of τ to F.

THEOREM 5. *Let $\sigma: F \to L$ be an embedding. Let $p(t)$ be an irreducible polynomial in $F[t]$. Let α be a root of p, and let β be a root of σp in L. Then there exists an embedding $\tau: F(\alpha) \to L$ which is an extension of σ, and such that $\tau\alpha = \beta$. Conversely, every extension τ of σ to $F(\beta)$ is such that $\tau\alpha$ is a root of σp.*

Proof. The second assertion follows from a remark we made previously. To prove the existence of τ, let f be any polynomial in $F[t]$, and define τ on the element $f(\alpha)$ to be $(\sigma f)(\beta)$. The same element $f(\alpha)$ has many representations as values $f(\alpha)$, for many polynomials f in $F[t]$. Thus we must show that our definition of τ does not depend on the choice of f. Suppose that $f, g \in F[t]$ are such that $f(\alpha) = g(\alpha)$. Then $(f - g)(\alpha) = 0$. Hence there exists a polynomial h in $F[t]$ such that $f - g = ph$. Then

$$\sigma f = \sigma g + (\sigma p)(\sigma h).$$

Hence

$$(\sigma f)(\beta) = (\sigma g)(\beta) + (\sigma p)(\beta) \cdot (\sigma h)(\beta)$$
$$= (\sigma g)(\beta).$$

This proves that our map is well defined. We used the fact that p is irreducible in an essential way! It is now a triviality to verify that τ is an embedding, and we leave it to the reader.

COROLLARY 1. *Let p be an irreducible polynomial over the field F. Let α be a root of p. Let*

$$\sigma: F \to \mathbf{C}$$

be an embedding of F into the complex numbers. Then the number of possible embeddings of $F(\alpha)$ into $\mathbf{C}$ which extend σ is equal to the degree of p (i.e. the degree of α over F).

Proof. Immediate consequence of Theorems 4 and 5.

COROLLARY 2. *Let E be a finite extension of F. Let n be the degree of E over F. Let $\sigma: F \to \mathbf{C}$ be an embedding of F into the complex numbers. Then the number of extensions of σ to an embedding of E into $\mathbf{C}$ is equal to n.*

Proof. We can write E in the form $E = F(\alpha_1, \ldots, \alpha_r)$. Consider the tower

$$F \subset F(\alpha_1) \subset F(\alpha_1, \alpha_2) \subset \cdots \subset F(\alpha_1, \ldots, \alpha_r).$$

Let $E_{r-1} = F(\alpha_1, \ldots, \alpha_{r-1})$. Suppose that we have proved by induction that the number of extensions of σ to E_{r-1} is equal to the degree $[E_{r-1} : F]$. Let $\sigma_1, \ldots, \sigma_m$ be the extensions of σ to E_{r-1}. Let d be the degree of α_r over E_{r-1}. For each $i = 1, \ldots, m$ we can find precisely d extensions of σ_i to E, say $\sigma_{i1}, \ldots, \sigma_{id}$. Then it is clear that the set $\{\sigma_{ij}\}$ $(i = 1, \ldots, m$ and $j = 1, \ldots, d)$ is the set of distinct extensions of σ to E. This proves our corollary.

Let α be algebraic over F. Let $p(t)$ be the irreducible polynomial of α over F. Let $\alpha_1, \ldots, \alpha_n$ be the roots of p. Then we call these roots the *conjugates* of α over F. For each α_i, there exists an embedding σ_i of $F(\alpha)$ which maps α on α_i, and which is the identity on F. This embedding is uniquely determined.

Example 1. Consider a root α of the polynomial $t^3 - 2$. We take α to be the real cube root of 2, written $\alpha = \sqrt[3]{2}$. Let $1, \omega, \omega^2$ be the three cube roots of unity. The polynomial $t^3 - 2$ is irreducible over $\mathbf{Q}$, because it has no root in $\mathbf{Q}$ (cf. Exercises 1, 2 of Chapter IV, §3). Hence there exist three embeddings of $\mathbf{Q}(\alpha)$ into $\mathbf{C}$, namely the three embeddings $\sigma_1, \sigma_2, \sigma_3$ such that

$$\sigma_1 \alpha = \alpha, \qquad \sigma_2 \alpha = \omega\alpha, \qquad \sigma_3 \alpha = \omega^2 \alpha.$$

Example 2. If $\alpha = 1 + \sqrt{2}$, there exist two embeddings of $\mathbf{Q}(\alpha)$ into $\mathbf{C}$, namely those sending α on $1 + \sqrt{2}$ and $1 - \sqrt{2}$ respectively.

THEOREM 6. *Let E be a finite extension of F. Then there exists an element γ of E such that $E = F(\gamma)$.*

Proof. It will suffice to prove that if $E = F(\alpha, \beta)$ with two elements α, β algebraic over F, then we can find γ in E such that $E = F(\gamma)$, for we can then proceed inductively. Let $[E : F] = n$. Let $\sigma_1, \ldots, \sigma_n$ be the n distinct embeddings of E into $\mathbf{C}$ extending the identity map on F. We shall first prove that we can find an element $c \in F$ such that the elements

$$\sigma_i \alpha + c\sigma_i \beta = \sigma_i(\alpha + c\beta)$$

are distinct, for $i = 1, \ldots, n$. We consider the polynomial

$$\prod_{i=1}^{n} \prod_{j \neq i} [\sigma_j \alpha - \sigma_i \alpha + t(\sigma_j \beta - \sigma_i \beta)].$$

It is not the zero polynomial, since each factor is different from 0. This polynomial has a finite number of roots. Hence we can certainly find an element c of F such that when we substitute c for t we don't get the value 0. This element c does what we want.

Now we assert that $E = F(\gamma)$, where $\gamma = \alpha + c\beta$. In fact, by construction, we have n distinct embeddings of $F(\gamma)$ into $\mathbf{C}$, extending the identity on F, namely $\sigma_1, \ldots, \sigma_n$. Hence $[F(\gamma) : F] \geq n$ by Corollary 1 of Theorem 5. Since $F(\gamma)$ is a subspace of E over F, and has the same dimension as E, it follows that $F(\gamma) = E$, and our theorem is proved.

Example 3.   Prove as an exercise that if $\alpha^3 = 2$ and β is a square root of 2, then $\mathbf{Q}(\alpha, \beta) = \mathbf{Q}(\gamma)$, where $\gamma = \alpha + \beta$.

EXERCISES

1. In each case, find an element γ such that $\mathbf{Q}(\alpha, \beta) = \mathbf{Q}(\gamma)$. Always prove all assertions which you make.
   (a) $\alpha = \sqrt{-5}, \beta = \sqrt{2}$ (b) $\alpha = \sqrt[3]{2}, \beta = \sqrt{2}$
   (c) $\alpha = $ root of $t^3 - t + 1, \beta = $ root of $t^2 - t - 1$
   (d) $\alpha = $ root of $t^3 - 2t + 3, \beta = $ root of $t^2 + t + 2$

2. Determine the degrees of the fields $\mathbf{Q}(\alpha, \beta)$ over $\mathbf{Q}$ in each one of the cases of Exercise 1.

3. Let E_1, E_2 be two extensions of a field F. Assume that $[E_2 : F] = 2$, and that $E_1 \cap E_2 = F$. Let $E_2 = F(\alpha)$. Show that $E_1(\alpha)$ has degree 2 over E_1.

4. Let $\alpha^3 = 2$, let ω be a complex cube root of unity, and let $\beta = \omega\alpha$. What is the degree of $\mathbf{Q}(\alpha, \beta)$ over $\mathbf{Q}$?

5. Let E_1 have degree p over F and E_2 have degree p', where p, p' are prime numbers. Show that either $E_1 = E_2$ or $E_1 \cap E_2 = F$.

6. Let E be a finite extension of F, of degree n. Let $\sigma_1, \ldots, \sigma_n$ be all distinct embeddings of E over F into the complex numbers. For $\alpha \in E$, define the trace and norm of α respectively (from E to F), by

$$\text{Tr}_F^E(\alpha) = \sum_{i=1}^{n} \sigma_i \alpha = \sigma_1 \alpha + \cdots + \sigma_n \alpha,$$

$$N_F^E(\alpha) = \prod_{i=1}^{n} \sigma_i \alpha = \sigma_1 \alpha \cdots \sigma_n \alpha.$$

(a) Show that the norm and trace of α lie in F.

(b) Show that the trace is an additive homomorphism, and that the norm is a multiplicative homomorphism.

7. Let α be algebraic over the field F, and let

$$p(t) = t^n + a_{n-1} t^{n-1} + \cdots + a_0$$

be the irreducible polynomial of α over F. Show that

$$N(\alpha) = (-1)^n a_0 \qquad \text{and} \qquad \text{Tr}(\alpha) = -a_{n-1}.$$

(The norm and trace are taken from $F(\alpha)$ to F.)

8. Let E be a finite extension of F, and let a be an element of F. Let $[E : F] = n$. What are the norm and trace of a from E to F?

§3. Splitting fields

Let E be a finite extension of F. Let σ be an embedding of F, and τ an extension of σ to an embedding of E. We shall also say that τ is *over* σ. If σ is the identity map, then we say that τ is an embedding of E over F. Thus τ is an embedding of E over F means that $\tau x = x$ for all $x \in F$. We also say that τ leaves F *fixed*.

By an *automorphism* of a field K we shall mean an isomorphism $\sigma : K \to K$ of K with itself. The context always makes it clear that we mean field-isomorphism (and not another kind of isomorphism, e.g. group, or vector space isomorphism).

Let σ be an embedding of a finite extension K of F, over F. Assume that $\sigma(K)$ is contained in K. Then $\sigma(K) = K$. Indeed, σ induces a linear map of the vector space of K over F, and is injective. Hence σ is surjective, and is therefore an isomorphism (of vector space or field), whence an automorphism.

We observe that the set of all automorphisms of a field K is a group. Trivial verification. We shall be concerned with certain subgroups.

Let G be a group of automorphisms of a field K. Let K^G be the set of all elements $x \in K$ such that $\sigma x = x$ for all $\sigma \in G$. Then K^G is a field. Indeed, K^G contains 0 and 1. If x, y are in K^G, then

$$\sigma(x + y) = \sigma x + \sigma y = x + y,$$
$$\sigma(xy) = \sigma(x)\sigma(y) = xy,$$

so $x + y$ and xy are in K^G. Also $\sigma(x^{-1}) = \sigma(x)^{-1} = x^{-1}$, so x^{-1} is in K^G. This proves that K^G is a field, called the *fixed field of G*.

If G is a group of automorphisms of K over a subfield F, then F is contained in the fixed field (by definition), but the fixed field may be bigger than F. For instance, G could consist of the identity alone, in which case its fixed field is K itself.

Example 1. The field of rational numbers has no automorphisms except identity. Proof?

Example 2. Prove that the field $\mathbf{Q}(\alpha)$ where $\alpha^3 = 2$ has no automorphism except the identity.

Example 3. Let F be a field, and $a \in F$. Assume that a is not a square in F, and let $\alpha^2 = a$. Then $F(\alpha)$ has precisely two automorphisms over F, namely the identity, and the automorphism which maps α on $-\alpha$.

A finite extension K of F will be said to be a *Galois extension* if every embedding of K over F is an automorphism of K.

A finite extension K of F is called a *splitting field* of a polynomial if $K = F(\alpha_1, \ldots, \alpha_n)$, where $\alpha_1, \ldots, \alpha_n$ are all the roots of the polynomial.

THEOREM 7. *A finite extension of F is Galois if and only if it is the splitting field of a polynomial.*

Proof. Let K be a Galois extension of F. Write $K = F(\alpha)$ for some element α (using Theorem 6). Let $p(t)$ be the irreducible polynomial of α over F. For each root α_1 of p, there exists a unique embedding σ_i of K over F such that $\sigma_i \alpha = \alpha_i$. Since each embedding is an automorphism, it follows that α_i is contained in K. Hence

$$K = F(\alpha) = F(\alpha_1, \ldots, \alpha_n),$$

and K is the splitting field of p.

Conversely, suppose that K is the splitting field of a polynomial $f(t)$, not necessarily irreducible, with roots $\alpha_1, \ldots, \alpha_n$. If σ is an embedding of K over F, then $\sigma \alpha_i$ must also be a root of F. Hence σ maps K into itself, and hence σ is an automorphism.

THEOREM 8. *Let K be a Galois extension of F. If $p(t)$ is a polynomial in $F[t]$, and is irreducible over F, and if p has one root in K, then p has all its roots in K.*

Proof. Let α be one root of p in K. Let β be another root. By Theorem 5 there exists an embedding σ of $F(\alpha)$ on $F(\beta)$ mapping α on β, and equal to the identity on F. Extend this embedding to K. Since an embedding of K over F is an automorphism, we must have $\sigma\alpha \in K$, and hence $\beta \in K$.

§4. Fundamental theorem

THEOREM 9. *Let K be a Galois extension of F. Let G be the group of automorphisms of K over F. Then F is the fixed field of G.*

Proof. Let F' be the fixed field. Then trivially, $F \subset F'$. Suppose $\alpha \in F'$ and $\alpha \notin F$. Then by Theorem 5 there exists an embedding σ_0 of $F(\alpha)$ over F such that $\sigma_0 \alpha \neq \alpha$. Extend σ_0 to an embedding σ of K over F (by Corollary 2 of Theorem 5). By hypothesis, σ is an automorphism of K over F, and $\sigma \alpha = \sigma_0 \alpha \neq \alpha$, thereby contradicting the assumption that $\alpha \in F'$ but $\alpha \notin F$. This proves our theorem.

THEOREM 10. *Let K be a Galois extension of F. To each intermediate field E, associate the subgroup $G_{K/E}$ of automorphisms of K leaving E fixed. Then K is Galois over E, and the map*

$$E \mapsto G_{K/E}$$

is an injective and surjective map from the set of intermediate fields, onto the set of subgroups of G, and E is the fixed field of $G_{K/E}$.

Proof. Every embedding of K over E is an embedding over F, and hence is an automorphism of K. It follows that K is Galois over E. Furthermore, E is the fixed field of $G_{K/E}$ by Theorem 9. This shows in particular that the map

$$E \mapsto G_{K/E}$$

is injective, i.e. if $E \neq E'$ then $G_{K/E} \neq G_{K/E'}$. Finally, let H be a subgroup of G. Write $K = F(\alpha)$ with some element α. Let $\{\sigma_1, \ldots, \sigma_r\}$ be the elements of H, and let

$$f(t) = (t - \sigma_1\alpha) \cdots (t - \sigma_r\alpha).$$

For any σ in H, we note that $\{\sigma\sigma_1, \ldots, \sigma\sigma_r\}$ is a permutation of $\{\sigma_1, \ldots, \sigma_r\}$. Hence from the expression

$$\sigma f(t) = (t - \sigma\sigma_1\alpha) \cdots (t - \sigma\sigma_r\alpha) = f(t),$$

we see that f has its coefficients in the fixed field E of H. Furthermore, $K = E(\alpha)$, and α is a root of a polynomial of degree r over E. Hence $[K : E] \leq r$. But K has r distinct embeddings over E (those of H), and hence by the standard argument, $[K : E] = r$, and $H = G_{K/E}$. This proves our theorem.

If K is a Galois extension of F, the group of automorphisms of $G_{K/F}$ is called the *Galois group* of K over F. If K is the splitting field of a polynomial $f(t)$ in $K[t]$, then we also say that $G_{K/F}$ is the *Galois group of f*.

Let $f(t) \in F[t]$, and let

$$f(t) = (t - \alpha_1) \cdots (t - \alpha_n).$$

Let $K = F(\alpha_1, \ldots, \alpha_n)$, and let σ be an element of $G_{K/F}$. Then $\{\sigma\alpha_1, \ldots, \sigma\alpha_n\}$ is a permutation of $\{\alpha_1, \ldots, \alpha_n\}$, which we may denote by π_σ. If $\sigma \neq \tau$, then $\pi_\sigma \neq \pi_\tau$, and clearly,

$$\pi_{\sigma\tau} = \pi_\sigma \circ \pi_\tau.$$

Hence we have represented the Galois group $G_{K/F}$ as a group of permutations of the roots of f. Of course, it is not always true that every permutation of $\{\alpha_1, \ldots, \alpha_n\}$ is represented by an element of $G_{K/F}$, even if f is irreducible over F. Cf. the next section for examples.

EXERCISES

1. By a *primitive n-th root of unity*, one means a number ω whose period is exactly n. For instance, $e^{2\pi i/n}$ is a primitive n-th root of unity. Show that every other primitive n-th root of unity is equal to a power $e^{2\pi i r/n}$ where r is an integer > 0 and relatively prime to n.

2. Let F be a field, and $K = F(\omega)$, where ω is a primitive n-th root of unity. Show that K is Galois over F, and that its Galois group is commutative. [*Hint:* For each embedding σ over F, note that $\sigma\omega = \omega^{r(\sigma)}$ with some integer $r(\sigma)$.] If τ is another embedding, what is $\tau\sigma\omega$, and $\sigma\tau\omega$?

3. Let K_1, K_2 be two Galois extensions of a field F. Say $K_1 = F(\alpha_1)$ and $K_2 = F(\alpha_2)$. Let $K = F(\alpha_1, \alpha_2)$. Show that K is Galois over F. Let G be its Galois group. Map G into the direct product $G_{K_1/F} \times G_{K_2/F}$ by associating with each σ in G the pair (σ_1, σ_2), where σ_1 is the restriction of σ to K_1, and σ_2 is the restriction of σ to K_2. Show that this mapping is an injective homomorphism.

4. Let K be a Galois extension of F, and let E be an intermediate field, $F \subset E \subset K$, such that E is Galois over F. Let G be the Galois group of K over F, and H the Galois group of K over E. For each $\sigma \in G$, let $\operatorname{res}_E\sigma$ be its restriction to E. Show that the map $\sigma \mapsto \operatorname{res}_E\sigma$ is a surjective homomorphism of G onto $G_{E/F}$ whose kernel is H. Hence $G_{E/F}$ is isomorphic to the factor group G/H.

5. Let F be a field containing $i = \sqrt{-1}$. Let K be a splitting field of the polynomial $t^4 - a$ with $a \in F$. Show that the Galois group of K over F is a subgroup of a cyclic group of order 4. If $t^4 - a$ is irreducible over F, show that this Galois group is cyclic of order 4. If α is a root of $t^4 - a$, express all the other roots in terms of α and i.

6. More generally, let F be a field containing all n-th roots of unity. Let K be a splitting field of the equation $t^n - a = 0$ with $a \in F$. Show that K is Galois over F, with a Galois group which is a subgroup of a cyclic group of order n.

7. Show that the Galois group of the polynomial $t^4 - 2$ over the rational numbers has order 8, and contains a cyclic subgroup of order 4. [*Hint:* Prove first that the polynomial is irreducible over $\mathbf{Q}$. Then, if α is a real fourth root of 2, consider $K = \mathbf{Q}(\alpha, i)$.]

§5. *Quadratic and cubic extensions*

We first summarize the properties of quadratic extensions. Let F be a field. Any irreducible polynomial $t^2 + bt + c$ over F has a splitting field $F(\alpha)$, with

$$\alpha = \frac{-b \pm \sqrt{b^2 - 4c}}{2}.$$

Thus $F(\alpha)$ is Galois over F, and its Galois group is cyclic of order 2. If we let $d = b^2 - 4c$, then $F(\alpha) = F(\sqrt{d})$. Conversely, the polynomial $t^2 - d$ is irreducible over F if and only if d is not a square in F.

Consider now the cubic case. After completing the square, a cubic polynomial in $F[t]$ can be brought into the form

$$f(t) = t^3 + bt + c = (t - \alpha_1)(t - \alpha_2)(t - \alpha_3)$$

with $b, c \in F$. The roots may or may not be in F. If f has no root in F, then f is irreducible. We find

$$\alpha_1 + \alpha_2 + \alpha_3 = 0, \qquad \alpha_1\alpha_2 + \alpha_1\alpha_3 + \alpha_2\alpha_3 = b, \qquad -\alpha_1\alpha_1\alpha_3 = c.$$

We let the *discriminant* of f be defined as

$$D = [(\alpha_2 - \alpha_1)(\alpha_3 - \alpha_1)(\alpha_3 - \alpha_2)]^2.$$

Any automorphism of $F(\alpha_1, \alpha_2, \alpha_3)$ leaves D fixed because it changes the product

$$\delta = (\alpha_2 - \alpha_1)(\alpha_3 - \alpha_1)(\alpha_3 - \alpha_2)$$

at most by a sign.

Let $K = F(\alpha_1, \alpha_2, \alpha_3)$ be the splitting field of f. Let G be the Galois group of K over F. Assume that f is irreducible. Then G is represented as a subgroup of the symmetric group S_3. Since K contains $F(\alpha)$ for any root α of f, it follows that $[K : F]$ is divisible by 3, and hence the order of G is 3 or 6. In the first case, it follows that $K = F(\alpha)$, and G is cyclic of order 3. In the second case G is isomorphic to S_3. As an exercise, prove:

THEOREM 11. *The group G is isomorphic to S_3 if and only if D is not a square in F. Thus if D is a square in F, then K has degree 3 over F.*

As another easy exercise (using what has already been said) prove:

THEOREM 12. *Let $f(t) = t^3 + at + b$ be an irreducible polynomial over F. Let K be the splitting field of f. Then $K = F(\sqrt{D}, \alpha)$ for any root α of f.*

Since D lies in F, we feel that there must be an expression of D in terms of a and b. With a little computation, you will find that

$$D = -4a^3 - 27b^2.$$

With all this information, the Galois group of a cubic polynomial can then be determined explicitly.

We emphasize that before doing anything else, one must *always* determine the irreducibility of f. For cubic polynomials, this can be done by Theorems 5 and 6 of Chapter IV, §5.

Example. We consider the polynomial $f(t) = t^3 - 3t + 1$. It has no integral root, and hence is irreducible over **Q**. Its discriminant is

$$D = -4a^3 - 27b^2 = 3^4.$$

The discriminant is a square in **Q**, and hence the Galois group of f over **Q** is cyclic of order 3. The splitting field is **Q**(α) for any root α.

Exercises

1. Determine the Galois groups of the following polynomials over the rational numbers.

(a) $t^2 - t + 1$ (b) $t^2 - 4$ (c) $t^2 + t + 1$ (d) $t^2 - 27$

2. Determine the Galois groups of the following polynomials over the rational numbers. Find the discriminants.

(a) $t^3 - 3t + 1$ (b) $t^3 + 3$ (c) $t^3 - 5$
(d) $t^3 - a$ where a is rational, $\neq 0$, and is not a cube of a rational number.
(e) $t^3 - 5t + 7$ (f) $t^3 + 2t + 2$ (g) $t^3 - t - 1$

3. Determine the Galois groups of the following polynomials over the indicated field.

(a) $t^3 - 10$ over $\mathbf{Q}(\sqrt{2})$ (b) $t^3 - 10$ over $\mathbf{Q}$
(c) $t^3 - t - 1$ over $\mathbf{Q}(\sqrt{-23})$ (d) $t^3 - 10$ over $\mathbf{Q}(\sqrt{-3})$
(e) $t^3 - 2$ over $\mathbf{Q}(\sqrt{-3})$ (f) $t^3 - 9$ over $\mathbf{Q}(\sqrt{-3})$
(g) $t^2 - 5$ over $\mathbf{Q}(\sqrt{-5})$ (h) $t^2 + 5$ over $\mathbf{Q}(\sqrt{-5})$

4. Let $f(t) = t^3 + at + b$. Let α be a root, and let β be a number such that

$$\alpha = \beta - \frac{a}{3\beta}.$$

Show that such a β can be found if $a \neq 0$. (Proof?) Show that

$$\beta^3 = -b/2 + \sqrt{-D/108}.$$

In this way we get an expression of α in terms of radicals.

§6. Solvability by radicals

Before considering the main theorem, we consider two special cases which will be typical of the general situation.

A Galois extension whose Galois group is abelian is said to be an *abelian extension*. Let K be a Galois extension of F, $K = F(\alpha)$. Let σ, τ be automorphisms of K over F. To verify that $\sigma\tau = \tau\sigma$ it suffices to verify that $\sigma\tau\alpha = \tau\sigma\alpha$. Indeed, any element of K can be written in the form

$$x = a_0 + a_1\alpha + \cdots + a_{d-1}\alpha^{d-1}$$

if d is the degree of α over K. Since $\sigma\tau a_i = \tau\sigma a_i$ for all i, it follows that if in addition $\sigma\tau\alpha = \tau\sigma\alpha$, then $\sigma\tau\alpha^i = \tau\sigma\alpha^i$ for all i, whence $\tau\sigma x = \sigma\tau x$. We shall describe two important cases.

(1) *Let F be a field and n a positive integer. Let ω be a primitive n-th root of unity, that is $\omega^n = 1$, and every n-th root of unity can be written in the form ω^r for some r, $0 \leq r < n$. Let $K = F(\omega)$. We shall prove that K is Galois*

and abelian over F. Let σ be an embedding of K over F. Then

$$(\sigma\omega)^n = \sigma(\omega)^n = 1.$$

Hence $\sigma\omega$ is also an n-th root of unity, and there exists an integer r such that $\sigma\omega = \omega^r$. In particular, K is Galois over F. Furthermore, if τ is another automorphism of K over F, then $\tau\omega = \omega^s$ for some s, and

$$\sigma\tau\omega = \sigma(\omega^s) = \sigma(\omega)^s = \omega^{rs} = \tau\sigma\omega.$$

Hence $\sigma\tau = \tau\sigma$, and the Galois group is abelian, as was to be shown.

(2) *Let F be a field and assume that the n-th roots of unity lie in F. Let $a \in F$. Let α be a root of the polynomial $t^n - a$, so $\alpha^n = a$, and let $K = F(\alpha)$. We shall again show that K is abelian over F.* Let σ be an embedding of K over F. Then

$$(\sigma\alpha)^n = \sigma(\alpha^n) = \sigma a = a.$$

Hence $\sigma\alpha$ is also a root of $t^n - a$, and

$$(\alpha/\sigma\alpha)^n = 1.$$

Hence if ω is a primitive n-th root of unity, there is some integer r such that

$$\sigma\alpha = \omega^r\alpha.$$

In particular, K is Galois over F. If τ is an automorphism of K over F, then for some integer s,

$$\tau\alpha = \omega^s\alpha,$$

whence

$$\sigma\tau\alpha = \sigma(\omega^s\alpha) = \omega^s\sigma\alpha = \omega^s\omega^r\alpha = \tau\sigma\alpha.$$

Hence $\sigma\tau = \tau\sigma$ and the Galois group is again abelian.

Let F be a field and f a polynomial of degree ≥ 1 over F. We shall say that F is *solvable by radicals* if its splitting field is contained in a Galois extension K which admits a sequence of subfields

$$F = F_0 \subset F_1 \subset F_2 \subset \cdots \subset F_m = K$$

such that:

(a) $F_1 = F(\omega)$ for some primitive n-th root of unity ω.

(b) For each i with $1 \leq i \leq m - 1$, the field F_{i+1} can be written in the form $F_{i+1} = F_i(\alpha_{i+1})$, where α_{i+1} is a root of some polynomial

$$t^d - a_i = 0,$$

where d divides n, and a_i is an element of F_i.

Observe that if d divides n, then $\omega^{n/d}$ is a primitive d-th root of unity (proof?) and hence by what we have seen, the extension F_{i+1} of F_i is abelian. We also have seen that F_1 is abelian over F. Thus K is decomposed into a sequence of abelian extensions. Let G_i be the Galois group of K over F_i. Then we obtain a corresponding sequence of groups

$$G \supset G_1 \supset G_2 \supset \cdots \supset G_m = \{e\}$$

such that G_{i+1} is normal in G_i, and the factor group G_i/G_{i+1} is abelian (cf. Exercise 4 of §4). Hence we have proved:

THEOREM 13. *If f is solvable by radicals, then its Galois group is solvable.*

It was a famous problem once to determine whether every polynomial is solvable by radicals. To show that this is not the case, it will suffice to exhibit a polynomial whose Galois group is the symmetric group S_5 (or S_n for $n \geqq 5$), according to Theorem 8 of Chapter II, §5. This is easily done:

THEOREM 14. *Let $x_1, \ldots, x_n$ be algebraically independent over a field F_0, and let*

$$f(t) = \prod_{i=1}^{n} (t - x_i) = t^n - s_1 t^{n-1} + \cdots + (-1)^n s_n,$$

where

$$s_1 = x_1 + \cdots + x_n, \ldots, \qquad s_n = x_1 \cdots x_n$$

are the coefficients of f. Let $F = F_0(s_1, \ldots, s_n)$. Let $K = F(x_1, \ldots, x_n)$. Then K is Galois over F, with Galois group S_n.

Proof. Certainly K is a Galois extension of F because

$$K = F(x_1, \ldots, x_n)$$

is the splitting field of f. Given any permutation σ of $\{1, \ldots, n\}$ we know that there is an automorphism π_σ of the field $F_0(x_1, \ldots, x_n)$ leaving F_0 fixed, and such that $\pi_\sigma(x_i) = x_{\sigma(i)}$. Since any permutation of $x_1, \ldots, x_n$ leaves the coefficients of f fixed, it follows that F is fixed under each π_σ for each $\sigma \in S_n$, and thus we see that the map $\sigma \mapsto \pi_\sigma$ gives an injective homomorphism of S_n into the Galois group of K over F. However, we have also seen that any automorphism of K over F can be represented as a permutation of the roots of F. It follows that S_n represents every automorphism of this Galois group, as was to be shown.

In the next section, we shall show that one can always select n complex numbers algebraically independent over **Q**.

§7. *Infinite extensions*

We begin by some cardinality statements concerning fields. We use only denumerable or finite sets in the present situation, and all that we need about such sets are the following:

If D is denumerable, then a finite product $D \times \cdots \times D$ is denumerable.

A denumerable union of denumerable sets is denumerable.

An infinite subset of a denumerable set is denumerable.

If D is denumerable, and $D \to S$ is a surjective map onto some set S which is not finite, then S is denumerable.

The reader will find simple self-contained proofs in Chapter VIII (cf. Theorem 3 and its corollaries), and for denumerable sets, these statements are nothing but simple exercises.

Let F be a field, and E an extension of F. We shall say that E is *algebraic* over F if every element of E is algebraic over F. Let $\overline{F}$ be the set of all complex numbers which are algebraic over F. Then $\overline{F}$ is a field, because we have seen that whenever α, β are algebraic, then $\alpha + \beta$ and $\alpha\beta$ are algebraic, being contained in the finite extension $F(\alpha, \beta)$ of F.

THEOREM 15. *Let F be a denumerable field. Then $\overline{F}$ is denumerable.*

Proof. We proceed stepwise. Let P_n be the set of irreducible polynomials of degree $n \geq 1$ with coefficients in F and leading coefficient 1. To each polynomial $f \in P_n$,

$$f(t) = t^n + a_{n-1}t^{n-1} + \cdots + a_0,$$

we associate its coefficients $(a_{n-1}, \ldots, a_0)$. We thus obtain an injection of P_n into $F \times \cdots \times F = F^n$, whence we conclude that P_n is denumerable.

Next, for each $f \in P_n$, we let $\alpha_{f,1}, \ldots, \alpha_{f,n}$ be its roots, in a fixed order. Let $J_n = \{1, \ldots, n\}$, and let

$$P_n \times \{1, \ldots, n\} \to \mathbf{C}$$

be the map of $P_n \times J_n$ into $\mathbf{C}$ such that

$$(f, i) \mapsto \alpha_{f,i}$$

for $i = 1, \ldots, n$ and $f \in P_n$. Then this map is a surjection of $P_n \times J_n$ onto the set of numbers of degree n over F, and hence this set is denumerable. Taking the union over all $n = 1, 2, \ldots$ we conclude that the set of all numbers algebraic over F is denumerable. This proves our theorem.

THEOREM 16. *Let F be a denumerable field. Then the field of rational functions $F(t)$ is denumerable.*

Proof. It will suffice to prove that the ring of polynomials $F[t]$ is denumerable, because we have a surjective map

$$F[t] \times F[t]_0 \to F(t),$$

where $F[t]_0$ denotes the set of non-zero elements of $F[t]$. The map is of course $(a, b) \mapsto a/b$. For each n, let P_n be the set of polynomials of degree $\leq n$ with coefficients in F. Then P_n is denumerable, and hence $F[t]$ is denumerable, being the denumerable union of $P_0, P_1, P_2, \ldots$ together with the single element 0.

COROLLARY. *Given an integer $n \geq 1$, there exist n algebraically independent complex numbers over* **Q**.

Proof. The field $\overline{\mathbf{Q}}$ is denumerable, and **C** is not. Hence there exists $x_1 \in \mathbf{C}$ which is transcendental over $\overline{\mathbf{Q}}$. Let $F_1 = \overline{\mathbf{Q}}(x_1)$. Then F_1 is denumerable. Proceeding inductively, we let x_2 be transcendental over $\overline{F}_1$, and so on, to find our desired elements $x_1, x_2, \ldots, x_n$.

Note: The fact that **C** (and even **R**) is not denumerable will be proved in the next chapter.

CHAPTER VII

The Real and Complex Numbers

§1. Ordering of rings

Let R be an entire ring. By an *ordering* of R one means a subset P of R satisfying the following conditions:

ORD 1. *For every* $x \in R$ *we have* $x \in P$, *or* $x = 0$, *or* $-x \in P$, *and these three possibilities are mutually exclusive.*

ORD 2. *If* $x, y \in P$ *then* $x + y \in P$ *and* $xy \in P$.

We also say that R is *ordered* by P, and call P the set of *positive* elements.

Let us assume that R is ordered by P. Since $1 \neq 0$, and $1 = 1^2 = (-1)^2$ we see that 1 is an element of P, i.e. 1 is positive. By ORD 2 and induction, it follows that $1 + \cdots + 1$ (sum taken n times) is positive. An element $x \in R$ such that $x \neq 0$ and $x \notin P$ is called *negative*. If x, y are negative elements of R, then xy is positive (because $-x \in P$, $-y \in P$, and hence $(-x)(-y) = xy \in P$). If x is positive and y is negative, then xy is negative, because $-y$ is positive, and hence $x(-y) = -xy$ is positive. For any $x \in R$, $x \neq 0$, we see that x^2 is positive.

Suppose that R is a field. If x is positive and $x \neq 0$ then $xx^{-1} = 1$, and hence by the preceding remarks, it follows that x^{-1} is also positive.

Let R be an arbitrary ordered entire ring again, and let R' be a subring. Let P be the set of positive elements in R, and let $P' = P \cap R$. Then it is clear that P' defines an ordering on R', which is called the *induced ordering*.

More generally, let R' and R be ordered rings, and let P', P be their sets of positive elements respectively. Let $f: R' \to R$ be an embedding (i.e. an injective homomorphism). We shall say that f is *order-preserving* if for every $x \in R'$ such that $x > 0$ we have $f(x) > 0$. This is equivalent to saying that $f^{-1}(P) = P'$ [where $f^{-1}(P)$ is the set of all $x \in R'$ such that $f(x) \in P$].

Let $x, y \in R$. We define $x < y$ (or $y > x$) to mean that $y - x \in P$. Thus to say that $x < 0$ is equivalent to saying that x is negative, or $-x$

120

is positive. One verifies easily the usual relations for inequalities, namely for $x, y, z \in R$:

IN 1. $x < y$ and $y < z$ *implies* $x < z$.
IN 2. $x < y$ and $z > 0$ *implies* $xz < yz$.
IN 3. $x < y$ *implies* $x + z < y + z$.

If R is a field, then

IN 4. $x < y$ and $x, y > 0$ *implies* $1/y < 1/x$.

As an example, we shall prove IN 2. We have $y - x \in P$ and $z \in P$, so that by ORD 2, $(y - x)z \in P$. But $(y - x)z = yz - xz$, so that by definition, $xz < yz$. As another example, to prove IN 4, we multiply the inequality $x < y$ by x^{-1} and y^{-1} to find the assertion of IN 4. The others are left as exercises.

If $x, y \in R$ we define $x \leq y$ to mean that $x < y$ or $x = y$. Then one verifies at once that IN 1, 2, 3 hold if we replace throughout the $<$ sign by $\leq$. Furthermore, one also verifies at once that if $x \leq y$ and $y \leq x$ then $x = y$.

In the next theorem, we see how an ordering on an entire ring can be extended to an ordering of its quotient field.

THEOREM 1. *Let R be an entire ring, ordered by P. Let K be its quotient field. Let P_K be the set of elements of K which can be written in the form a/b with $a, b \in R$, $b > 0$ and $a > 0$. Then P_K defines an ordering on K.*

Proof. Let $x \in K$, $x \neq 0$. Multiplying a numerator and denominator of x by -1 if necessary, we can write x in the form $x = a/b$ with $a, b \in R$ and $b > 0$. If $a > 0$ then $x \in P_K$. If $-a > 0$ then $-x = -a/b \in P_K$. We cannot have both x and $-x \in P_K$, for otherwise, we could write

$$x = a/b \qquad \text{and} \qquad -x = c/d$$

with $a, b, c, d \in R$ and $a, b, c, d > 0$. Then

$$-a/b = c/d,$$

whence $-ad = bc$. But $bc \in P$ and $ad \in P$, a contradiction. This proves that P_K satisfies ORD 1. Next, let $x, y \in P_K$ and write

$$x = a/b \qquad \text{and} \qquad y = c/d$$

with $a, b, c, d \in R$ and $a, b, c, d > 0$. Then $xy = ac/bd \in P_K$. Also

$$x + y = \frac{ad + bc}{bd}$$

lies in P_K. This proves that P_K satisfies ORD 2, and proves our theorem.

Theorem 1 shows in particular how one extends the usual ordering on the ring of integers $\mathbf{Z}$ to the field of rational numbers $\mathbf{Q}$. How one defines the integers, and the ordering on them, will be discussed in an appendix.

Let R be an ordered ring as before. If $x \in R$, we define

$$|x| = \begin{cases} x & \text{if } x \geq 0, \\ -x & \text{if } x < 0. \end{cases}$$

We then have the following characterization of the function $x \mapsto |x|$, which is called the *absolute value:*

For every $x \in R$, $|x|$ is the unique element $z \in R$ such that $z \geq 0$ and $z^2 = x^2$.

To prove this, observe first that certainly $|x|^2 = x^2$, and $|x| \geq 0$ for all $x \in R$. On the other hand, given $a \in R$, $a > 0$ there exist at most two elements $z \in R$ such that $z^2 = a$ because the polynomial $t^2 - a$ has at most two roots. If $w^2 = a$ then $w \neq 0$ and $(-w)^2 = w^2 = a$ also. Hence there is at most one positive element $z \in R$ such that $z^2 = a$. This proves our assertion.

We define the symbol $\sqrt{a}$ for $a \geq 0$ in R to be the element $z \geq 0$ in R such that $z^2 = a$, if such z exists. Otherwise, $\sqrt{a}$ is not defined. It is now easy to see that if $a, b \geq 0$ and $\sqrt{a}, \sqrt{b}$ exist, then $\sqrt{ab}$ exists and

$$\sqrt{ab} = \sqrt{a}\,\sqrt{b}.$$

Indeed, if $z, w \geq 0$ and $z^2 = a$, $w^2 = b$, then $(zw)^2 = z^2 w^2 = ab$. Thus we may express the definition of the absolute value by means of the expression $|x| = \sqrt{x^2}$.

The absolute value satisfies the following rules:

AV 1. *For all $x \in R$, we have $|x| \geq 0$, and $|x| > 0$ if $x \neq 0$.*

AV 2. *$|xy| = |x|\,|y|$ for all $x, y \in R$.*

AV 3. *$|x + y| \leq |x| + |y|$ for all $x, y \in R$.*

The first one is obvious. As to AV 2, we have

$$|xy| = \sqrt{(xy)^2} = \sqrt{x^2 y^2} = \sqrt{x^2}\,\sqrt{y^2} = |x|\,|y|.$$

For AV 3, we have

$$\begin{aligned} |x + y|^2 = (x + y)^2 &= x^2 + xy + xy + y^2 \\ &\leq |x|^2 + 2|xy| + |y|^2 \\ &= |x|^2 + 2|x|\,|y| + |y|^2 \\ &= (|x| + |y|)^2. \end{aligned}$$

Taking square roots yields what we want. (We have used implicitly two properties of inequalities, cf. Exercise 1.)

1. Let R be an ordered entire ring. (a) Prove that $x \leq |x|$ for all $x \in R$.
(b) If $a, b \geq 0$ and $a \leq b$, and if $\sqrt{a}$, $\sqrt{b}$ exist, show that $\sqrt{a} \leq \sqrt{b}$.

2. Let K be an ordered field. Let P be the set of polynomials

$$f(t) = a_n t^n + \cdots + a_0$$

over K, with $a_n > 0$. Show that P defines an ordering on $K[t]$.

3. Let R be an ordered entire ring. If $x, y \in R$, prove that $|-x| = |x|$,

$$|x - y| \geq |x| - |y|$$

and also

$$|x + y| \geq |x| - |y|.$$

Also prove that $|x| \leq |x + y| + |y|$.

4. Let K be an ordered field and $f \colon \mathbf{Q} \to K$ an embedding of the rational numbers into K. Show that f is necessarily order preserving.

§2. *Preliminaries*

Let K be an ordered field. From Exercise 4 of the preceding section, we know that the embedding of $\mathbf{Q}$ in K is order preserving. We shall identify $\mathbf{Q}$ as a subfield of K.

We recall formally a definition. Let S be a set. A *sequence* of elements of S is simply a mapping

$$\mathbf{Z}^+ \to S$$

from the positive integers into S. One usually denotes a sequence with the notation

$$\{x_1, x_2, \ldots\}$$

or

$$\{x_n\}_{n \geq 1}$$

or simply

$$\{x_n\}$$

if there is no danger of confusing this with the set consisting of the single element x_n.

A sequence $\{x_n\}$ in K is said to be a *Cauchy sequence* if given an element $\epsilon > 0$ in K, there exists a positive integer N such that for all integers $m, n \geq N$ we have

$$|x_n - x_m| \leq \epsilon.$$

(For simplicity, we agree to let N, n, m denote positive integers unless otherwise specified. We also agree that ϵ denotes elements of K.)

To avoid the use of excessively many symbols, we shall say that a certain statement S concerning positive integers holds for all *sufficiently large* integers if there exists N such that the statement $S(n)$ holds for all $n \geq N$. It is clear that if $S_1, \ldots, S_r$ is a finite number of statements, each holding for all sufficiently large integers, then they are valid simultaneously for all sufficiently large integers. Indeed, if

$$S_1(n) \text{ is valid for } n \geq N_1, \ldots, S_r(n) \text{ is valid for } n \geq N_r,$$

we let N be the maximum of $N_1, \ldots, N_r$ and see that each $S_i(n)$ is valid for $n \geq N$.

We shall say that a statement holds for *arbitrarily large* integers if given N, the statement holds for some $n \geq N$.

A sequence $\{x_n\}$ in K is said to *converge* if there exists an element $x \in K$ such that, given $\epsilon > 0$ we have

$$|x - x_n| \leq \epsilon$$

for all sufficiently large n.

An ordered field in which every Cauchy sequence converges is said to be *complete*. We observe that the number x above, if it exists, is uniquely determined, for if $y \in K$ is such that

$$|y - x_n| \leq \epsilon$$

for all sufficiently large n, then

$$|x - y| \leq |x - x_n + x_n - y| \leq |x - x_n| + |x_n - y| \leq 2\epsilon.$$

This is true for every $\epsilon > 0$ in K, and it follows that $x - y = 0$, that is $x = y$. We call this number x the *limit of the sequence* $\{x_n\}$.

An ordered field K will be said to be *archimedean* if given $x \in K$ there exists a positive integer n such that $x \leq n$. It then follows that given $\epsilon > 0$ in K, we can find an integer $m > 0$ such that $1/\epsilon < m$, whence $1/m < \epsilon$.

It is easy to see that the field of rational numbers is not complete. For instance, one can construct Cauchy sequences of rationals whose square approaches 2, but such that the sequence has no limit in $\mathbf{Q}$ (otherwise, $\sqrt{2}$ would be rational). In the next section, we shall construct an archimedean complete field, which will be called the real numbers. Here, we prove one property of such fields, which is taken as the starting point of analysis.

Let S be a subset of K. By an *upper bound* for S one means an element $z \in K$ such that $x \leq z$ for all $x \in S$. By a *least upper bound* of S one means an element $w \in K$ such that w is an upper bound, and such that, if z is an upper bound, then $w \leqq z$. If w_1, w_2 are least upper bounds of S, then $w_1 \leqq w_2$ and $w_2 \leqq w_1$ so that $w_1 = w_2$: A least upper bound is uniquely determined.

THEOREM 2. *Let K be a complete archimedean ordered field. Then every non-empty subset S of K which has an upper bound also has a least upper bound.*

Proof. For each positive integer n we consider the set T_n consisting of all integers y such that for all $x \in S$, we have $nx \leqq y$ (and consequently, $x \leqq y/n$). Then T_n is bounded from below by any element nx (with $x \in S$), and is not empty because if b is an upper bound for S, then any integer y such that $nb \leqq y$ will be in T_n. (We use the archimedean property.) Let y_n be the smallest element of T_n. Then there exists an element x_n of S such that

$$y_n - 1 < nx_n \leqq y_n$$

(otherwise, y_n is not the smallest element of T_n). Hence

$$\frac{y_n}{n} - \frac{1}{n} < x_n \leqq \frac{y_n}{n}.$$

Let $z_n = y_n/n$. We contend that the sequence $\{z_n\}$ is Cauchy. To prove this, let m, n be positive integers and say $y_n/n \leqq y_m/m$. We contend that

$$\frac{y_m}{m} - \frac{1}{m} < \frac{y_n}{n} \leqq \frac{y_m}{m}.$$

Otherwise

$$\frac{y_n}{n} \leqq \frac{y_m}{m} - \frac{1}{m}$$

and

$$\frac{y_m}{m} - \frac{1}{m}$$

is an upper bound for S, which is not true because x_m is bigger. This proves our contention, from which we see that

$$\left| \frac{y_n}{n} - \frac{y_m}{m} \right| \leqq \frac{1}{m}.$$

For m, n sufficiently large, this is arbitrarily small, and we have proved that our sequence $\{z_n\}$ is Cauchy.

Let w be its limit. We first prove that w is an upper bound for S. Suppose there exists $x \in S$ such that $w < x$. There exists an n such that

$$|z_n - w| \leqq \frac{x - w}{2}.$$

Then

$$x - z_n = x - w + w - z_n \geqq x - w - |w - z_n|$$
$$\geqq x - w - \frac{x - w}{2}$$
$$\geqq \frac{x - w}{2} > 0,$$

so $x > z_n$, contradicting the fact that z_n is an upper bound for S.

We now show that w is a least upper bound for S. Let $u < w$. There exists some n such that

$$|z_n - x_n| \leqq \frac{1}{n} < \frac{w - u}{4}.$$

(Just select n sufficiently large.) We can also select n sufficiently large so that

$$|z_n - w| \leqq \frac{w - u}{4}$$

since w is the limit of $\{z_n\}$. Now

$$x_n - u = w - u + x_n - z_n + z_n - w$$
$$\geqq w - u - |x_n - z_n| - |z_n - w|$$
$$\geqq w - u - \frac{w - u}{4} - \frac{w - u}{4}$$
$$\geqq \frac{w - u}{2} > 0,$$

whence $u < x_n$. Hence u is not an upper bound. This proves that w is the least upper bound, and concludes the proof of the theorem.

§3. Construction of the real numbers

We start with the rational numbers $\mathbf{Q}$ and their ordering obtained from the ordering of the integers $\mathbf{Z}$ as in Theorem 1 of §1. We wish to define the real numbers. In elementary school, one uses the real numbers as infinite decimals, like

$$\sqrt{2} = 1.414 \ldots$$

Such an infinite decimal is nothing but a sequence of rational numbers, namely

$$1, \ 1.4, \ 1.41, \ 1.414, \ \ldots$$

and it should be noted that there exist other sequences which "approach" $\sqrt{2}$. If one wishes to *define* $\sqrt{2}$, it is then reasonable to take as definition an equivalence class of sequences of rational numbers, under a suitable concept of equivalence. We shall do this for all real numbers.

We start with our ordered field **Q** and Cauchy sequences in **Q**. Let $\gamma = \{c_n\}$ be a sequence of rational numbers. We say that γ is a *null sequence* if given a rational number $\epsilon > 0$ we have

$$|c_n| \leqq \epsilon$$

for all sufficiently large n. Unless otherwise specified we deal with rational ϵ in what follows, and our sequences are sequences of rational numbers.

If $\alpha = \{a_n\}$ and $\beta = \{b_n\}$ are sequences of rational numbers, we define $\alpha + \beta$ to be the sequence $\{a_n + b_n\}$, i.e. the sequence whose n-th term is $a_n + b_n$. We define the product $\alpha\beta$ to be the sequence whose n-th term is $a_n b_n$. Thus the set of sequences of rational numbers is nothing but the ring of all mappings of $\mathbf{Z}^+$ into **Q**. We shall see in a moment that the Cauchy sequences form a subring.

LEMMA 1. *Let $\alpha = \{a_n\}$ be a Cauchy sequence. There exists a positive rational number B such that $|a_n| \leqq B$ for all n.*

Proof. Given 1 there exists N such that for all $n \geqq N$ we have

$$|a_n - a_N| \leqq 1.$$

Then for all $n \geqq N$,

$$|a_n| \leqq |a_N| + 1.$$

We let B be the maximum of $|a_1|, |a_2|, \ldots, |a_{N-1}|, |a_N| + 1$.

LEMMA 2. *The Cauchy sequences form a commutative ring.*

Proof. Let $\alpha = \{a_n\}$ and $\beta = \{b_n\}$ be Cauchy sequences. Given $\epsilon > 0$, we have

$$|a_n - a_m| \leqq \frac{\epsilon}{2}$$

for all m, n sufficiently large, and also

$$|b_n - b_m| \leqq \frac{\epsilon}{2}$$

for all m, n sufficiently large. Hence for all m, n sufficiently large, we have

$$|a_n + b_n - (a_m + b_m)| = |a_n - a_m + b_n - b_m|$$
$$\leqq |a_n - a_m| + |b_n - b_m|$$
$$\leqq \frac{\epsilon}{2} + \frac{\epsilon}{2} = \epsilon.$$

Hence the sum $\alpha + \beta$ is a Cauchy sequence. One sees at once that

$$-\alpha = \{-a_n\}$$

is a Cauchy sequence. As for the product, we have

$$|a_n b_n - a_m b_m| = |a_n b_n - a_n b_m + a_n b_m - a_m b_m|$$
$$\leqq |a_n| \, |b_n - b_m| + |a_n - a_m| \, |b_m|.$$

By Lemma 1, there exists $B_1 > 0$ such that $|a_n| \leqq B_1$ for all n, and $B_2 > 0$ such that $|b_n| \leqq B_2$ for all n. Let $B = \max(B_1, B_2)$. For all m, n sufficiently large, we have

$$|a_n - a_m| \leqq \frac{\epsilon}{2B} \qquad \text{and} \qquad |b_n - b_m| \leqq \frac{\epsilon}{2B},$$

and consequently

$$|a_n b_n - a_m b_m| \leqq \frac{\epsilon}{2} + \frac{\epsilon}{2} = \epsilon.$$

So the product $\alpha\beta$ is a Cauchy sequence. It is clear that the sequence $e = \{1, 1, 1, \ldots\}$ is a Cauchy sequence. Hence Cauchy sequences form a ring, and a subring of the ring of all mappings of $\mathbf{Z}^+$ into $\mathbf{Q}$. This ring is obviously commutative.

LEMMA 3. *The null sequences form an ideal in the ring of Cauchy sequences.*

Proof. Let $\beta = \{b_n\}$ and $\gamma = \{c_n\}$ be null sequences. Given $\epsilon > 0$, for all n sufficiently large we have

$$|b_n| \leqq \frac{\epsilon}{2} \qquad \text{and} \qquad |c_n| \leqq \frac{\epsilon}{2}.$$

Hence for all n sufficiently large, we have

$$|b_n + c_n| \leqq \epsilon$$

so $\beta + \gamma$ is a null sequence. It is clear that $-\beta$ is a null sequence.

By Lemma 1, given a Cauchy sequence $\alpha = \{a_n\}$, there exists a rational number $B > 0$ such that $|a_n| \leqq B$ for all n. For all n sufficiently large, we have

$$|b_n| \leqq \frac{\epsilon}{B},$$

whence

$$|a_n b_n| \leqq B \frac{\epsilon}{B} = \epsilon,$$

so that $\alpha\beta$ is a null sequence. This proves that null sequences form an ideal, as desired.

Let R be the ring of Cauchy sequences and M the ideal of null sequences. We then have the notion of congruence, that is if α, $\beta \in R$, we had defined $\alpha \equiv \beta \pmod{M}$ to mean $\alpha - \beta \in M$, or in other words $\alpha = \beta + \gamma$ for some null sequence γ. We define a *real number* to be a congruence class of Cauchy sequences. As we know from constructing arbitrary factor rings, the set of such congruence classes is itself a ring, denoted by R/M, but which we shall also denote by **R**. The congruence class of the sequence α will be denoted by $\bar{\alpha}$ for the moment. Then by definition,

$$\overline{\alpha + \beta} = \bar{\alpha} + \bar{\beta}, \qquad \overline{\alpha\beta} = \bar{\alpha}\,\bar{\beta}.$$

The unit element of **R** is the class of the Cauchy sequence $\{1, 1, 1, \ldots\}$.

THEOREM 3. *The ring $R/M = $ **R** of real numbers is in fact a field.*

Proof. We must prove that if α is a Cauchy sequence, and is not a null sequence, then there exists a Cauchy sequence β such that $\alpha\beta \equiv e \pmod{M}$, where $e = \{1, 1, 1, \ldots\}$. We need a lemma on null sequences.

LEMMA 4. *Let α be a Cauchy sequence, and not a null sequence. Then there exists N_0 and a rational number $c > 0$ such that $|a_n| \geq c$ for all $n \geq N_0$.*

Proof. Suppose otherwise. Let $\alpha = \{a_n\}$. Then given $\epsilon > 0$, there exists an infinite sequence $n_1 < n_2 < \cdots$ of positive integers such that

$$|a_{n_i}| < \frac{\epsilon}{3}$$

for each $i = 1, 2, \ldots$. By definition, there exists N such that for $m, n \geq N$ we have

$$|a_n - a_m| \leq \frac{\epsilon}{3}.$$

Let $n_i \geq N$. We have for $m \geq N$,

$$|a_m| \leq |a_m - a_{n_i}| + |a_{n_i}| \leq \frac{2\epsilon}{3},$$

and for $m, n \geq N$,

$$|a_n| \leq |a_m| + \frac{\epsilon}{3} \leq \epsilon.$$

This shows that α is a null sequence, contrary to hypothesis, and proves our lemma.

We return to the proof of the theorem. By Lemma 4, there exists N_0 such that for $n \geq N_0$ we have $a_n \neq 0$. Let $\beta = b_n$ be the sequence such that $b_n = 1$ if $n < N_0$, and $b_n = a_n^{-1}$ if $n \geq N_0$. Then $\beta\alpha$ differs from e only in a finite number of terms, and so $\beta\alpha - e$ is certainly a null sequence. There remains to prove that β is a Cauchy sequence. By Lemma 4, we can select N_0 such that for all $n \geq N_0$ we have $a_n \geq c > 0$. It follows that

$$\frac{1}{|a_n|} \leq \frac{1}{c}.$$

Given $\epsilon > 0$, there exists N (which we can take $\geqq N_0$) such that for all $m, n \geqq N$ we have

$$|a_n - a_m| \leqq \epsilon c^2.$$

Then for $m, n \geqq N$ we get

$$\left| \frac{1}{a_n} - \frac{1}{a_m} \right| = \left| \frac{a_m - a_n}{a_m a_n} \right| \leqq \frac{\epsilon c^2}{c^2} = \epsilon,$$

thereby proving that β is a Cauchy sequence, and concluding the proof of our theorem.

We have constructed the field of real numbers.

Observe that we have a natural ring-homomorphism of $\mathbf{Q}$ into $\mathbf{R}$, obtained by mapping each rational number a on the class of the Cauchy sequence $\{a, a, a, \ldots\}$. This is a composite of two homomorphisms, first the map

$$a \mapsto \{a, a, a, \ldots\}$$

of $\mathbf{Q}$ into the ring of Cauchy sequences, followed by the map $R \to R/M$. Since this is not the zero homomorphism, it follows that it is an isomorphism of $\mathbf{Q}$ onto its image.

The next lemma is designed for the purpose of defining an ordering on the real numbers.

LEMMA 5. *Let* $\alpha = \{a_n\}$ *be a Cauchy sequence. Exactly one of the following possibilities holds:*

(1) α *is a null sequence.*
(2) *There exists a rational* $c > 0$ *such that for all n sufficiently large,* $a_n \geqq c$.
(3) *There exists a rational* $c < 0$ *such that for all n sufficiently large,* $a_n \leqq c$.

Proof. It is clear that if α satisfies one of the three possibilities, then it cannot satisfy any other, i.e. the possibilities are mutually exclusive. What we must show is that at least one of the possibilities holds. Suppose that α is not a null sequence. By Lemma 4, there exists N_0 and a rational number $c > 0$ such that $|a_n| \geqq c$ for all $n \geqq N_0$. Thus $a_n \geqq c$ if a_n is positive, and $-a_n \geqq c$ if a_n is negative. Suppose that there exist arbitrarily large integers n such that a_n is positive, and arbitrarily large integers m such that a_m is negative. Then for such m, n we have

$$a_n - a_m \geqq 2c > 0,$$

thereby contradicting the fact that α is a Cauchy sequence. This proves that (2) or (3) must hold, and concludes the proof of the lemma.

LEMMA 6. *Let* $\alpha = \{a_n\}$ *be a Cauchy sequence and let* $\beta = \{b_n\}$ *be a null sequence. If* α *satisfies property* (2) *of Lemma* 5, *then* $\alpha + \beta$ *also satisfies this property, and if* α *satisfies property* (3) *of Lemma* 5, *then* $\alpha + \beta$ *also satisfies property* (3).

Proof. Suppose that α satisfies property (2). For all n sufficiently large, by definition of a null sequence, we have $|b_n| \leq c/2$. Hence for sufficiently large n,

$$a_n + b_n \geq |a_n| - |b_n| \geq c/2.$$

A similar argument proves the analogue for Property (3). This proves the lemma.

We may now define an ordering on the real numbers. We let P be the set of real numbers which can be represented by a Cauchy sequence α having property (2), and prove that P defines an ordering.

Let α be a Cauchy sequence representing a real number. If α is not null and does not satisfy (2), then $-\alpha$ obviously satisfies (2). By Lemma 6, every Cauchy sequence representing the same real number as α also satisfies (2). Hence P satisfies condition ORD 1.

Let $\alpha = \{a_n\}$ and $\beta = \{b_n\}$ be Cauchy sequences representing real numbers in P, and satisfying (2). There exists $c_1 > 0$ such that $a_n \geq c_1$ for all sufficiently large n, and there exists $c_2 > 0$ such that $b_n \geq c_2$ for all sufficiently large n. Hence $a_n + b_n \geq c_1 + c_2 > 0$ for sufficiently large n, thereby proving that $\alpha + \beta$ is also in P. Furthermore,

$$a_n b_n \geq c_1 c_2 > 0$$

for all sufficiently large n, so that $\alpha\beta$ is in P. This proves that P defines an ordering on the real numbers.

We recall that we had obtained an isomorphism of $\mathbf{Q}$ onto a subfield of $\mathbf{R}$, given by the map

$$a \mapsto \overline{\{a, a, a, \ldots\}}.$$

In view of Exercise 4, §1 this map is order preserving, but this is also easily seen directly from our definitions. For a while, we shall not identify a with its image in $\mathbf{R}$, and we denote by $\bar{a}$ the class of the Cauchy sequence $\{a, a, a, \ldots\}$.

THEOREM 4. *The ordering of* $\mathbf{R}$ *is archimedean.*

Proof. Let A be a real number, represented by a Cauchy sequence $\alpha = \{a_n\}$. By Lemma 1, we can find a rational number r such that $a_n \leq r$ for all n, and multiplying r by a positive denominator, we see that there exists an integer b such that $a_n \leq b$ for all n. Then $\bar{b} - \bar{\alpha}$ is represented by the sequence $\{b - a_n\}$ and $b - a_n \geq 0$ for all n. By definition, it follows that

$$\bar{b} - \bar{a} \geq 0,$$

whence $\bar{a} \leq \bar{b}$, as desired.

The following lemma gives us a criterion for inequalities between real numbers in terms of Cauchy sequences.

LEMMA 7. *Let* $\gamma = \{c_n\}$ *be a Cauchy sequence of rational numbers, and let* c *be a rational number* > 0. *If* $|c_n| \leq c$ *for all n sufficiently large, then* $|\bar{\gamma}| \leq \bar{c}$.

Proof. If $\bar{\gamma} = 0$, our assertion is trivial. Suppose $\bar{\gamma} \neq 0$, and say $\bar{\gamma} > 0$. Then $|\bar{\gamma}| = \bar{\gamma}$, and thus we must show that $\bar{c} - \bar{\gamma} \geq 0$. But for all n sufficiently large, we have

$$c - c_n \geq 0.$$

Since $\bar{c} - \bar{\gamma} = \overline{\{c - c_n\}}$, it follows from our definition of the ordering in R that $\bar{c} - \bar{\gamma} \geq 0$. The case when $\bar{\gamma} < 0$ is proved by considering $-\bar{\gamma}$.

Given a real number $\epsilon > 0$, by Theorem 4 there exists a rational number $\epsilon_1 > 0$ such that $0 < \bar{\epsilon}_1 < \epsilon$. Hence in the definition of limit, when we are given the ϵ, it does not matter whether we take it real or rational.

LEMMA 8. *Let* $\alpha = \{a_n\}$ *be a Cauchy sequence of rational numbers. Then* $\bar{\alpha}$ *is the limit of the sequence* $\{\bar{a}_n\}$.

Proof. Given a *rational* number $\epsilon > 0$, there exists N such that, for $m, n \geq N$ we have

$$|a_n - a_m| \leq \epsilon.$$

Then for all $m \geq N$ we have by Lemma 7, for all $n \geq N$,

$$|\bar{\alpha} - \bar{a}_m| = |\overline{\{a_n - a_m\}}| \leq \bar{\epsilon}.$$

This proves our assertion.

THEOREM 5. *The field of real numbers is complete.*

Proof. Let $\{A_n\}$ be a Cauchy sequence of real numbers. For each n, by Lemma 8, we can find a rational number a_n such that

$$|A_n - \bar{a}_n| \leq \frac{1}{n}.$$

(Strictly speaking, we still should write $1/\bar{n}$ on the right-hand side!) Furthermore, by definition, given $\epsilon > 0$ there exists N such that for all $m, n \geq N$ we have

$$|A_n - A_m| \leq \frac{\epsilon}{3}.$$

Let N_1 be an integer $\geq N$, and such that $1/N_1 \leq \epsilon/3$. Then for all $m, n \geq N_1$ we get

$$
\begin{aligned}
|\bar{a}_n - \bar{a}_m| &= |\bar{a}_n - A_n + A_n - A_m + A_m - \bar{a}_m| \\
&\leq |\bar{a}_n - A_n| + |A_n - A_m| + |A_m - \bar{a}_m| \\
&\leq \frac{\epsilon}{3} + \frac{\epsilon}{3} + \frac{\epsilon}{3} = \epsilon.
\end{aligned}
$$

This proves that $\{\bar{a}_n\}$ is a Cauchy sequence of rational numbers. Let A be its limit. For all n, we have

$$|A_n - A| \leq |A_n - \bar{a}_n| + |\bar{a}_n - A|.$$

If we take n sufficiently large, we see that A is also the limit of the sequence $\{A_n\}$, thereby proving our theorem.

EXERCISES

1. Let p be a prime number. If x is a non-zero rational number, written in the form $x = p^r a/b$ where r is an integer, a, b are integers not divisible by p, we define

$$|x|_p = 1/p^r.$$

Define $|0|_p = 0$. Show that for all rational x, y we have

$$|xy|_p = |x|_p |y|_p \qquad \text{and} \qquad |x + y|_p \leq |x|_p + |y|_p.$$

2. Define Cauchy sequences with respect to the function $|\ |_p$, and construct a completion of $\mathbf{Q}$ with respect to this function, which is called the *p-adic absolute value*.

3. Prove that every positive real number has a positive square root in $\mathbf{R}$. Since the polynomial $t^2 - a$ has at most two roots in a field, and since for any root α, the number $-\alpha$ is also a root, it follows that for every $a \in \mathbf{R}$, $a \geq 0$, there exists a unique $\alpha \in \mathbf{R}$, $\alpha \geq 0$ such that $\alpha^2 = a$. [*Hint:* For the above proof, let α be the least upper bound of the set of rational numbers b such that $b^2 \leq a$.]

§4. Decimal expansions

THEOREM 6. *Let d be an integer ≥ 2, and let m be an integer ≥ 0. Then m can be written in a unique way in the form*

(1) $$m = c_0 + c_1 d + \cdots + c_n d^n$$

with integers c_i such that $0 \leq c_i < d$.

Proof. This is easily seen from the Euclidean algorithm, and we shall give the proof. For the existence, if $m < d$, we let $c_0 = m$ and $c_i = 0$ for $i > 0$. If $m \geq d$ we write

$$m = qd + c_0$$

with $0 \leq c_0 < d$, using the Euclidean algorithm. Then $q < m$, and by induction, there exist integers c_i ($0 \leq c_i < d$ and $i \geq 1$) such that

$$q = c_1 + c_2 d + \cdots + c_k d^k.$$

Substituting this value for q yields what we want. As for uniqueness, suppose that

(2) $$m = b_0 + b_1 d + \cdots + b_n d^n$$

with integers b_i satisfying $0 \leq b_i < d$. (We can use the same n simply by adding terms with coefficients $b_i = 0$ or $c_i = 0$ if necessary.) Say $a_0 \leq b_0$. Then $b_0 - a_0 \geq 0$, and $b_0 - a_0 < d$. On the other hand, $b_0 - a_0 = de$ for some integer e [as one sees subtracting (2) from (1)]. Hence $b_0 - a_0 = 0$ and $b_0 = a_0$. Assume by induction that we have shown $a_i = b_i$ for $0 \leq i \leq s$ and $s < n$. Then

$$a_{s+1} d^{s+1} + \cdots + a_n d^n = b_{s+1} d^{s+1} + \cdots + b_n d^n.$$

Dividing both sides by d^{s+1}, we obtain

$$a_{s+1} + \cdots + a_{n-s-1} d^{n-s-1} = b_{s+1} + \cdots + b_{n-s-1} d^{n-s-1}.$$

By what we have just seen, it follows that $a_{s+1} = b_{s+1}$, and thus we have proved uniqueness by induction, as desired.

Let x be a positive real number, and d an integer ≥ 2. Then x has a unique expression of the form

$$x = m + \alpha,$$

where $0 \leq \alpha < 1$. Indeed, we let m be the largest integer $\leq x$. Then $x < m + 1$, and hence $0 \leq x - m < 1$. We shall now describe a d-decimal expansion for real numbers between 0 and 1.

THEOREM 7. *Let x be a real number, $0 \leq x < 1$. Let d be an integer ≥ 2. For each positive integer n there is a unique expression*

(3) $$x = \frac{a_1}{d} + \frac{a_2}{d^2} + \cdots + \frac{a_n}{d^n} + \alpha_n$$

with integers a_i satisfying $0 \leq a_i < d$ and $0 \leq \alpha_n < 1/d^n$.

Proof. Let m be the largest integer $\leq d^n x$. Then $m \geq 0$ and

$$d^n x = m + \alpha_n$$

with some number α_n such that $0 \leq \alpha_n < 1$. We apply Theorem 6 to m, and then divide by d^n to obtain the desired expression. Conversely, given such an expression (3), we multiply it by d^n and apply the uniqueness part of Theorem 6 to obtain the uniqueness of (3). This proves our theorem.

When $d = 10$, the numbers $a_1, a_2, \ldots$ in Theorem 7 are precisely those of the decimal expansion of x, which is written

$$x = 0.a_1 a_2 a_3 \ldots$$

since time immemorial.

Conversely:

THEOREM 8. *Let d be an integer ≥ 2. Let $a_1, a_2, \ldots$ be a sequence of integers, $0 \leq a_i < d$ for all i, and assume that given a positive integer N there exists some $n \geq N$ such that $a_n \neq d - 1$. Then there exists a real number x such that for each $n \geq 1$ we have*

$$x = \frac{a_1}{d} + \frac{a_2}{d^2} + \cdots + \frac{a_n}{d^n} + \alpha_n,$$

where α_n is a number with $0 \leq \alpha_n < 1/d^n$.

Proof. We shall use freely some simple properties of limits and infinite sums, treated in any standard beginning course of analysis. Let

$$y_n = \frac{a_1}{d} + \cdots + \frac{a_n}{d^n}.$$

Then the sequence $y_1, y_2, \ldots$ is increasing, and easily shown to be bounded from above. Let x be its least upper bound. Then x is a limit of the sequence, and

$$x = y_n + \alpha_n,$$

where

$$\alpha_n = \sum_{\nu=n+1}^{\infty} \frac{a_\nu}{d^\nu}.$$

Let

$$\beta_n = \sum_{\nu=n+1}^{\infty} \frac{d-1}{d^\nu}.$$

By hypothesis, we have $\alpha_n < \beta_n$ because there is some a_ν with $\nu \geq n + 1$

such that $a_\nu \neq d - 1$. On the other hand,

$$\beta_n = \frac{d-1}{d^{n+1}} \sum_{\nu=0}^{\infty} \frac{1}{d^\nu} = \frac{d-1}{d^{n+1}} \frac{1}{1 - \dfrac{1}{d}} = \frac{1}{d^n}.$$

Hence $0 \leq \alpha_n < 1/d^n$, as was to be proved.

COROLLARY. *The real numbers are not denumerable.*

Proof. Consider the subset of real numbers consisting of all decimal sequences

$$0.a_1 a_2 \ldots$$

with $0 \leq a_i \leq 8$, taking $d = 10$ in Theorems 7 and 8. It will suffice to prove that this subset is not denumerable. Suppose it is, and let

$$\alpha_1 = 0.a_{11} a_{12} a_{13} \ldots,$$
$$\alpha_2 = 0.a_{21} a_{22} a_{23} \ldots,$$
$$\alpha_3 = 0.a_{31} a_{32} a_{33} \ldots,$$
$$\ldots$$

be an enumeration of this subset. Let

$$\alpha = 0.a_{11} a_{22} a_{33} \ldots.$$

Then α is not equal to any one of the α_n ($n = 1, 2, \ldots$) and all the integers in its decimal expansion are ≥ 0 and ≤ 8, contradicting the hypothesis that we had an enumeration of our subset, and proving our corollary. (*Note:* The simple facts concerning the terminology of denumerable sets used in this proof will be dealt with systematically in the next chapter.)

EXERCISE

Look up a text on diophantine approximations or continued fractions, to see how one can define by means of the Euclidean algorithm a more canonical sequence of rational numbers converging to a given real number x, not depending on a particular decimal system.

§5. *The complex numbers*

Our purpose in this section is to identify the real numbers with a subfield of some field in which the equation $t^2 = -1$ has a root. As is usual in these matters, we define the bigger field in a way designed to make this equation obvious, and must then prove all desired properties.

We define a *complex number* to be a pair (x, y) of real numbers. If $z = (x, y)$ we define multiplication of z by a real number a to be

$$az = (ax, ay).$$

Thus the set of complex numbers, denoted by $\mathbf{C}$, is nothing so far but $\mathbf{R}^2$, and can be viewed already as a vector space over $\mathbf{R}$. We let $e = (1, 0)$ and $i = (0, 1)$. Then every complex number can be expressed in a unique way as a sum $xe + yi$ with $x, y \in \mathbf{R}$. We must still define the multiplication of complex numbers. If $z = xe + yi$ and $w = ue + vi$ are complex numbers with $x, y, u, v \in \mathbf{R}$ we *define*

$$zw = (xu - yv)e + (xv + yu)i.$$

Observe at once that $ez = ze = z$ for all $z \in \mathbf{C}$, and $i^2 = -e$. We now contend that $\mathbf{C}$ is a field. We already know that it is an additive (abelian) group. If $z_1 = x_1e + y_1i$, $z_2 = x_2e + y_2i$, and $z_3 = x_3e + y_3i$, then

$$\begin{aligned}
(z_1z_2)z_3 &= ((x_1x_2 - y_1y_2)e + (y_1x_2 + x_1y_2)i)(x_3e + y_3i) \\
&= (x_1x_2x_3 - y_1y_2x_3 - y_1x_2y_3 - x_1y_2y_3)e \\
&\quad + (y_1x_2x_3 + x_1y_2x_3 + x_1x_2y_3 - y_1y_2y_3)i.
\end{aligned}$$

A similar computation of $z_1(z_2z_3)$ shows that one gets the same value as for $(z_1z_2)z_3$. Furthermore, letting $w = u + vi$ again, we have

$$\begin{aligned}
w(z_1 + z_2) &= (ue + vi)((x_1 + x_2)e + (y_1 + y_2)i) \\
&= (u(x_1 + x_2) - v(y_1 + y_2))e + (v(x_1 + x_2) + u(y_1 + y_2))i \\
&= (ux_1 - vy_1 + ux_2 - vy_2)e + (vx_1 + uy_1 + vx_2 + uy_2)i.
\end{aligned}$$

Computing $wz_1 + wz_2$ directly shows that one gets the same thing as $w(z_1 + z_2)$. We also have obviously $wz = zw$ for all $w, z \in \mathbf{C}$, and hence $(z_1 + z_2)w = z_1w + z_2w$. This proves that the complex numbers form a commutative ring.

The map $x \mapsto (x, 0)$ is immediately verified to be an injective homomorphism of $\mathbf{R}$ into $\mathbf{C}$, and from now on, we identify $\mathbf{R}$ with its image in $\mathbf{C}$, that is we write x instead of xe for $x \in \mathbf{R}$.

If $z = x + iy$ is a complex number, we define its *complex conjugate*

$$\bar{z} = x - iy.$$

Then from our multiplication rule, we see that

$$z\bar{z} = x^2 + y^2.$$

If $z \neq 0$, then at least one of the real numbers x or y is not equal to 0, and one sees that

$$\lambda = \frac{\bar{z}}{x^2 + y^2}$$

is such that $z\lambda = \lambda z = e$, because

$$z\frac{\bar{z}}{x^2 + y^2} = \frac{z\bar{z}}{x^2 + y^2} = 1.$$

Hence every non-zero element of **C** has an inverse, and consequently **C** is a field, which contains **R** as a subfield [taking into account our identification of x with $(x, 0)$].

We define the *absolute value* of a complex number $z = x + iy$ to be

$$|z| = \sqrt{a^2 + b^2}$$

and in terms of the absolute value, we can write the inverse of a non-zero complex number z in the form

$$z^{-1} = \frac{\bar{z}}{|z|^2}.$$

If z, w are complex numbers, it is easily shown that

$$|z + w| \leq |z| + |w| \quad \text{and} \quad |zw| = |z| \, |w|.$$

Furthermore, $\overline{z + w} = \bar{z} + \bar{w}$ and $\overline{zw} = \bar{z}\bar{w}$. We leave these properties as exercises. We have thus brought the theory of complex numbers to the point where the analysts take over.

In particular, using the exponential function, one proves that every positive real number r has a real n-th root, and that in fact any complex number w has an n-th root, for any positive integer n. This is done by using the polar form,

$$w = re^{i\theta}$$

with real θ, in which case $r^{1/n}e^{i\theta/n}$ is such an n-th root.

Aside from this fact, we shall use that a continuous real-valued function on a closed, bounded set of complex numbers has a maximum. All of this is proved in elementary courses in analysis.

Using these facts, we shall now prove that *the complex numbers are algebraically closed, in other words, that every polynomial $f \in \mathbf{C}[t]$ of degree ≥ 1 has a root in* **C**.

We may write

$$f(t) = a_n t^n + a_{n-1}t^{n-1} + \cdots + a_0$$

with $a_n \neq 0$. For every real $R > 0$, the function $|f|$ such that

$$t \mapsto |f(t)|$$

is continuous on the closed disc of radius R, and hence has a minimum value on this disc. On the other hand, from the expression

$$f(t) = a_n t^n \left(1 + \frac{a_{n-1}}{a_n t} + \cdots + \frac{a_0}{a_n t^n} \right)$$

we see that when $|t|$ becomes large, then $|f(t)|$ also becomes large, i.e. given $C > 0$ there exists $R > 0$ such that if $|t| > R$ then $|f(t)| > C$. Consequently, there exists a positive number R_0 such that, if z_0 is a minimum point of $|f|$ on the closed disc of radius R_0, then

$$|f(t)| \geqq |f(z_0)|$$

for all complex numbers t. In other words, z_0 is an absolute minimum for $|f|$. We shall prove that $f(z_0) = 0$.

We express f in the form

$$f(t) = c_0 + c_1(t - z_0) + \cdots + c_n(t - z_0)^n$$

with constants c_i. If $f(z_0) \neq 0$, then $c_0 = f(z_0) \neq 0$. Let $z = t - z_0$, and let m be the smallest integer > 0 such that $c_m \neq 0$. This integer m exists because f is assumed to have degree $\geqq 1$. Then we can write

$$f(t) = f_1(z) = c_0 + c_m z^m + z^{m+1} g(z)$$

for some polynomial g, and some polynomial f_1 (obtained from f by changing the variable). Let z_1 be a complex number such that $z_1^m = -c_0/c_m$, and consider values of z of type

$$z = \lambda z_1$$

where λ is real, $0 \leqq \lambda \leqq 1$. We have

$$\begin{aligned}
f(t) = f_1(\lambda z_1) &= c_0 - \lambda^m c_0 + \lambda^{m+1} z_1^{m+1} g(\lambda z_1) \\
&= c_0[1 - \lambda^m + \lambda^{m+1} z_1^{m+1} c_0^{-1} g(\lambda z_1)].
\end{aligned}$$

There exists a number $C > 0$ such that for all λ with $0 \leqq \lambda \leqq 1$ we have $|z_1^{m+1} c_0^{-1} g(\lambda z_1)| \leqq C$, and hence

$$|f_1(\lambda z_1)| \leqq |c_0|(1 - \lambda^m + C\lambda^{m+1}).$$

If we can now prove that for sufficiently small λ with $0 < \lambda < 1$ we have

$$0 < 1 - \lambda^m + C\lambda^{m+1} < 1,$$

then for such λ we get $|f_1(\lambda z_1)| < |c_0|$, thereby contradicting the hypothesis that $|f(z_0)| \leqq |f(t)|$ for all complex numbers t. The left inequality is of course obvious since $0 < \lambda < 1$. The right inequality amounts to $C\lambda^{m+1} < \lambda^m$, or equivalently $C\lambda < 1$, which is certainly satisfied for sufficiently small λ. This concludes the proof.

Remark. The idea of the proof is quite simple. We have our polynomial

$$f_1(z) = c_0 + c_m z^m + z^{m+1} g(z),$$

and $c_m \neq 0$. If $g = 0$, we simply adjust $c_m z^m$ so as to subtract a term in the same direction as c_0, to shrink it towards the origin. This is done by extracting the suitable m-th root as above. Since $g \neq 0$ in general, we have to do a slight amount of analytic juggling to show that the third term is very small compared to $c_m z^m$, and that it does not disturb the general idea of the proof in an essential way.

EXERCISES

1. Assuming the result just proved about the complex numbers, prove that every irreducible polynomial over the real numbers has degree 1 or 2. [*Hint:* Split the polynomial over the complex numbers and pair off complex conjugate roots.]

2. Prove that an irreducible polynomial of degree 2 over **R**, with leading coefficient 1, can be written in the form

$$(t - a)^2 + b^2$$

with $a, b \in \mathbf{R}, b > 0$.

CHAPTER VIII

Sets

§1. More terminology

This chapter is the most abstract of the book, and is the one dealing with objects having the least structure, namely just sets. The remarkable thing is that interesting facts can be proved with so little at hand.

We shall first define some terminology. Let S and I be sets. By a *family of elements of S, indexed by I,* one means simply a map $f: I \to S$. However, when we speak of a family, we write $f(i)$ as f_i, and also use the notation $\{f_i\}_{i \in I}$ to denote the family.

Example 1. Let S be the set consisting of the single element 3. Let $I = \{1, \ldots, n\}$ be the set of integers from 1 to n. A family of elements of S, indexed by I, can then be written $\{a_i\}_{i=1,\ldots,n}$ with each $a_i = 3$. Note that a family is different from a subset. The same element of S may receive distinct indices.

A family of elements of a set S indexed by positive integers, or non-negative integers, is also called a *sequence*.

Example 2. A sequence of real numbers is written frequently in the form

$$\{x_1, x_2, \ldots\} \qquad \text{or} \qquad \{x_n\}_{n \geq 1}$$

and stands for the map $f: \mathbf{Z}^+ \to \mathbf{R}$ such that $f(i) = x_i$. As before, note that a sequence can have all its elements equal to each other, that is

$$\{1, 1, 1, \ldots\}$$

is a sequence of integers, with $x_i = 1$ for each $i \in \mathbf{Z}^+$.

We define a *family of sets indexed by a set I* in the same manner, that is, a family of sets indexed by I is an assignment

$$i \mapsto S_i$$

which to each $i \in I$ associates a set S_i. The sets S_i may or may not have elements in common, and it is conceivable that they may all be equal. As before, we write the family $\{S_i\}_{i \in I}$.

141

We can define the intersection and union of families of sets, just as for the intersection and union of a finite number of sets. Thus, if $\{S_i\}_{i\in I}$ is a family of sets, we define the *intersection* of this family to be the set

$$\bigcap_{i\in I} S_i$$

consisting of all elements x which lie in all S_i. We define the *union*

$$\bigcup_{i\in I} S_i$$

to be the set consisting of all x such that x lies in some S_i.

If S, S' are sets, we define $S \times S'$ to be the set of all pairs (x, y) with $x \in S$ and $y \in S'$. We can define finite products in a similar way. If $S_1, S_2, \ldots$ is a sequence of sets, we define the product

$$\prod_{i=1}^{\infty} S_i$$

to be the set of all sequences $(x_1, x_2, \ldots)$ with $x_i \in S_i$. Similarly, if I is an indexing set, and $\{S_i\}_{i\in I}$ a family of sets, we define the product

$$\prod_{i\in I} S_i$$

to be the set of all families $\{x_i\}_{i\in I}$ with $x_i \in S_i$.

Let X, Y, Z be sets. We have the formula

$$(X \cup Y) \times Z = (X \times Z) \cup (Y \times Z).$$

To prove this, let $(w, z) \in (X \cup Y) \times Z$ with $w \in X \cup Y$ and $z \in Z$. Then $w \in X$ or $w \in Y$. Say $w \in X$. Then $(w, z) \in X \times Z$. Thus

$$(X \cup Y) \times Z \subset (X \times Z) \cup (Y \times Z).$$

Conversely, $X \times Z$ is contained in $(X \cup Y) \times Z$ and so is $Y \times Z$. Hence their union is contained in $(X \cup Y) \times Z$, thereby proving our assertion.

We say that two sets X, Y are *disjoint* if their intersection is empty. We say that a union $X \cup Y$ is *disjoint* if X and Y are disjoint. Note that if X, Y are disjoint, then $(X \times Z)$ and $(Y \times Z)$ are disjoint.

We can take products with arbitrary families. For instance, if $\{X_i\}_{i\in I}$ is a family of sets, then

$$\left(\bigcup_{i\in I} X_i\right) \times Z = \bigcup_{i\in I} (X_i \times Z).$$

If the family $\{X_i\}_{i \in I}$ is disjoint (that is $X_i \cap X_j$ is empty if $i \neq j$ for $i, j \in I$), then the sets $X_i \times Z$ are also disjoint.

We have similar formulas for intersections. For instance,

$$(X \cap Y) \times Z = (X \cap Z) \times (Y \cap Z).$$

We leave the proof to the reader.

Let X be a set and Y a subset. The *complement* of Y in X, denote by $\mathcal{C}_X Y$, or $X - Y$, is the set of all elements $x \in X$ such that $x \notin Y$. If Y, Z are subsets of X, then we have the following formulas:

$$\mathcal{C}_X(Y \cup Z) = \mathcal{C}_X Y \cap \mathcal{C}_X Z,$$

$$\mathcal{C}_X(Y \cap Z) = \mathcal{C}_X Y \cup \mathcal{C}_X Z.$$

These are essentially reformulations of definitions. For instance, suppose $x \in X$ and $x \notin (Y \cup Z)$. Then $x \notin Y$ and $x \notin Z$. Hence $x \in \mathcal{C}_X Y \cap \mathcal{C}_X Z$. Conversely, if $x \in \mathcal{C}_X Y \cap \mathcal{C}_X Z$, then x lies neither in Y nor Z, and hence $x \in \mathcal{C}_X(Y \cup Z)$. This proves the first formula. We leave the second to the reader. Exercise: Formulate these formulas for the complement of the union of a family of sets, and the complement of the intersection of a family of sets.

Let A, B be sets and $f: A \to B$ a mapping. If Y is a subset of B, we define $f^{-1}(Y)$ to be the set of all $x \in A$ such that $f(x) \in Y$. It may be that $f^{-1}(Y)$ is empty, of course. We call $f^{-1}(Y)$ the *inverse image of* Y (under f). If f is injective, and Y consists of one element y, then $f^{-1}(\{y\})$ is either empty, or has precisely one element. We shall give certain simple properties of the inverse image as exercises.

EXERCISES

1. If $f: A \to B$ is a map, and Y, Z are subsets of B, prove the following formulas:

$$f^{-1}(Y \cup Z) = f^{-1}(Y) \cup f^{-1}(Z).$$

$$f^{-1}(Y \cap Z) = f^{-1}(Y) \cap f^{-1}(Z).$$

2. Formulate and prove the analogous properties of Exercise 1 for families of subsets, e.g. if $\{Y_i\}_{i \in I}$ is a family of subsets of B, show that

$$f^{-1}\left(\bigcup_{i \in I} Y_i\right) = \bigcup_{i \in I} f^{-1}(Y_i).$$

3. Let $f: A \to B$ be a surjective map. Show that there exists an injective map of B into A.

§2. Zorn's lemma

In order to deal efficiently with infinitely many sets simultaneously, one needs a special axiom. To state it, we need some more terminology.

Let S be a set. A *partial ordering* (also called an ordering) of S is a relation, written $x \leq y$, among some pairs of elements of S, having the following properties.

PO 1. *We have* $x \leq x$.

PO 2. *If* $x \leq y$ *and* $y \leq z$ *then* $x \leq z$.

PO 3. *If* $x \leq y$ *and* $y \leq x$ *then* $x = y$.

Note that we don't require that the relation $x \leq y$ or $y \leq x$ hold for every pair of elements (x, y) of S. Some pairs may not be comparable. We sometimes write $y \geq x$ for $x \leq y$.

Example 1. Let G be a group. Let S be the set of subgroups. If H, H' are subgroups of G, we define

$$H \leq H'$$

if H is a subgroup of H'. One verifies immediately that this relation defines a partial ordering on S. Given two subgroups H, H' of G, we do not necessarily have $H \leq H'$ or $H' \leq H$.

Example 2. Let R be a ring, and let S be the set of left ideals of R. We define a partial ordering in S in a way similar to the above, namely if L, L' are left ideals of R, we define

$$L \leq L'$$

if $L \subset L'$.

Example 3. Let X be a set, and S the set of subsets of X. If Y, Z are subsets of X, we define $Y \leq Z$ if Y is a subset of Z. This defines a partial ordering on S.

In all these examples, the relation of partial ordering is said to be that of inclusion.

In a partially ordered set, if $x \leq y$ and $x \neq y$ we then write $x < y$.

Remark. We have not defined the word "relation". This can be done in terms of sets as follows. We define a *relation* between pairs of elements of a set A to be a subset R of the product $A \times A$. If $x, y \in A$ and $(x, y) \in R$, then we say that x, y *satisfy our relation*. Using this formulation, we can restate our conditions for a partial ordering relation in the following form. For all $x, y, z \in A$:

PO 1. *We have* $(x, x) \in R$.

PO 2. *If $(x, y) \in R$ and $(y, z) \in R$ then $(x, z) \in R$.*

PO 3. *If $(x, y) \in R$ and $(y, x) \in R$ then $x = y$.*

The notation we used previously is, however, much easier to use, and having shown how this notation can be explained only in terms of sets, we shall continue to use it as before.

Let A be a partially ordered set, and B a subset. Then we can define a partial ordering on B by defining $x \leqq y$ for $x, y \in B$ to hold if and only if $x \leqq y$ in A. In other words, if $R \subset A \times A$ is the subset of $A \times A$ defining our relation of partial ordering in A, we let $R_0 = R \cap (B \times B)$, and then R_0 defines a relation of partial ordering in B. We shall say that R_0 is the partial ordering on B *induced* by R, or is the *restriction* to B of the partial ordering of A.

Let S be a partially ordered set. By a *least* element of S (or a *smallest* element) one means an element $a \in S$ such that $a \leqq x$ for all $x \in S$. Similarly, by a *greatest element* one means an element b such that $x \leqq b$ for all $x \in S$.

By a *maximal element* m of S one means an element such that if $x \in S$ and $x \geqq m$, then $x = m$. Note that a maximal element need not be a greatest element. There may be many maximal elements in S, whereas if a greatest element exists, then it is unique (proof?).

Let S be a partially ordered set. We shall say that S is *totally ordered* if given $x, y \in S$ we have necessarily $x \leqq y$ or $y \leqq x$.

Example 4.   The integers **Z** are totally ordered by the usual ordering. So are the real numbers.

Let S be a partially ordered set, and T a subset. An *upper bound* of T (in S) is an element $b \in S$ such that $x \leqq b$ for all $x \in T$. A *least upper bound* of T in S is an upper bound b such that, if c is another upper bound, then $b \leqq c$. We shall say that S is *inductively ordered* if every non-empty totally ordered subset has an upper bound.

We shall say that S is *strictly* inductively ordered if every non-empty totally ordered subset has a least upper bound.

In Examples 1, 2, 3, in each case, the set is strictly inductively ordered. To prove this, let us take Example 2. Let T be a non-empty totally ordered subset of the set of subgroups of G. This means that if $H, H' \in T$, then $H \subset H'$ or $H' \subset H$. Let U be the union of all sets in T. Then:

(1) U is a subgroup. *Proof:* If $x, y \in U$, there exist subgroups $H, H' \in T$ such that $x \in H$ and $y \in H'$. If, say, $H \subset H'$, then both $x, y \in H'$ and hence $xy \in H'$. Hence $xy \in U$. Also, $x^{-1} \in H'$, so $x^{-1} \in U$. Hence U is a subgroup.

(2) U is an upper bound for each element of T. *Proof:* Every $H \in T$ is contained in U, so $H \leq U$ for all $H \in T$.

(3) U is a least upper bound for T. *Proof:* Any subgroup of G which contains all the subgroups $H \in T$ must then contain their union U.

The proof that the sets in Examples 2, 3 are strictly inductively ordered is entirely similar.

We can now state the axiom mentioned at the beginning of the section.

ZORN'S LEMMA. *Let S be a non-empty inductively ordered set. Then there exists a maximal element in S.*

We shall see by two examples how one applies Zorn's lemma.

THEOREM 1. *Let R be a commutative ring with unit element $1 \neq 0$. Then there exists a maximal ideal in R.*

(Recall that a maximal ideal is an ideal M such that $M \neq R$, and if J is an ideal such that $M \subset J \subset R$, then $J = M$ or $J = R$.)

Proof. Let S be the set of proper ideals of R, that is ideals J such that $J \neq R$. Then S is not empty, because the zero ideal is in S. Furthermore, S is inductively ordered by inclusion. To see this, let T be a non-empty totally ordered subset of S. Let U be the union of all ideals in T. Then U is an ideal (the proof being similar to the proof we gave before concerning Example 1). The crucial thing here, however, is that U is not equal to R. Indeed, if $U = R$, then $1 \in U$, and hence there is some ideal $J \in T$ such that $1 \in J$ because U is the union of such ideals J. This is impossible since S is a set of *proper* ideals. Hence U is in S, and is obviously an upper bound for T (even a least upper bound), as was to be shown.

Let V be a non-zero vector space over a field K. Let $\{v_i\}_{i \in I}$ be a family of elements of V. If $\{a_i\}_{i \in I}$ is a family of elements of K, such that $a_i = 0$ for all but a finite number of indices i, then we can form the sum

$$\sum_{i \in I} a_i v_i.$$

If $i_1, \ldots, i_n$ those indices for which $a_i \neq 0$, then the above sum is defined to be

$$a_{i_1} v_{i_1} + \cdots + a_{i_n} v_{i_n}.$$

We shall say that family $\{v_i\}_{i \in I}$ is *linearly independent* if, whenever we have a family $\{a_i\}_{i \in I}$ with $a_i \in K$, all but a finite number of which are 0, and

$$\sum_{i \in I} a_i v_i = 0,$$

then all $a_i = 0$. For simplicity, we shall abbreviate "all but a finite number" by "almost all." We say that a family $\{v_i\}_{i \in I}$ of elements of V *generates* V if every element $v \in V$ can be written in the form

$$v = \sum_{i \in I} a_i v_i$$

for some family $\{a_i\}_{i \in I}$ of elements of K, almost all a_i being 0. A family $\{v_i\}_{i \in I}$ which is linearly independent and generates V is called a *basis* of V.

If U is a subset of V, we may view U as a family, indexed by its own elements. Thus if for each $v \in U$ we are given an element $a_v \in K$, almost all $a_v = 0$, we can form the sum

$$\sum_{v \in U} a_v v.$$

In this way, we can define what it means for a subset of V to generate V and to be linearly independent. We can define a basis of V to be a subset of V which generates V and is linearly independent.

THEOREM 2. *Let V be a non-zero vector space over the field K. Then there exists a basis of V.*

Proof. Let S be the set of linearly independent subsets of V. Then S is not empty, because for any $v \in V$, $v \neq 0$, the set $\{v\}$ is linearly independent. If B, B' are elements of S, we define $B \leqq B'$ if $B \subset B'$. Then S is partially ordered, and is inductively ordered, because if T is a totally ordered subset of S, then

$$\bigcup_{B \in T} B$$

is an upper bound for T in S. Let M be a maximal element of S, by Zorn's lemma. Let $v \in V$. Since M is maximal, if $v \notin M$, the set $M \cup \{v\}$ is not linearly independent. Hence there exist elements $a_w \in K$ ($w \in M$) and $b \in K$ not all 0, but almost all 0, such that

$$bv + \sum_{w \in M} a_w w = 0.$$

If $b = 0$, then we contradict the fact that M is linearly independent. Hence $b \neq 0$, and

$$v = \sum_{w \in M} -b^{-1} a_w w$$

is a linear combination of elements of M. If $v \in M$, then trivially, v is a linear combination of elements of M. Hence M generates V, and is therefore the desired basis of V.

EXERCISES

1. Write out in detail the proof that the sets of Examples 2, 3 are inductively ordered.

2. In the proof of Theorem 2, write out in detail the proof of the statement: "it is easily checked that U is linearly independent".

3. Let R be a ring and E a finitely generated module over R, i.e. a module with a finite number of generators $v_1, \ldots, v_n$. Assume that E is not the zero module. Show that E has a maximal submodule, i.e. a submodule $M \neq E$ such that if N is a submodule, $M \subset N \subset E$, then $M = N$ or $N = E$.

4. Let R be a commutative ring and S a subset of R, S not empty, and $0 \notin S$. Show that there exists an ideal M whose intersection with S is empty, and is maximal with respect to this property. We then say that M is a maximal ideal not meeting S.

§3. Cardinal numbers

Let A, B be sets. We shall say that the *cardinality of A is the same as the cardinality of B*, and write

$$\operatorname{card}(A) = \operatorname{card}(B)$$

if there exists a bijection of A onto B.

We say $\operatorname{card}(A) \leq \operatorname{card}(B)$ if there exists an injective mapping (injection) $f: A \to B$. We also write $\operatorname{card}(B) \geq \operatorname{card}(A)$ in this case. It is clear that if $\operatorname{card}(A) \leq \operatorname{card}(B)$ and $\operatorname{card}(B) \leq \operatorname{card}(C)$, then

$$\operatorname{card}(A) \leq \operatorname{card}(C).$$

This amounts to saying that a composite of injective mappings is injective. Similarly, if $\operatorname{card}(A) = \operatorname{card}(B)$ and $\operatorname{card}(B) = \operatorname{card}(C)$ then

$$\operatorname{card}(A) = \operatorname{card}(C).$$

This amounts to saying that a composite of bijective mappings is bijective. Finally, we clearly have $\operatorname{card}(A) = \operatorname{card}(A)$.

We shall first discuss denumerable sets. A set D is called *denumerable* if there exists a bijection of D with the positive integers, and such a bijection is called an *enumeration* of the set D.

Any infinite subset of a denumerable set is denumerable.

One proves this easily by induction. (We sketch the proof: It suffices to prove that any infinite subset of the positive integers is denumerable. Let $D = D_1$ be such a subset. Then D_1 has a least element a_1. Suppose inductively that we have defined D_n for an integer $n \geq 1$. Let D_{n+1} be the set of all elements of D_n which are greater than the least element of D_n. Then we get an injective mapping

$$n \mapsto a_n$$

of $\mathbf{Z}^+$ into D, and one sees at once that this map is surjective.)

THEOREM 3. *Let D be a denumerable set. Then $D \times D$ is denumerable.*

Proof. It suffices to prove that $\mathbf{Z}^+ \times \mathbf{Z}^+$ is denumerable. Consider the map

$$(m, n) \mapsto 2^m 3^n.$$

It is an injective map of $\mathbf{Z}^+ \times \mathbf{Z}^+$ into $\mathbf{Z}^+$, and hence $\mathbf{Z}^+ \times \mathbf{Z}^+$ has the same cardinality as an infinite subset of $\mathbf{Z}^+$, whence $\mathbf{Z}^+ \times \mathbf{Z}^+$ is denumerable, as was to be shown.

In this proof, we have used the factorization of integers. One can also give a proof without using this fact. The idea for such a proof is illustrated in the following diagram:

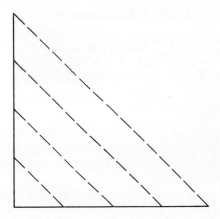

We must define a bijection $\mathbf{Z}^+ \to \mathbf{Z}^+ \times \mathbf{Z}^+$. We map 1 on $(1, 1)$. Inductively, suppose that we have defined an injective map

$$f: \{1, \ldots, n\} \to \mathbf{Z}^+ \times \mathbf{Z}^+.$$

We wish to define $f(n + 1)$.

If $f(n) = (1, k)$ then we let $f(n + 1) = (k + 1, 1)$.
If $f(n) = (r, k)$ with $r \neq 1$ then we let $f(n + 1) = (r - 1, k + 1)$.

It is then routinely checked that we obtain an injection of $\{1, \ldots, n + 1\}$ into $\mathbf{Z}^+ \times \mathbf{Z}^+$. By induction, we obtain a map of $\mathbf{Z}^+$ into $\mathbf{Z}^+ \times \mathbf{Z}^+$ which is also routinely verified to be a bijection. In the diagram, our map f can be described as follows. We start in the corner $(1, 1)$, and then move towards the inside of the quadrant, starting on the horizontal axis, moving diagonally leftwards until we hit the vertical axis, and then starting on the horizontal axis one step further, repeating the process. Geometrically, it is then clear that our map goes through every point (i, j) of $\mathbf{Z}^+ \times \mathbf{Z}^+$.

COROLLARY 1. *For every positive integer* n, *the product* $D \times \cdots \times D$ *taken* n *times is denumerable.*

Proof. Induction.

COROLLARY 2. *Let* $\{D_1, D_2, \ldots\}$ *be a sequence of denumerable sets, also written* $\{D_i\}_{i \in \mathbf{Z}^+}$. *Then the union*

$$U = \bigcup_{i=1}^{\infty} D_i$$

is denumerable.

Proof. For each i we have an enumeration of the elements of D_i, say

$$D_i = \{a_{i1}, a_{i2}, \ldots\}.$$

Then the map

$$(i, j) \mapsto a_{ij}$$

is a map from $\mathbf{Z}^+ \times \mathbf{Z}^+$ into U, and is in fact surjective. Let

$$f: \mathbf{Z}^+ \times \mathbf{Z}^+ \to U$$

be this map. For each $a \in U$ there exists an element $x \in \mathbf{Z}^+ \times \mathbf{Z}^+$ such that $f(x) = a$, and we can write this element x in the form x_a. The association $a \mapsto x_a$ is an injection of U into $\mathbf{Z}^+ \times \mathbf{Z}^+$, and we can now apply the theorem to conclude the proof.

In the preceding proof, we used a special case of a cardinality statement which it is useful to state in general:

Let $f: A \to B$ *be a surjective map of a set* A *onto a set* B. *Then*

$$\operatorname{card}(B) \leqq \operatorname{card}(A).$$

This is easily seen, because for each $y \in B$ there exists an element $x \in A$, denoted by x_y, such that $f(x_y) = y$. Then the association $y \mapsto x_y$ is an injective mapping of B into A, whence by definition,

$$\operatorname{card}(B) \leqq \operatorname{card}(A).$$

In dealing with arbitrary cardinalities, one needs a theorem which is somewhat less trivial than in the denumerable case.

THEOREM 4 (Schroeder-Bernstein). *Let A, B be sets, and suppose that* $\operatorname{card}(A) \leqq \operatorname{card}(B)$, *and* $\operatorname{card}(B) \leqq \operatorname{card}(A)$. *Then*

$$\operatorname{card}(A) = \operatorname{card}(B).$$

Proof. Let $f\colon A \to B$ and $g\colon B \to A$ be injective maps. We separate A into two disjoint sets A_1 and A_2. We let A_1 consist of all $x \in A$ such that, when we lift back x by a succession of inverse maps,

$$x, \quad g^{-1}(x), \quad f^{-1} \circ g^{-1}(x), \quad g^{-1} \circ f^{-1} \circ g^{-1}(x), \ldots,$$

then at some stage we reach an element of A which cannot be lifted back to B by g. We let A_2 be the complement of A_1, in other words, the set of $x \in A$ which can be lifted back indefinitely, or such that we get stopped in B (i.e. reach an element of B which has no inverse image in A by f). Then $A = A_1 \cup A_2$. We shall define a bijection h of A onto B.

If $x \in A_1$, we define $h(x) = f(x)$.

If $x \in A_2$, we define $h(x) = g^{-1}(x) =$ unique element $y \in B$ such that $g(y) = x$.

Then trivially, h is injective. We must prove that h is surjective. Let $b \in B$. If, when we try to lift back b by a succession of maps

$$\cdots \circ f^{-1} \circ g^{-1} \circ f^{-1} \circ g^{-1} \circ f^{-1}(b)$$

we can lift back indefinitely, or if we get stopped in B, then $f(b)$ belongs to A_2 and consequently $b = h(g(b))$, so b lies in the image of h. On the other hand, if we cannot lift back b indefinitely, and get stopped in A, then $f^{-1}(b)$ is defined (i.e. b is in the image of f), and $f^{-1}(b)$ lies in A_1. In this case, $b = h(f^{-1}(b))$ is also in the image of h, as was to be shown.

Next we consider theorems concerning sums and products of cardinalities.

We shall reduce the study of cardinalities of products of arbitrary sets to the denumerable case, using Zorn's lemma. Note first that an infinite set A always contains a denumerable set. Indeed, since A is infinite, we can first select an element $a_1 \in A$, and the complement of $\{a_1\}$ is infinite. Inductively, if we have selected distinct elements $a_1, \ldots, a_n$ in A, the complement of $\{a_1, \ldots, a_n\}$ is infinite, and we can select a_{n+1} in this complement. In this way, we obtain a sequence of distinct elements of A, giving rise to a denumerable subset of A.

Let A be a set. By a *covering* of A one means a set Γ of subsets of A such that the union

$$\bigcup_{C \in \Gamma} C$$

of all the elements of Γ is equal to A. We shall say that Γ is a *disjoint covering* if whenever C, $C' \in \Gamma$, and $C \neq C'$, then the intersection of C and C' is empty.

LEMMA. *Let A be an infinite set. Then there exists a disjoint covering of A by denumerable sets.*

Proof. Let S be the set whose elements are pairs (B, Γ) consisting of a subset B of A, and a disjoint covering of B by denumerable sets. Then S is not empty. Indeed, since A is infinite, A contains a denumerable set D, and the pair $(D, \{D\})$ is in S. If (B, Γ) and (B', Γ') are elements of S, we define

$$(B, \Gamma) \leqq (B', \Gamma')$$

to mean that $B \subset B'$, and $\Gamma \subset \Gamma'$. Let T be a totally ordered non-empty subset of S. We may write $T = \{(B_i, \Gamma_i)\}_{i \in I}$ for some indexing set I. Let

$$B = \bigcup_{i \in I} B_i \quad \text{and} \quad \Gamma = \bigcup_{i \in I} \Gamma_i.$$

If C, $C' \in \Gamma$, $C \neq C'$, then there exists some indices i, j such that $C \in \Gamma_i$ and $C' \in \Gamma_j$. Since T is totally ordered, we have, say,

$$(B_i, \Gamma_i) \leqq (B_j, \Gamma_j).$$

Hence in fact, C, C' are both elements of Γ_j, and hence C, C' have an empty intersection. On the other hand, if $x \in B$, then $x \in B_i$ for some i, and hence there is some $C \in \Gamma_i$ such that $x \in C$. Hence Γ is a disjoint covering of B. Since the elements of each Γ_i are denumerable subsets of A, it follows that Γ is a disjoint covering of B by denumerable sets, so (B, Γ) is in S, and is obviously an upper bound for T. Therefore S is inductively ordered.

Let (M, Δ) be a maximal element of S, by Zorn's lemma. Suppose that $M \neq A$. If the complement of M in A is infinite, then there exists a denumerable set D contained in this complement. Then

$$(M \cup D, \Delta \cup \{D\})$$

is a bigger pair than (M, Δ), contradicting the maximality of (M, Δ). Hence the complement of M in A is a finite set F. Let D_0 be an element of Δ. Let $D_1 = D_0 \cup F$. Then D_1 is denumerable. Let Δ_1 be the set consisting of all elements of Δ, except D_0, together with D_1. Then Δ_1 is a disjoint covering of A by denumerable sets, as was to be shown.

THEOREM 5. *Let A be an infinite set, and let D be a denumerable set. Then*

$$\text{card}(A \times D) = \text{card}(A).$$

Proof. By the lemma, we can write

$$A = \bigcup_{i \in I} D_i$$

as a disjoint union of denumerable sets. Then

$$A \times D = \bigcup_{i \in I} (D_i \times D).$$

For each $i \in I$, there is a bijection of $D_i \times D$ on D_i by Theorem 3. Since the sets $D_i \times D$ are disjoint, we get in this way a bijection of $A \times D$ on A, as desired.

COROLLARY 1. *If F is a finite non-empty set, then*

$$\text{card}(A \times F) = \text{card}(A).$$

Proof. We have

$$\text{card}(A) \leq \text{card}(A \times F) \leq \text{card}(A \times D) = \text{card}(A).$$

We can then use Theorem 4 to get what we want.

COROLLARY 2. *Let A, B be non-empty sets, A infinite, and suppose* $\text{card}(B) \leq \text{card}(A)$. *Then*

$$\text{card}(A \cup B) = \text{card}(A).$$

Proof. We can write $A \cup B = A \cup C$ for some subset C of B, such that C and A are disjoint. (We let C be the set of all elements of B which are not elements of A.) Then $\text{card}(C) \leq \text{card}(A)$. We can then construct an injection of $A \cup C$ into the product

$$A \times \{1, 2\}$$

of A with a set consisting of 2 elements. Namely, we have a bijection of A with $A \times \{1\}$ in the obvious way, and also an injection of C into $A \times \{2\}$. Thus

$$\text{card}(A \cup C) \leq \text{card}(A \times \{1, 2\}).$$

We conclude the proof by Corollary 1 and Theorem 4.

THEOREM 6. *Let A be an infinite set. Then*

$$\text{card}(A \times A) = \text{card}(A).$$

Proof. Let S be the set consisting of pairs (B, f) where B is an infinite subset of A, and $f: B \to B \times B$ is a bijection of B onto $B \times B$. Then S is not empty because if D is a denumerable subset of A, we can always find a bijection of D on $D \times D$. If (B, f) and (B', f') are in S, we define $(B, f) \leq (B', f')$ to mean $B \subset B'$, and the restriction of f' to B is equal to f. Then S is partially ordered, and we contend that S is inductively ordered. Let T be a non-empty totally ordered subset of S, and say T consists of the pairs (B_i, f_i) for i in some indexing set I. Let

$$M = \bigcup_{i \in I} B_i.$$

We shall define a bijection $g: M \to M \times M$. If $x \in M$, then x lies in some B_i. We define $g(x) = f_i(x)$. This value $f_i(x)$ is independent of the choice of B_i in which x lies. Indeed, if $x \in B_j$ for some $j \in I$, then say

$$(B_i, f_i) \leq (B_j, f_j).$$

By assumption, $B_i \subset B_j$, and $f_j(x) = f_i(x)$, so g is well defined. To show g is surjective, let $x, y \in M$ and $(x, y) \in M \times M$. Then $x \in B_i$ for some $i \in I$ and $y \in B_j$ for some $j \in I$. Again since T is totally ordered, say $(B_i, f_i) \leq (B_j, f_j)$. Thus $B_i \subset B_j$, and $x, y \in B_j$. There exists an element $b \in B_j$ such that $f_j(b) = (x, y) \in B_j \times B_j$. By definition, $g(b) = (x, y)$, so g is surjective. We leave the proof that g is injective to the reader to conclude the proof that g is a bijection. We then see that (M, g) is an upper bound for T in S, and therefore that S is inductively ordered.

Let (M, g) be a maximal element of S, and let C be the complement of M in A. If $\text{card}(C) \leq \text{card}(M)$, then

$$\text{card}(M) \leq \text{card}(A) = \text{card}(M \cup C) = \text{card}(M)$$

by Corollary 2 of Theorem 5, and hence $\text{card}(M) = \text{card}(A)$ by Bernstein's Theorem. Since $\text{card}(M) = \text{card}(M \times M)$, we are done with the proof in this case. If $\text{card}(M) \leq \text{card}(C)$, then there exists a subset M_1 of C having the same cardinality as M. We consider

$$(M \cup M_1) \times (M \cup M_1)$$
$$= (M \times M) \cup (M_1 \times M) \cup (M \times M_1) \cup (M_1 \times M_1).$$

By the assumption on M and Corollary 2 of Theorem 5, the last three sets in parentheses on the right of this equation have the same cardinality as M. Thus

$$(M \cup M_1) \times (M \cup M_1) = (M \times M) \cup M_2$$

where M_2 is disjoint from $M \times M$, and has the same cardinality as M. We now define a bijection

$$g_1 : M \cup M_1 \to (M \cup M_1) \times (M \cup M_1).$$

We let $g_1(x) = g(x)$ if $x \in M$, and we let g_1 on M_1 be any bijection of M_1 on M_2. In this way we have extended g to $M \cup M_1$, and the pair $(M \cup M_1, g_1)$ is in S, contradicting the maximality of (M, g). The case $\mathrm{card}(M) \leqq \mathrm{card}(C)$ therefore cannot occur, and our theorem is proved.

COROLLARY 1. *If A is an infinite set, and $A^{(n)} = A \times \cdots \times A$ is the product taken n times, then*

$$\mathrm{card}(A^{(n)}) = \mathrm{card}(A).$$

Proof. Induction.

COROLLARY 2. *If $A_1, \ldots, A_n$ are non-empty sets, and*

$$\mathrm{card}(A_i) \leqq \mathrm{card}(A_n)$$

for $i = 1, \ldots, n$, then

$$\mathrm{card}(A_1 \times \cdots \times A_n) = \mathrm{card}(A_n).$$

Proof. We have

$$\mathrm{card}(A_n) \leqq \mathrm{card}(A_1 \times \cdots \times A_n) \leqq \mathrm{card}(A_n \times \cdots \times A_n)$$

and we use Corollary 1 and the Schroeder-Bernstein Theorem to conclude the proof.

COROLLARY 3. *Let A be an infinite set, and let Φ be the set of finite subsets of A. Then*

$$\mathrm{card}(\Phi) = \mathrm{card}(A).$$

Proof. Let Φ_n be the set of subsets of A having exactly n elements, for each integer $n = 1, 2, \ldots$. We first show that $\mathrm{card}(\Phi_n) \leqq \mathrm{card}(A)$. If F is an element of Φ_n, we order the elements of F in any way, say

$$F = \{x_1, \ldots, x_n\},$$

and we associate with F the element $(x_1, \ldots, x_n) \in A^{(n)}$,

$$F \mapsto (x_1, \ldots, x_n).$$

If G is another subset of A having n elements, say $G = \{y_1, \ldots, y_n\}$, and $G \neq F$, then

$$(x_1, \ldots, x_n) \neq (y_1, \ldots, y_n).$$

Hence our map

$$F \mapsto (x_1, \ldots, x_n)$$

of Φ_n into $A^{(n)}$ is injective. By Corollary 1, we conclude that

$$\mathrm{card}(\Phi_n) \leqq \mathrm{card}(A).$$

Now Φ is the disjoint union of the Φ_n for $n = 1, 2, \ldots$ and it is an exercise to show that $\mathrm{card}(\Phi) \leqq \mathrm{card}(A)$ (cf. Exercise 1). Since

$$\mathrm{card}(A) \leqq \mathrm{card}(\Phi),$$

because in particular, $\mathrm{card}(\Phi_1) = \mathrm{card}(A)$, we see that our corollary is proved.

In the next theorem, we shall see that given a set, there always exists another set whose cardinality is bigger.

THEOREM 7. *Let A be an infinite set, and T the set consisting of two elements $\{0, 1\}$. Let M be the set of all maps of A into T. Then*

$$\mathrm{card}(A) \leqq \mathrm{card}(M) \qquad and \qquad \mathrm{card}(A) \neq \mathrm{card}(M).$$

Proof. For each $x \in A$ we let

$$f_x \colon A \to \{0, 1\}$$

be the map such that $f_x(x) = 1$ and $f_x(y) = 0$ if $y \neq x$. Then $x \mapsto f_x$ is obviously an injection of A into M, so that $\mathrm{card}(A) \leqq \mathrm{card}(M)$. Suppose that $\mathrm{card}(A) = \mathrm{card}(M)$. Let

$$x \mapsto g_x$$

be a bijection between A and M. We define a map $h \colon A \to \{0, 1\}$ by the rule

$$h(x) = 0 \qquad \text{if} \quad g_x(x) = 1,$$
$$h(x) = 1 \qquad \text{if} \quad g_x(x) = 0.$$

Then certainly $h \neq g_x$ for any x, and this contradicts the assumption that $x \mapsto g_x$ is a bijection, thereby proving Theorem 7.

COROLLARY. *Let A be an infinite set, and let S be the set of all subsets of A. Then $\mathrm{card}(A) \leqq \mathrm{card}(S)$ and $\mathrm{card}(A) \neq \mathrm{card}(S)$.*

Proof. We leave it as an exercise. [*Hint:* If B is a non-empty subset of A, use the characteristic function φ_B such that

$$\varphi_B(x) = 1 \qquad \text{if} \quad x \in B,$$

$$\varphi_B(x) = 0 \qquad \text{if} \quad x \notin B.$$

What can you say about the association $B \mapsto \varphi_B$?]

EXERCISES

1. Prove the statement made in the proof of Corollary 3, Theorem 6.

2. If A is an infinite set, and Φ_n is the set of subsets of A having exactly n elements, show that
$$\text{card}(A) \leq \text{card}(\Phi_n)$$
for $n \geq 1$.

3. Let A_i be infinite sets for $i = 1, 2, \ldots$ and assume that

$$\text{card}(A_i) \leq \text{card}(A)$$

for some set A, and all i. Show that

$$\text{card}\left(\bigcup_{i=1}^{\infty} A_i \right) \leq \text{card}(A).$$

4. Let K be a subfield of the complex numbers. Show that for each integer $n \geq 1$, the cardinality of the set of extensions of K of degree n in $\mathbf{C}$ is $\leq \text{card}(K)$.

5. Let K be an infinite field, and E an algebraic extension of K. Show that $\text{card}(E) = \text{card}(K)$.

6. Finish the proof of the Corollary of Theorem 7.

7. If A, B are sets, denote by $M(A, B)$ the set of all maps of A into B. If B, B' are sets with the same cardinality, show that $M(A, B)$ and $M(A, B')$ have the same cardinality. If A, A' have the same cardinality, show that $M(A, B)$ and $M(A', B)$ have the same cardinality.

8. Let A be an infinite set and abbreviate $\text{card}(A)$ by α. If B is an infinite set, abbreviate $\text{card}(B)$ by β. Define $\alpha\beta$ to be $\text{card}(A \times B)$. Let B' be a set disjoint from A such that $\text{card}(B) = \text{card}(B')$. Define $\alpha + \beta$ to be $\text{card}(A \cup B')$. Denote by B^A the set of all maps of A into B, and denote $\text{card}(B^A)$ by β^α. Let C be an infinite set and abbreviate $\text{card}(C)$ by γ. Prove the following statements: (a) $\alpha(\beta + \gamma) = \alpha\beta + \alpha\gamma$. (b) $\alpha\beta = \beta\alpha$. (c) $\alpha^{\beta+\gamma} = \alpha^\beta \alpha^\gamma$.

9. Let K be an infinite field. Prove that there exists an algebraically closed field $\overline{K}$ containing K as a subfield, and algebraic over K. [*Hint:* Let Ω be a set of cardinality strictly greater than the cardinality of K, and containing K. Consider the set S of all pairs (E, φ) where E is a subset of Ω such that $K \subset E$,

and φ denotes a law of addition and multiplication on E which makes E into a field such that K is a subfield, and E is algebraic over K. Define a partial ordering on S in an obvious way; show that S is inductively ordered, and that a maximal element is algebraic over K and algebraically closed. You will need Exercise 5 in the last step.]

10. Let K be an infinite field. Show that the field of rational functions $K(t)$ has the same cardinality as K.

11. Let J_n be the set of integers $\{1, \ldots, n\}$. Let $\mathbf{Z}^+$ be the set of positive integers. Show that the following sets have the same cardinality:
    (a) The set of all maps $M(\mathbf{Z}^+, J_n)$.
    (b) The set of all maps $M(\mathbf{Z}^+, J_2)$.
    (c) The set of all real numbers x such that $0 \leqq x < 1$.
    (d) The set of all real numbers.
[*Hint:* Use decimal expansions.]

12. If you have read about continued fractions for real numbers, show that $M(\mathbf{Z}^+, \mathbf{Z}^+)$ has the same cardinality as the real numbers.

§4. Well-ordering

A set A is said to be *well-ordered* if it is totally ordered, and if every non-empty subset B has a least element, i.e. an element $a \in B$ such that $a \leqq x$ for all $x \in B$.

Example 1.   The set of positive integers $\mathbf{Z}^+$ is well-ordered. Any finite set can be well-ordered, and a denumerable set D can be well-ordered: Any bijection of D with $\mathbf{Z}^+$ will give rise to a well-ordering of D.

Example 2.   Let D be a denumerable set which is well ordered. Let b be an element of some set, and $b \notin D$. Let $A = D \cup \{b\}$. We define $x \leqq b$ for all $x \in D$. Then A is totally ordered, and is in fact well-ordered. *Proof:* Let B be a non-empty subset of A. If B consists of b alone, then b is a least element of B. Otherwise, B contains some element $a \in A$. Then $B \cap A$ is not empty, and hence has a least element, which is obviously also a least element for B.

Example 3.   Let D_1, D_2 be two denumerable sets, each one well-ordered, and assume that $D_1 \cap D_2$ is empty. Let $A = D_1 \cup D_2$. We define a total ordering in A by letting $x < y$ for all $x \in D_1$ and all $y \in D_2$. Using the same type of argument as in Example 2, we see that A is well-ordered.

Example 4.   Proceeding inductively, given a sequence of disjoint denumerable sets $D_1, D_2, \ldots$ we let $A = \bigcup D_i$, and we can define a well-ordering on A by ordering each D_i like $\mathbf{Z}^+$, and then defining $x < y$

for $x \in D_i$ and $y \in D_{i+1}$. One may visualize this situation as follows:

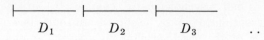

$$D_1 \qquad\qquad D_2 \qquad\qquad D_3 \qquad \ldots$$

THEOREM 8. *Every non-empty infinite set A can be well-ordered.*

Proof. Let S be the set of all pairs (X, R) where X is a subset of A, and R is a total ordering of X such that X is well-ordered. Then S is not empty, since given a denumerable subset D of A, we can always well order it like the positive integers. If (X, R) and (Y, Q) are elements of S, we define $(X, R) \leqq (Y, Q)$ if $X \subset Y$, if the restriction of Q to X is equal to R, and if every element $y \in Y$, $y \notin X$ is such that $x < y$ for all $x \in X$. Then S is partially ordered. To show that S is inductively ordered, let T be a totally ordered non-empty subset of S, say $T = \{(X_i, R_i)\}_{i \in I}$. Let

$$M = \bigcup_{i \in I} X_i.$$

Let $x, y \in M$. There exists $i, j \in I$ such that $x \in X_i$ and $y \in X_j$. Since T is totally ordered, say $(X_i, R_i) \leqq (X_j, R_j)$. Then both $x, y \in X_j$. We define $x \leqq y$ in M if $x \leqq y$ in X_j. This is easily seen to be independent of the choice of (X_j, R_j) such that $x, y \in X_j$, and it is then trivially verified that we have defined a total ordering on M, which we denote by (M, P). We contend that this total ordering on M is a well-ordering. To see this, let N be a non-empty subset of M. Let $x_0 \in N$. Then there exists some $i_0 \in I$ such that $x_0 \in X_{i_0}$. The subset $M \cap X_{i_0}$ is not empty. Let a be a least element. We contend that a is in fact a least element of M. Let $x \in M$. Then x lies in some X_i. Since T is totally ordered, we have

$$(X_i, R_i) \leqq (X_{i_0}, R_{i_0}) \qquad \text{or} \qquad (X_{i_0}, R_{i_0}) \leqq (X_i, R_i).$$

In the first case, $x \in X_i \subset X_{i_0}$ and hence $a \leqq x$. In the second case, if $x \notin X_{i_0}$ then by definition, $a < x$. This proves that (M, P) is a well-ordering.

We have therefore proved that S is inductively ordered. By Zorn's lemma, let (M, P) be a maximal element of S. Then M is well-ordered, and all that remains to be shown is that $M = A$. Suppose $M \neq A$, and let z be an element of A and $z \notin M$. Let $M' = M \cup \{z\}$. We define a total ordering on M' by defining $x < z$ for all $x \in M$. Then M' is well-ordered, for let N be a totally ordered non-empty subset of M'. If $N \cap M$ is not empty, then $N \cap M$ has a least element a, which is obviously a least element for N. If $N \cap M$ is empty, then $N = \{z\}$, and then z itself is a least element for N. This contradicts the fact that M is maximal in S. Hence $M = A$, and our theorem is proved.

§5. *Proof of Zorn's lemma*

Zorn's lemma is not psychologically completely satisfactory as an axiom, because its statement is too involved, and one does not visualize easily the existence of the maximal element asserted in that statement. In this section, we show how one can prove Zorn's lemma from other properties of sets which everyone would immediately grant as acceptable psychologically.

From now on to the end of the proof of Theorem 9, we let A be a non-empty partially ordered and strictly inductively ordered set. We recall that *strictly inductively ordered* means that every non-empty totally ordered subset has a least upper bound. We assume given a map $f: A \to A$ such that for all $x \in A$ we have $x \leq f(x)$. We could call such a map an *increasing* map.

Let $a \in A$. Let B be a subset of A. We shall say that B is *admissible* if:

(1) B contains a.

(2) We have $f(B) \subset B$.

(3) Whenever T is a totally ordered subset of B, the least upper bound of T in A lies in B.

Then B is also strictly inductively ordered, by the induced ordering of A. We shall prove:

THEOREM 9 (Bourbaki). *Let A be a non-empty partially ordered and strictly inductively ordered set. Let $f: A \to A$ be an increasing mapping. Then there exists an element $x_0 \in A$ such that $f(x_0) = x_0$.*

Proof. Suppose that A were totally ordered. By assumption, it would have a least upper bound $b \in A$, and then

$$b \leq f(b) \leq b,$$

so that in this case, our theorem is clear. The whole problem is to reduce the theorem to that case. In other words, what we need to find is a totally ordered admissible subset of A.

If we throw out of A all elements $x \in A$ such that x is not $\geq a$, then what remains is obviously an admissible subset. Thus without loss of generality, we may assume that A has a least element a, that is $a \leq x$ for all $x \in A$.

Let M be the intersection of all admissible subsets of A. Note that A itself is an admissible subset, and that all admissible subsets of A contain a, so that M is not empty. Furthermore, M is itself an admissible subset of A. To see this, let $x \in M$. Then x is in every admissible subset, so $f(x)$ is also in every admissible subset, and hence $f(x) \in M$. Hence $f(M) \subset M$. If T is a totally ordered non-empty subset of M, and b is the least upper bound of T in A, then b lies in every admissible subset of A, and hence lies in M. It follows that M is the smallest admissible subset of A, and that any admissible subset of A contained in M is equal to M.

We shall prove that M is totally ordered, and thereby prove Theorem 9.

[First we make some remarks which don't belong to the proof, but will help in the understanding of the subsequent lemmas. Since $a \in M$, we see that $f(a) \in M$, $f \circ f(a) \in M$, and in general $f^n(a) \in M$. Furthermore,

$$a \leqq f(a) \leqq f^2(a) \leqq \cdots .$$

If we had an equality somewhere, we would be finished, so we may assume that the inequalities hold. Let D_0 be the totally ordered set $\{f^n(a)\}_{n \geqq 0}$. Then D_0 looks like this:

$$a < f(a) < f^2(a) < \cdots < f^n(a) < \cdots .$$

Let a_1 be the least upper bound of D_0. Then we can form

$$a_1 < f(a_1) < f^2(a_1) < \cdots$$

in the same way to obtain D_1, and we can continue this process, to obtain

$$D_1, D_2, \ldots .$$

It is clear that $D_1, D_2, \ldots$ are contained in M. If we had a precise way of expressing the fact that we can establish a never-ending string of such denumerable sets, then we would obtain what we want. The point is that we are now trying to prove Zorn's lemma, which is the natural tool for guaranteeing the existence of such a string. However, given such a string, we observe that its elements have two properties: If c is an element of such a string and $x < c$, then $f(x) \leqq c$. Furthermore, there is no element between c and $f(c)$, that is if x is an element of the string, then $x \leqq c$ or $f(c) \leqq x$. We shall now prove two lemmas which show that elements of M have these properties.]

Let $c \in M$. We shall say that c is an *extreme point* of M if whenever $x \in M$ and $x < c$, then $f(x) \leqq c$. For each extreme point $c \in M$ we let

$$M_c = \text{set of } x \in M \quad \text{such that} \quad x \leqq c \quad \text{or} \quad f(c) \leqq x.$$

Note that M_c is not empty because a is in it.

LEMMA 1. *We have $M_c = M$ for every extreme point c of M.*

Proof. It will suffice to prove that M_c is an admissible subset. Let $x \in M_c$. If $x < c$ then $f(x) \leqq c$ so $f(x) \in M_c$. If $x = c$ then $f(x) = f(c)$ is again in M_c. If $f(c) \leqq x$, then $f(c) \leqq x \leqq f(x)$, so once more $f(x) \in M_c$. Thus we have proved that $f(M_c) \subset M_c$.

Let T be a totally ordered subset of M_c and let b be the least upper bound of T in M. If all elements $x \in T$ are $\leq c$, then $b \leq c$ and $b \in M_c$. If some $x \in T$ is such that $f(c) \leq x$, then $f(c) \leq x \leq b$, and so b is in M_c. This proves our lemma.

LEMMA 2. *Every element of M is an extreme point.*

Proof. Let E be the set of extreme points of M. Then E is not empty because $a \in E$. It will suffice to prove that E is an admissible subset. We first prove $f(E) \subset E$. Let $c \in E$. Let $x \in M$ and suppose $x < f(c)$. We must prove that $f(x) \leq f(c)$. By Lemma 1, $M = M_c$, and hence we have $x < c$, or $x = c$, or $f(c) \leq x$. This last possibility cannot occur because $x < f(c)$. If $x < c$ then $f(x) \leq c \leq f(c)$.

If $x = c$ then $f(x) = f(c)$ whence $f(E) \subset E$. Finally let T be a totally ordered subset of E. Let b be its least upper bound in M. Let $x \in M$, $x < b$. We must show $f(x) \leq b$. By Lemma 1, we know that for each $t \in T$ we have $M_t = M$ whence $x \leq t$ or $f(t) \leq x$. If for some $t \in T$ we have $x \leq t$, then $f(x) \leq f(t) \leq b$ and we are done. Otherwise for all $t \in T$ we have $f(t) \leq x$ whence x is an upper bound for T and $b \leq x$ which is impossible. This proves that E is admissible, and our lemma is proved.

We now see trivially that M is totally ordered. For let $x, y \in M$. Then x is an extreme point of M by Lemma 2, and $y \in M_x$ so $y \leq x$ or

$$x \leq f(x) \leq y,$$

thereby proving that M is totally ordered. As remarked previously, this concludes the proof of Theorem 9.

We shall obtain Zorn's lemma essentially as a corollary of Theorem 9. We first obtain Zorn's lemma in a slightly weaker form.

COROLLARY 1. *Let A be a non-empty strictly inductively ordered set. Then A has a maximal element.*

Proof. Suppose that A does not have a maximal element. Then for each $x \in A$ there exists an element $y_x \in A$ such that $x < y_x$. Let $f: S \to S$ be the map such that $f(x) = y_x$ for all $x \in S$. Then A, f satisfy the hypotheses of Theorem 9, and applying Theorem 9 yields a contradiction.

The only difference between Corollary 1 and Zorn's lemma is that in Corollary 1, we assume that a non-empty totally ordered subset has a *least* upper bound, rather than an upper bound. It is, however, a simple matter to reduce Zorn's lemma to the seemingly weaker form of Corollary 1. We do this in the second corollary.

COROLLARY 2 (Zorn's Lemma). *Let S be a non-empty inductively ordered set. Then S has a maximal element.*

Proof. Let A be the set of non-empty totally ordered subsets of S. Then A is not empty since any subset of S with one element belongs to A. If X, $Y \in A$, we define $X \leq Y$ to mean $X \subset Y$. Then A is partially ordered, and is in fact strictly inductively ordered. For let $T = \{X_i\}_{i \in I}$ be a totally ordered subset of A. Let

$$Z = \bigcup_{i \in I} X_i.$$

Then Z is totally ordered. To see this, let x, $y \in Z$. Then $x \in X_i$ and $y \in X_j$ for some $i, j \in I$. Since T is totally ordered, say $X_i \subset X_j$. Then x, $y \in X_j$ and since X_j is totally ordered, $x \leq y$ or $y \leq x$. Thus Z is totally ordered, and is obviously a least upper bound for T in A. By Corollary 1, we conclude that A has a maximal element X_0. This means that X_0 is a maximal totally ordered subset of S (non-empty). Let m be an upper bound for X_0 in S. Then m is the desired maximal element of S. For if $x \in S$ and $m \leq x$ then $X_0 \cup \{x\}$ is totally ordered, whence equal to X_0 by the maximality of X_0. Thus $x \in X_0$ and $x \leq m$. Hence $x = m$, as was to be shown.

Remark. It is an elaborate matter to axiomatize the theory of sets beyond the point where we have carried it in the arguments of this chapter. Since all the arguments of the chapter are easily acceptable to working mathematicians, it is a reasonable policy to stop at this point without ever looking at the deeper foundations.

One may, however, be interested in these foundations for their own sake, as a matter of taste. We refer the reader to technical books on the subject if he is so inclined. However, we make one additional remark on the proof of Zorn's lemma. If the reader looks at Corollary 1, we said "Let $f: S \to S$ be the map such that $f(x) = y_x$." In laying the foundations of set theory, one needs a special axiom which guarantees the existence of such a map. This axiom is called the *axiom of choice*, so what we have shown is that the axiom of choice implies Zorn's lemma. Stated independently, the axiom of choice runs as follows:

Let $\{S_i\}_{i \in I}$ be a family of sets, and assume that each S_i is not empty. Then there exists a family of elements $\{x_i\}_{i \in I}$ with each $x_i \in S_i$.

In Corollary 1, for each $x \in A$ we let B_x be the set of $y \in A$ such that $x < y$. If each B_x is not empty, taking $A = I$, we get the existence of our family $\{y_x\}_{x \in A}$. But as said at the beginning of the section, who would question this?

APPENDIX

§1. *The natural numbers*

The purpose of this appendix is to show how the integers can be obtained axiomatically using only the terminology and elementary properties of sets. The rules of the game from now allow us to use only sets and mappings.

We assume given once for all a set $\mathbf{N}$ called the set of *natural numbers,* and a map $\sigma\colon \mathbf{N} \to \mathbf{N}$, satisfying the following (Peano) axioms:

NN 1. *There is an element* $0 \in \mathbf{N}$.

NN 2. *We have* $\sigma(0) \neq 0$ *and if we let* $\mathbf{N}^+$ *denote the subset of* $\mathbf{N}$ *consisting of all* $n \in \mathbf{N}$, $n \neq 0$, *then the map* $x \mapsto \sigma(x)$ *is a bijection between* $\mathbf{N}$ *and* $\mathbf{N}^+$.

NN 3. *If S is a subset of* $\mathbf{N}$, *if* $0 \in S$, *and if* $\sigma(n)$ *lies in S whenever n lies in S, then $S = \mathbf{N}$.*

We often denote $\sigma(n)$ by n' and think of n' as the successor of n. The reader will recognize NN 3 as induction.

We denote $\sigma(0)$ by 1.

Our next task is to define addition between natural numbers.

LEMMA 1. *Let $f\colon \mathbf{N} \to \mathbf{N}$ and $g\colon \mathbf{N} \to \mathbf{N}$ be maps such that*

$$f(0) = g(0) \qquad and \qquad \begin{cases} f(n') = f(n)', \\ g(n') = g(n)'. \end{cases}$$

Then $f = g$.

Proof. Let S be the subset of $\mathbf{N}$ consisting of all n such that $f(n) = g(n)$. Then S obviously satisfies the hypotheses of induction, so $S = \mathbf{N}$, thereby proving the lemma.

For each $m \in \mathbf{N}$, we wish to define $m + n$ with $n \in \mathbf{N}$ such that

$$(1_m) \quad m + 0 = m \qquad \text{and} \qquad m + n' = (m + n)' \qquad \text{for all } n \in \mathbf{N}.$$

By Lemma 1, this is possible in only one way.

If $m = 0$, we define $0 + n = n$ for all $n \in \mathbf{N}$. Then (1_m) is obviously satisfied. Let T be the set of $m \in \mathbf{N}$ for which one can define $m + n$ for all $n \in \mathbf{N}$ in such a way that (1_m) is satisfied. Then $0 \in T$. Suppose

$m \in T$. We define for all $n \in \mathbf{N}$,

$$m' + 0 = m' \qquad \text{and} \qquad m' + n = (m + n)'.$$

Then

$$m' + n' = (m + n')' = ((m + n)')' = (m' + n)'.$$

Hence $(1_{m'})$ is satisfied, so $m' \in T$. This proves that $T = \mathbf{N}$, and thus we have defined addition for all pairs (m, n) of natural numbers.

The properties of addition are easily proved.

Commutativity: Let S be the set of all natural numbers m such that

(2_m) $$m + n = n + m \qquad \text{for all} \quad n \in \mathbf{N}.$$

Then 0 is obviously in S, and if $m \in S$, then

$$m' + n = (m + n)' = (n + m)' = n + m',$$

thereby proving that $S = \mathbf{N}$, as desired.

Associativity. Let S be the set of natural numbers m such that

(3_m) $$(m + n) + k = m + (n + k) \qquad \text{for all} \quad n, k \in \mathbf{N}.$$

Then 0 is obviously in S. Suppose $m \in S$. Then

$$(m' + n) + k = (m + n)' + k = ((m + n) + k)'$$
$$= (m + (n + k))' = m' + (n + k),$$

thereby proving that $S = \mathbf{N}$, as desired.

Cancellation law. Let m be a natural number. We shall say that the *cancellation law holds for m* if for all $k, n \in \mathbf{N}$ satisfying $m + k = m + n$ we must have $k = n$. Let S be the set of m for which the cancellation law holds. Then obviously $0 \in S$, and if $m \in S$, then

$$m' + k = m' + n \qquad \text{implies} \qquad (m + k)' = (m + n)'.$$

Since the mapping $x \mapsto x'$ is injective, it follows that $m + k = m + n$, whence $k = n$. By induction, $S = \mathbf{N}$.

For multiplication, and other applications, we need to generalize Lemma 1.

LEMMA 2. *Let S be a set, and $\varphi \colon S \to S$ a map of S into itself. Let f, g be maps of $\mathbf{N}$ into S. If*

$$f(0) = g(0) \qquad \text{and} \qquad \begin{cases} f(n') = \varphi \circ f(n), \\ g(n') = \varphi \circ g(n) \end{cases}$$

for all $n \in \mathbf{N}$, then $f = g$.

Proof. Trivial by induction.

For each natural number m, it follows from Lemma 2 that there is at most one way of defining a product mn satisfying

$$m0 = 0 \qquad \text{and} \qquad mn' = mn + m \qquad \text{for all } n \in \mathbf{N}.$$

We in fact define the product this way in the same inductive manner that we did for addition, and then prove in a similar way that this product is *commutative, associative, and distributive,* that is

$$m(n + k) = mn + mk$$

for all m, n, $k \in \mathbf{N}$. We leave the details to the reader.

In this way, we obtain all the properties of a ring, *except* that $\mathbf{N}$ is not an additive group: We lack additive inverses. Note that 1 is a unit element for the multiplication, that is $1m = m$ for all $m \in \mathbf{N}$.

It is also easy to prove the *multiplicative cancellation law,* namely if $mk = mn$ and $m \neq 0$, then $k = n$. We also leave this to the reader. In particular, if $mn \neq 0$, then $m \neq 0$ and $n \neq 0$.

We recall that an *ordering* in a set X is a relation $x \leq y$ between certain pairs (x, y) of elements of X, satisfying the conditions (for all $x, y, z \in X$):

PO 1. *We have $x \leq x$.*

PO 2. *If $x \leq y$ and $y \leq z$, then $x \leq z$.*

PO 3. *If $x \leq y$ and $y \leq x$, then $x = y$.*

The ordering is called a *total ordering* if given $x, y \in X$ we have $x \leq y$ or $y \leq x$. We write $x < y$ if $x \leq y$ and $x \neq y$.

We can define an ordering in $\mathbf{N}$ by defining $n \leq m$ if there exists $k \in \mathbf{N}$ such that $m = n + k$. The proof that this is an ordering is routine and left to the reader. *This is in fact a total ordering,* and we give the proof for that. Given a natural number m, let C_m be the set of $n \in \mathbf{N}$ such that $n \leq m$ or $m \leq n$. Then certainly $0 \in C_m$. Suppose that $n \in C_m$. If $n = m$, then $n' = m + 1$, so $m \leq n'$. If $n < m$, then $m = n + k'$ for some $k \in \mathbf{N}$, so that

$$m = n + k' = (n + k)' = n' + k,$$

and $n' \leq m$. If $m \leq n$, then for some k, we have $n = m + k$, so that $n + 1 = m + k + 1$ and $m \leq n + 1$. By induction, $C_m = \mathbf{N}$, thereby showing our ordering is total.

It is then easy to prove standard statements concerning inequalities, e.g.

$$m < n \quad \text{if and only if} \quad m + k < n + k \quad \text{for some } k \in \mathbf{N},$$

$$m < n \quad \text{if and only if} \quad mk < nk \quad \text{for some } k \in \mathbf{N}, k \neq 0.$$

One can also replace "for some" by "for all" in these two assertions. The proofs are left to the reader. It is also easy to prove that if m, n are natural numbers and $m \leq n \leq m + 1$, then $m = n$ or $n = m + 1$. We leave the proof to the reader.

We now prove the first property of integers mentioned in Chapter I, §2, namely the well-ordering: *Every non-empty subset S of $\mathbf{N}$ has a least element.*

To see this, let T be the subset of $\mathbf{N}$ consisting of all n such that $n \leq x$ for all $x \in S$. Then $0 \in T$, and $T \neq \mathbf{N}$. Hence there exists $m \in T$ such that $m + 1 \notin T$ (by induction!). Then $m \in S$ (otherwise $m < x$ for all $x \in S$, so $m + 1 \leq x$ for all $x \in S$ which is impossible). It is then clear that m is the smallest element of S, as desired.

In Chapter VIII, we assumed known the properties of finite cardinalities. We shall prove these here. For each natural number $n \neq 0$ let J_n be the set of natural numbers x such that $1 \leq x \leq n$.

If $n = 1$, then $J_n = \{1\}$, and there is only a single map of $\mathbf{N}_1$ into itself. This map is obviously bijective. We recall that sets A, B are said to have the same cardinality if there is a bijection of A onto B. Since a composite of bijections is a bijection, it follows that if

$$\mathrm{card}(A) = \mathrm{card}(B) \qquad \text{and} \qquad \mathrm{card}(B) = \mathrm{card}(C),$$

then $\mathrm{card}(A) = \mathrm{card}(C)$.

Let m be a natural number ≥ 1 and let $k \in J_{m'}$. Then there is a bijection between

$$J_{m'} - \{k\} \qquad \text{and} \qquad J_m$$

defined in the obvious way: We let $f: J_{m'} - \{k\} \to J_m$ be such that

$$f: x \mapsto x \qquad \text{if} \quad x < k,$$

$$f: x \mapsto \sigma^{-1}(x) \qquad \text{if} \quad x > k.$$

We let $g: J_m \to J_{m'} - \{k\}$ be such that

$$g: x \mapsto x \qquad \text{if} \quad x < k,$$

$$g: x \mapsto \sigma(x) \qquad \text{if} \quad x \geq k.$$

Then $f \circ g$ and $g \circ f$ are the respective identities, so f, g are bijections.

We conclude that for all natural numbers $m \geq 1$, if

$$h: J_m \to J_m$$

is an injection, then h is a bijection. Indeed, this is true for $m = 1$, and by induction, suppose the statement true for some $m \geq 1$. Let

$$\varphi: J_{m'} \to J_{m'}$$

be an injection. Let $r \in \mathbf{N}_{m'}$ and let $s = \varphi(r)$. Then we can define a map

$$\varphi_0 \colon J_{m'} - \{r\} \to J_{m'} - \{s\}$$

by $x \mapsto \varphi(x)$. The cardinality of each set $J_{m'} - \{r\}$ and $J_{m'} - \{s\}$ is the same as the cardinality of J_m. By induction, it follows that φ_0 is a bijection, whence φ is a bijection, as desired.

We conclude that if $1 \leqq m < n$, *then a map*

$$f \colon J_n \to J_m$$

cannot be injective. For otherwise by what we have seen, $f(J_m) = J_m$, and hence $f(n) = f(x)$ for some x such that $1 \leqq x \leqq m$, so f is not injective.

Given a set A, we shall say that $\operatorname{card}(A) = n$ (or the *cardinality of* A is n, or A has n elements) for a natural number $n \geqq 1$, if there is a bijection of A with J_n. By the above results, it follows that such a natural number n is uniquely determined by A. We also say that A has cardinality 0 if A is empty. We say that A is *finite* if A has cardinality n for some natural number n. It is then an exercise to prove the following statements:

If A, B are finite sets, and $A \cap B$ is empty, then

$$\operatorname{card}(A) + \operatorname{card}(B) = \operatorname{card}(A \cup B).$$

Furthermore,

$$\operatorname{card}(A) \operatorname{card}(B) = \operatorname{card}(A \times B).$$

We leave the proofs to the reader.

§2. *The integers*

Having the natural numbers, we wish to define the integers. We do this the way it is done in elementary school; there is no better way.

For each natural number $n \neq 0$ we select a new symbol denoted by $-n$, and we denote by $\mathbf{Z}$ the set consisting of the union of $\mathbf{N}$ and all the symbols $-n$ for $n \in \mathbf{N}$, $n \neq 0$. We must define addition in $\mathbf{Z}$. If $x, y \in \mathbf{N}$ we use the same addition as before. For all $x \in \mathbf{Z}$, we define

$$0 + x = x + 0 = x.$$

This is compatible with the addition defined in §1 when $x \in \mathbf{N}$.

Let $m, n \in \mathbf{N}$ and neither n nor $m = 0$. If $m = n + k$ with $k \in \mathbf{N}$ we define:

(a) $m + (-n) = (-n) + m = k.$
(b) $(-m) + n = n + (-m) = -k$ if $k \neq 0$, and $= 0$ if $k = 0$.
(c) $(-m) + (-n) = -(m + n).$

Given x, $y \in \mathbf{Z}$, if not both x, y are natural numbers, then at least one of the situations (a), (b), (c) applies to their addition.

It is then tedious but routine to verify that $\mathbf{Z}$ is an additive group.

Next we define multiplication in $\mathbf{Z}$. If x, $y \in \mathbf{N}$ we use the same multiplication as before. For all $x \in \mathbf{Z}$ we define $0x = x0 = 0$.

Let m, $n \in \mathbf{N}$ and neither n nor $m = 0$. We define:

$$(-m)n = n(-m) = -(mn) \qquad \text{and} \qquad (-m)(-n) = mn.$$

Then it is routinely verified that $\mathbf{Z}$ is a commutative ring, and is in fact entire, its unit element being the element 1 in $\mathbf{N}$. In this way we get the integers.

Observe that $\mathbf{Z}$ is an ordered ring in the sense of Chapter VII, §1 because the set of natural numbers $n \neq 0$ satisfies all the conditions given in that chapter, as one sees directly from our definitions of multiplication and addition.

§3. Infinite sets

A set A is said to be *infinite* if it is not finite (and in particular, not empty).

We shall prove that *an infinite set A contains a denumerable subset.* For each nonempty subset T of A, let x_T be a chosen element of T. We prove by induction that for each positive integer n we can find uniquely determined elements $x_1, \ldots, x_n \in A$ such that $x_1 = x_A$ is the chosen element corresponding to the set A itself, and for each $k = 1, \ldots, n-1$, the element x_{k+1} is the chosen element in the complement of $\{x_1, \ldots, x_k\}$. When $n = 1$, this is obvious. Assume the statement probed for $n > 1$. Then we let x_{n+1} be the chosen element in the complement of $\{x_1, \ldots, x_n\}$. If $x_1, \ldots, x_n$ are already uniquely determined, so is x_{n+1}. This proves what we wanted. In particular, since the elements $x_1, \ldots, x_n$ are distinct for all n, it follows that the subset of A consisting of all elements x_n is a denumerable subset, as desired.

Index